Ronnie

Found this book in
Areopoli & thought
you'd like it.

Happy Birthday 2014.

David

COLONEL LEAKE IN THE MANI

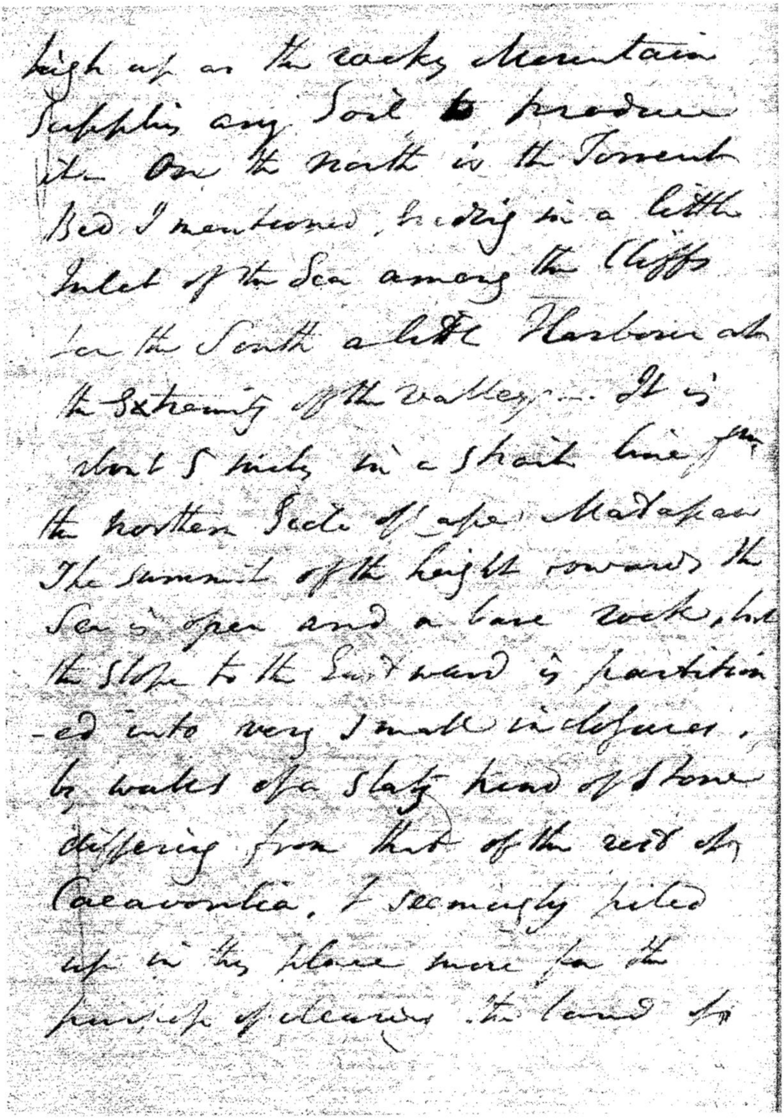
high up as the rocky Mountain
supplies any Soil to produce
it. On the north is the Torrent
Bed I mentioned, ending in a little
Inlet of the Sea among the Cliffs
on the South a little Harbour at
the Extremity of the valley... It is
about 5 miles in a short line from
the northern Side of Cape Matapan
The summit of the height towards the
Sea is open and a bare rock, but
the Slope to the Eastward is partition
-ed into very small inclosures,
by walls of a slaty kind of Stone
differing from that of the red stony
Cacavoulea, & seemingly piled
up in this place more for the
purpose of clearing the land for

Figure 1 Facsimile of a page of Leake's handwritten notes.

COLONEL LEAKE IN THE MANI

A Digest of Chapters 7, 8 and 9 of
William Martin Leake's Travels in the Morea
(London, 1830)

Martin Jones

Book Guild Publishing
Sussex, England

First published in Great Britain in 2012 by
The Book Guild Ltd
Pavilion View
19 New Road
Brighton, BN1 1UF

Typesetting in Garamond by
YHT Ltd, London

Printed and bound in Great Britain by
CPI Antony Rowe

A catalogue record for this book is available from
The British Library.

ISBN 978 1 84624 784 2

Contents

List of Maps and Illustration

Acknowledgements & Sources.

Front Cover: © National Portrait Gallery, London.
Rear Cover: Plate XII, O.M. Stackelberg, *Costumes et Usages des peuples de la Grèce Moderne.* Rome 1825. © British Library.
Figure 1. With kind permission of the Faculty of Classics, Cambridge.
Figure 5. With kind permission of Melissa Books, Athens.
Figure 6. Henri Bel, Trois Années en Grèce. Paris 1881.
Figure 7. J. Galt, *Voyages & Travels in the years 1809, 1810 & 1811*, London 1815. © British Library.
Figures 8, 13 & 14. Plates XI, XXVII & XXVIII, O.M. Stackelberg, idem © British Library.
Figures 4 & 9-12. *Expédition Scientifique de Morée.* Travaux de la Section des Sciences Physiques. Paris/Strasbourg 1835. © British Library.

TRAVELS

IN

THE MOREA.

WITH

A MAP AND PLANS.

BY

WILLIAM MARTIN LEAKE,

F.R.S. ETC.

IN THREE VOLUMES.

VOL. I.

LONDON:
JOHN MURRAY, ALBEMARLE STREET.

MDCCCXXX.

PREFACE.

The very limited success of the principal works descriptive of Greece, which have lately been published, shew how difficult it is to render travels in that country agreeable to the general reader, and may serve in part to explain the long delay which has occurred in the publication of the present volumes. The new condition of the Peloponnesus will equally account for their being now submitted to the public. Greece, in fact, abstracted from its ancient history, has, until very recently, been no more than the thinly peopled province of a semi-barbarous empire, presenting the usual results of Ottoman bigotry and despotism, relieved only by the occasional resistance of particular districts to their rapacious governors, or of armed bandits to the established authority. It was almost entirely by connexion with ancient history that Greece, or its inhabitants, or even its natural productions, could long detain the traveller by furnishing matter of interest to his inquiries, whence arises a continual reference to the Greek and Roman authors, and a frequent necessity for citing even their words, which gives to travels in Greece a *learned aspect,* by no means calculated to obtain for them that success which is indicated by an extensive circulation, more especially as the demand for such works on the continent of Europe is speedily supplied by translations, published at a much smaller expense than is possible in England.

When the journeys were undertaken, of which the following pages contain a diary, the Peloponnesus had been very little explored, and no description of it had been made public, except those by Wheler and Chandler, of some small portions adjacent to the sea coast. The real topography of the interior was unknown, and the map of ancient Greece was formed only by inference from its historians and geographers, although, having been densely populated, divided into numerous small states, and in a high state of improvement in the arts of peace and war, it is, above all others, the country which particularly requires a minute geographical examination for the elucidation of its literature, or, in other words, a map upon a large scale, formed from actual surveys. The delineation of the Peloponnesus, which accompanies the present volumes, is very far from attaining these requisites : nevertheless, it is the result of more than fifteen hundred measurements with the sextant and theodolite, made from every important geodæsic station, which circumstances would admit of my employing, corrected or confirmed by a few good observations of latitude. The coast line has been adopted from the nautical surveys executed under the orders of the Admiralty by Captains Smyth and Copeland, of the Royal Navy, as far as their surveys extended. The unsurveyed coast, which comprehends the entire Argolic Gulf northward of Cape Iéraka, together with the Straits of Petza and Ýdhra, will undoubtedly require considerable correction.

The reader will not be long in discovering, that the critical remarks on ancient history or geography which occur in the following pages, are not taken from the Author's manuscript journal exactly in the form in which they are now submitted to the public. The itinerary itself has received only such emendations as a compressed diary requires, to be intelligible; but the commentaries just alluded to, although their basis was laid in the form of notes in the journeys described, and by confronting the text of the ancient authors with the actual locality to which they relate, have been amplified and brought

into their present form at the Author's leisure.
In defence of the frequent occurrence of translated extracts it may be remarked, that in general such extracts afford the most perspicuous
and even the shortest mode of resolving the
questions which arise out of the authority cited ;
and that of the two authors most frequently
quoted, namely, Strabo and Pausanias, there
exists no translation in the English language of
the former, and of the latter only one, which
scarcely deserves the name.

Although the description of the ancient cities
of Peloponnesus, which I have extracted in an
abridged form from Pausanias, relate in some
instances to places, of which not a vestige now
remains to illustrate the Greek topographer, I
have nevertheless introduced them all, because,
by the addition of a few pages, the present work
is thus rendered more complete, and because
the reader is thus enabled to compare every
part of Peloponnesus as Pausanias found it,
with the view which it presented to the fol-
lower of his steps, after an interval of sixteen
centuries. I am, moreover, much inclined to
believe, that the descriptions which the ancient
traveller has given of the cities of Greece—of
their distribution, mode of decoration, monuments, and productions of art, would, if better
known, be useful to the cultivators of the

fine arts in general; that they might have a ten-
dency to assist the public discrimination on these
subjects; and that they are particularly worthy
of the attention of those upon whom depends
the erection of monuments and public works of
every kind, in regard to which few persons will
be so hardy as to assert, that the good taste of
this nation has kept pace with its wealth and
expenditure.

Note to the Reader

The three volume work *Travels in the Morea* was published by John Murray in 1830 and has never been reprinted, except in a facsimile form. Copies of the original are rare and correspondingly expensive. For the average reader, interested in obtaining a first hand glimpse of what, in effect, is eighteenth century Mani, the only way is to consult such copies as are held in the world's major libraries. This is in spite of Leake's travels being referred to in the great majority of accounts of Greece during the years leading up to the War of Independence. One further reason for Leake's low visibility is that his only biography was a memoir published soon after his death, written by his stepson.[1]

My book is an attempt to make more accessible Leake's remarkable description of life in the Mani two hundred years ago. Wherever possible the author's original text has been retained. He wrote almost constantly in the present tense and gives the impression of having made his notes whilst on horseback and with his chronometer in the other hand.

I have used to the best of my ability Leake's text, letting him speak directly whenever possible, but have been to an extent selective. I hope that I have never falsified the original nor made

---

[1] Marsden, J. H. *A brief memoir of the life and writings of the late Lt. Col. William Martin Leake.* London 1864

any un-warranted alterations. I have omitted fairly lengthy digressions that Leake made when interpreting Pausanias' texts, my objective being to concentrate on Leake's actual travels and his comments on the Mani two centuries ago.

Leake's spelling of place and family names is not always consistent and does not agree with the present day conventions for Greek transliteration into English. In his foreword he was at great pains to explain to the reader how he transcribed Greek into English. Wherever possible I have retained Leake's spelling, making changes only where they simplify or improve the sense. To anyone familiar with the area, Leake's grasp and description of the geography is remarkably accurate, especially as he had no reliable maps at his disposal, but many place names have changed since his time.

Anyone who takes the trouble to compare this text with the original will see that relevant parts of Chapters 7, 8 and 9 have been considerably condensed. In Leake's original text these run to 125 pages compared with about 90 in this volume. The reason for this is that I have eliminated virtually all Leake's digressions concerning Pausanias' description of the Mani. Today's reader has several excellent translations of Pausanias available, Leake had only the original Greek.

Acknowledgements

This project would never have seen the light of day without the invaluable help of John Saumarez-Smith in locating, in almost pristine condition, a copy of the three volumes of Leake's *Travels in the Morea*. Subsequently, it was Roger Matthew's journalistic 'nose' for a story that persuaded me to follow in some of Leake's footsteps in the Peloponnese. Once a preliminary text had been written the late Fred Gearing made very pertinent suggestions based on his many years experience in the Outer Mani. I am sorry that he is no longer with us to see the final result. John Rendall's publishing qualifications, together with his wide knowledge of Greece, were of great help.

Marikaiti Georgota, Richard Marre and John Humphries patiently read the draft and offered much useful advice. My wife Jeswyn's superior skills in the English language helped to bring the text to its final shape and smooth over some rather rough edges. I also gratefully acknowledge the invaluable expert help of Joanna Bentley and her colleagues at Book Guild Publishing in bringing this book to fruition.

Figure 2 Map of Southern Peloponnese, *Travels in the Morea*

Chronology

The Mani and W. M. Leake

YEAR	Events
Circa 880 Basil I	Mani was pagan until evangelised by the Byzantine Emperor Basil I.
1204–1261	Latin Byzantine Empire.
1205 The Franks arrive after the fourth Crusade.	The Peloponnese conquered by 100 French and Burgundian knights. Established castles in the Mani at Beaufort (Stoupa), Tigani and Maina.
1259 Franks defeated by Byzantine army	Geoffrey de Villehardouin forced to give up his castles at Tigani, Maina and Mistras. The Mani reverts to Byzantine control with exception of Venetian outposts.
1320–1430 The entire Peloponnese under control of Palaeologian Despots	Mani governed from Mistras
1460 Turkish invasion	The Ottoman empire controls the Peloponnese with the exception of Venetian possessions.
1601 Spanish invasion	Aided by the Greek Orthodox Church a Spanish army occupies the Mani.
1614 Turks repulse the Spanish	The Capitain Pasha garrisons certain locations in the Mani and demands regular payments of tribute.
1685 Venetian invasion	Venetians conquer the Peloponnese and occupy the Mani.

1715 Turks return to the Peloponnese and expel the Venetians.	Mani placed under the nominal government of the Pasha of Morea, based in Tripoli.
1770 The Orloff uprising	Russian invasion (the Orlofica) of the Peloponnese, landing at Navarino, Nafplio, Patras and the Mani.
1776 Turks squash the rebellion with help from Albanian mercenaries.	Mani transferred to the direct control of the Kapitain Pasha. First Bey of Mani installed.
1777 The Mani given autonomy.	The Turks demand, in return, the payment of an annual tribute.
1777 William Henry Leake born 14 January, second son of John Martin Leake.	
1779 Turks expel Albanians.	Last of Albanian mercenaries driven out of the Peloponnese.
1786 French plans for the Balkans	The French foreign office contemplates the seizure of the Peloponnese.
1792 Leake enters Royal Military Academy, Woolwich as a Gentleman Cadet.	The French Revolution, monarchy deposed.
1794 Commissioned as 2nd Lieutenant in the Royal Artillery. Posted to Antigua.	
1795 Record of first English-speaking traveller in the Mani.	J.B.S. Morritt of Rokesby visits the Mani with the botanist Dr Sibthorp.
1797 Napoleon's interest in Greece	Napoleon, via the Treaty of Campo Formeo, gains joint control of the Ionian Islands with the Russians. Sends Dimo and Nicolo Stephanopoli to explore Greece, including the Mani.
1798 July. Leake returned to a posting at RMA Woolwich. October. Selected to join a Military Mission to Turkey. Promoted to brevet Captain. December. Leake posted to Istanbul.	July. French Army, with Napoleon, lands in Egypt. August, Nelson defeats French fleet at Abou Kir. The Military Mission, headed by Sir John Moore, sets out for Jaffa to support the Ottoman Empire against the French Army.

CHRONOLOGY

1799 2 April. Leake leaves Britain.
May. Napoleon quits Egypt.
14 June Leake arrives in Istanbul.

Russian/Turkish fleets seize Ionian Islands.

1800 18 January. Leake departs to join Turkish forces in Syria.
February, reaches Cyprus, Mission is cancelled and Leake ordered to return to Istanbul.
March. Leake falls ill with jaundice, unable to depart with Mission.
April. Sets off alone by sea for Istanbul.
June. Reaches Istanbul, finds Mission has left for Palestine.
October. Leake arrives in Jaffa.

French, at the convention of El Arish, agree to evacuate their forces from Egypt.

1801 May. Leake in command of 3 guns. Helps defeat of the French by Turkish army at Gaza.
11 July. Reaches Cairo with Military Mission.

January. Sir John Moore meets Grand Vizier in Jaffa.
February, Ottoman army launches attack on French army in Egypt.

1801/1802 Makes General Survey of Egypt.

1802 April. Sets out for Greece via Lebanon and Syria.
16 September. Leake sails from Piraeus with Elgin marbles. Shipwrecked off Kythira.

1803 Leake reaches London in January and is promoted to Lt. Colonel

Britain's war with France resumes. The French land gunpowder and lead for cannon balls at Gythio. The Turks capture Gythio to recover these armaments.

1804 April

John Philip Morier appointed by British government as Consul General for 'Albania, Morea and adjacent lands' and is based in Patras.

1804 July (?)

Morier arrives in Corfu to take up post and is briefed by Spiridon Foresti, whom he is replacing. Jack Morier, brother of John, meets Zanet Bey in Corfu. Foresti describes him as a great friend of the British.

1804 28 August, The PM, William Pitt
jnr, instructs Leake to make a
survey of the Peloponnese and N.
Greece.
September. Leake leaves on his
mission via Malta, Corfu and
Zakynthos.

1805 22 February, Leake sails from
Zakynthos for Gastuni and starts
his travels in the Morea.
30 May, reaches Patras at end of 1st
tour.
June, Leake moves to N. Greece to   October, Battle of Trafalgar, Nelson's
start his survey there and remains   death.
for rest of year.

1806 16 February, starts 2nd tour from
Patras.
Morea tour is complete by 5 April.
May, Leake returns to complete his
survey of N. Greece.

1807 February, Leake is imprisoned in   War breaks out between Britain and the
Salonika.   Turks.
12 November, Leake meets Ali   In Treaty of Tilsit the Russians cede rights
Pasha at Nicopolis.   to Ionian Isles to the British.

1808 Leake returns to England.
November. Leake leaves England
with artillery and stores for Ali
Pasha.

1809 February. Leake lands at Prevyza en   Byron meets Ali Pasha at Tepelene.
route for meeting with Ali Pasha.   Britain annexes Corfu and other Ionian
March. Leake has moved on to   Islands.
Ioannina.   Byron is visiting Ali Pasha, no record of
                                          him meeting Leake.

1810 Leake returns to England.

1860 6 January. Leake dies in Brighton, a
minister of Greek king attends
funeral.

Introduction

In mediaeval times the Peloponnese was referred to as the Morea. The name is derived from the Greek word for the mulberry leaf, since its outline is considered to resemble that of the Peloponnese. Leake retained this name although it was already going out of use at the time he was writing. The Mani is situated at the southern extremity of the middle peninsula which ends at Cape Matapan (nowadays known as Tenaro). A good description of the Mani and its coastline is found in a nineteenth century guide for those in yachts touring the Mediterranean '... a very forest of pinnacles, peak after peak, one pointed summit after another...culminates at last in the graceful spire of S. Elias that rises dominant over the whole of the southern Peloponnese. And if this range decreases in altitude towards the south, in wild grandeur it increases still, till in Cape Matapan it has a termination for precipitous boldness and savage desolation scarcely equalled in Europe. The character of the inhabitants of this wild region corresponds well with the scenery. Maina (the old name for the Mani), as it is called, has been for centuries the refuge of a race, half-patriot, half-brigand, in whom something of the character, as also of the language, of the ancient Sparta still survives.'[1]

---

[1] Playfair, Sir Robert Lambert, *Murray's Hand-Book to the Mediterranean* (London: John Murray, 1890): p.243.

1

There are several recorded visits to the Mani by Englishmen at the end of the eighteenth and in the first decade of the nineteenth century. This was mainly the result of the Napoleonic wars rendering travel in France and Italy (classic destinations for the Grand Tour), if not impossible, at least very difficult. As a result Greece became for the first time a preferred destination for young noblemen. Philhellenism had already in 1770 become, as William St Clair describes in his book[2], accepted as a self evident truth. He goes on: '...the conventions of the poets and the essayists were repeated in the travel books, and the ideas which had started life as literary conceits seemed to be confirmed by direct observation. Travelling in Greece was expensive and dangerous and the authors tended to regard themselves as belonging to a club. They drew shamelessly on their predecessors to eke out their own information and often devoted part of their book to discussing the inadequacies of their rivals. Only a few were equipped to make more than superficial observation and many indulged in sweeping generalizations on the strength of a few weeks' visit.' At that time there were two types of philhellenism, the classic variety and that of the 'romantic' movement which favoured revolution to bring about the independence of both Italy and Greece, and of which Byron was one of the most outspoken protagonists. This second group of travellers was motivated by the twin strands of classical archaeology along with a political interest in the current conditions of the Turkish domination and every day life in Greece.

Very few travellers in Greece had ventured as far as the Mani before Leake. One of the earliest recorded English visitors to the Mani was the Earl of Sandwich who in 1738 sailed round the

---

[2] St Clair, William, *That Greece Might Still Be Free, The Philhellenes in the War of Independence*, 2nd edition, Cambridge 2008.

coast of the Southern Peloponnese but never landed! The account of his travels was ghost written and not published until 1799. In April 1795 John Morritt of Rokeby in his tour of the Ottoman Empire had travelled to Kalamata, Kitries, Kardamyli, Oitylo and Gythio. There were two other English visitors that year, John Sibthorp, the famous Oxford botanist who with John Hawkins, a geologist, when travelling in Greece and Cyprus went into the Taygetos to collect plant specimens to complete his study of Greek flora. France, which had annexed neighbouring Kythera from the Venetians, was eyeing the Mani and Napoleon commissioned a visit to the Mani by Dimo and Nicolo Stephanopoli in 1797–98 to gain more information on local conditions.

Sir William Gell, a topographer and antiquarian, made two visits to the Peloponnese (1801–02 and 1805–06). In March 1805 he had been to Kalamata and Kitries, just one month before Leake's arrival there. It is highly probable that Gell and Leake later compared notes of their experiences. Of rather more significance, in relation to Leake's travels, was the journey made by John Philip Morier to Kalamata and Kitries from 30th April to 26th May 1804, just one year before Leake.[3] There is more than circumstantial evidence to suppose that Leake and Morier were working closely together and that they met both in Corfu and Patras in the period during Leake's travels. However, Leake was the first Western European traveller for several centuries to explore the Mani so thoroughly and to describe his travels with such a wealth of detail and observations. Another traveller was William Galt who recorded his travels across the Mediterranean over three years (1809, 1810 and 1811) and sailed into Gythio in 1810. He did not venture far into the Mani, but turned towards

---

[3] 'John Philip Morier's Account of the Mani, 1804' by J. M. Wagstaff, *Actes du Colloque, Limeni, Areopolis 4–7 Novembre 1993* (Athens: Institut de Recherches Néohelléniques, F.N.R.S., 1996).

Mistras, Sparta and Tripoli. William Galt gives a very vivid and lively account of life in Gythio but the most thorough and detailed visit to the Mani at that time was made by W. M. Leake.

William Martin Leake was born in 1777 to John Martin Leake in the family house in Mayfair, the second son in a family that would be described today as upper middle class. His grandfather had occupied an important post in the Admiralty and various relations had served in the army and navy. It was, therefore, not surprising that the young Leake should be enrolled as a gentleman cadet when he reached the age of 15 in the Royal Military Academy in Woolwich. This was the sole institution at that time for the training of professional army officers. Two years later at the age of 17 Leake was commissioned as 2nd Lieutenant in the Royal Artillery and was sent to the West Indies for his first posting. He spent four years in the tropics before returning in July 1798 to a posting at Woolwich.

The year 1798 was one of the turning points in the Napoleonic wars and also a turning point in Leake's career. Contrary to popular belief, Napoleon had never seriously intended to invade the British Isles. As a ruse to foster this belief he had made a widely reported visit to Boulogne-sur-Mer where he was said to have gazed over the Channel. In fact, the French, since pre-revolutionary times, were planning to dislodge Britain's hold on India. A minutely prepared plan was finally put into effect in the spring of 1798.[4] Napoleon set sail from Toulon on 19th May with an impressive fleet of seventeen warships, eight frigates and an armada of other vessels carrying 40,000 troops, the élite of the French army. The destination was Alexandria and Egypt, where (with the agreement of the Turks) the French planned to launch an attack on India via the Red Sea.

---

[4] See François Charles-Roux, *L'Angleterre et l'Expédition Française en Egypte*, (Cairo: Royal Egyptian Geographic Society, 1925).

The French troops reached Alexandria on 1st July 1798 having, en route, captured Malta. This move took the Prime Minister (then William Pitt the younger) and the British government virtually by surprise. But luckily the Navy was blockading Cadiz, commanded by Admiral Jarvis, and Nelson, under his command, had a fleet of warships in the western Mediterranean shadowing the French fleet based in Toulon. Exactly one month later on 1st August Nelson took six hours to destroy the French fleet at anchor in Abou Kir bay, near Alexandria. When the news finally reached London on 1st October Nelson was made a lord and given an annual pension of £2,000 per year. Upon hearing of this victory the Turks immediately declared war on France and became allies of the British!

To counter the presence of Napoleon's land forces now established in Egypt, an Army Military Mission, headed by Brigadier General Koehler, was formed to give support to the Ottoman Empire. The Mission precipitately left Britain in December 1798 for Constantinople. Leake, as a rising and promising professional soldier with artillery experience, had been appointed to join the Mission in October 1798 with the rank of brevet Captain. He had just celebrated his 21st birthday. But it was only in April 1799 that Leake was able to join the Mission in Constantinople with the rearguard party of the force. Napoleon meanwhile was hemmed into Egypt with his army and, rapidly conquering Egypt and advancing into Syria, on 16th March 1799 his army laid siege to Acre which was in Turkish hands. Just two months later Napoleon abandoned the siege and retreated to Cairo. Shortly after this he deserted his army in Egypt and fled with a few officers for France.

On 19th January 1800 Leake, with the Military Mission, headed by Sir John Moore, left Constantinople to join Turkish forces in Syria by way of Cyprus. But on arriving in Cyprus in

February the Mission was cancelled and the troops returned to Constantinople. However, Leake had contracted jaundice and was unable to return. He stayed on in Cyprus until he recovered, then made his own way back to Constantinople by land and sea, only to find that the Mission had already departed for Palestine! He immediately set out again and by October had reached Jaffa.

The Ottoman army moved onto the offensive on 25th February 1801 against the French army led by General Kleber. Leake was put in command of three guns and participated in the defeat of the French at Gaza. Three months later, under further Ottoman attack, the French fell back and evacuated their forces from Egypt. On 11th July 1801 Leake arrived in Cairo with the British Mission and was quartered in the house used previously by the French to house their Institut d'Égypte. Leake was charged with making a General Survey of Egypt with Richard William Hamilton, a diplomat who had been secretary to Lord Elgin, the British ambassador in Constantinople. The next eight months were spent very pleasantly exploring Egypt, gathering information for this survey. In April 1802, the survey of Egypt complete, Leake made his way through the Lebanon, Syria and Asia Minor to Greece, accompanied by Hamilton (in 1833 Hamilton became one of the founding members of the Royal Geographical Society). The latter had already made his reputation whilst in Egypt when, in 1801, he had discovered that the French were trying to smuggle the Rosetta stone out of the country and had boarded a French boat to recover it.

It was on this trip through Asia Minor that Leake formed the habit of writing a journal of his travels. After the summer in Athens, Leake joined Hamilton, still the secretary of Lord Elgin, who had requested his employee to escort to Britain the famous marbles from the acropolis in Athens. On 19th September both Hamilton and Leake sailed in the brigantine *Mentor* from Piraeus

for England carrying a cargo of antiquities collected by Lord
Elgin in Egypt, Turkey and Greece. Among these were the
marbles, packed in seventeen cases. The vessel encountered a
storm off Cape Malea and sought shelter in the bay of Avole-
mona on the neighbouring island of Kythera but foundered there.
Luckily, there was no loss of life but the Elgin marbles went to
the bottom of the sea. Sixteen of the cases were later recovered
intact by Hamilton, who ensured that they were safely trans-
ported to England together with his text of the Survey of Egypt;
sadly, however, Leake's diaries of his journey through Asia Minor
were lost in the wreck. Nevertheless, Leake was able to rewrite an
account of the journey, and meanwhile made his own way back to
Britain overland by way of Trieste, Venice and Paris.

In 1803 we find Leake back in London, having been promoted
to the rank of Lt. Colonel, and involved with military intelligence
and diplomacy. Britain's war with France had resumed in 1804
and the Foreign Office obtained intelligence from Paris that the
French were actively looking towards the Balkans and working to
gain a foothold in Southern Greece after Napoleon's set back in
the Near East. Napoleon circulated a false story that his ancestors
had come from Oitylo before fleeing to Corsica. He even went so
far as to send two agents to the Mani, Dimo Stephanopoli and his
nephew, whom he asked to deliver a letter to Tzanet Bey, the
Maniot leader, replying to his appeal for French support in
overthrowing Turkish domination. The Stephanopoli were also
required to gather information on both the Mani and the Epirus,
in the event that French troops were landed in either of these
regions. The account of their two missions was 'ghost written' by
a certain Professor A. Sérieys and then published[5] in Paris and

[5] Stephanopoli, Dimo, *Voyage de Dimo et Nicolo Stephanopoli en Grèce pendant les années 1797 et 1798*, (Paris, 1800).

7

London in 1800 entitled *Travels in Greece*![6] There was consternation in Whitehall that Britain had virtually no knowledge of the geography of Greece apart from the Royal Navy maritime charts which were concerned only with coastal areas. As a result, in instructions dated 28th August 1804 issued by the prime minister (William Pitt the younger), Col. Leake was despatched on a topographical reconnaissance to Greece. He was also desired to take all the note he could of sites of classical interest, consistent with the objectives of his mission.

In September 1804 Leake left Britain not only with this remit but also with instructions from the Foreign Office to treat with the governors of European Turkey and encourage them to defend their frontiers against the French. He visited first Malta and then Corfu, where he was briefed on the current situation in Greece. After a short stop in Zakynthos, Leake arrived in the Peloponnese at Kylini near Gastouni on the 22nd February 1805 and started the mammoth task of travelling on horseback throughout the Morea and Northern Greece. His remit was to describe the terrain, noting rivers, towns and possible harbours, in order to allow maps to be prepared for the eventuality of a military campaign in the country. Leake was given every facility by the occupying Turks to travel where he wished. One senses that this is a task Leake relished, both from the aspect of his military training and also from his great interest in classical history. Greece had already become a focus of interest for antiquarians and there was a great move to collect ancient artefacts. Leake saw this as a heaven-sent opportunity to become a leading expert on Greek remains and to solve many of the puzzles that existed at that time in pinpointing the sites described in classical texts (in

---

[6] *Handbook for Travellers in Greece,* 5th Edition (John Murray, London, 1884) p. 495.

particular, Pausanias's travels across Greece in second century AD).

Further evidence of the potential French interest in the Peloponnese is given by Leake soon after he arrived there in March 1805. He was travelling from Kyparissia (on the west coast of the Peloponnese) to Tripolis. On an overnight halt he met a Turk who, on learning that Leake was freshly arrived, asked him for the latest news, having already learnt that the French fleet had set out. Leake recounts: '. . .the Turks of the Morea are conscious of their weakness and are excessively alarmed lest the French should endeavour to excite an insurrection of the Greeks and make a landing for that purpose in the Peninsula; and this fear acting on their cruel disposition renders (them) capable of committing any excesses against the Greeks, who are therefore as much alarmed at such reports as the Turks themselves.'[7]

Leake had completed his first tour of the Peloponnese by the end of May at Patras and immediately started his tour of Northern Greece. However, he fell seriously ill in November 1805 but recovered and returned to Patras on his second tour of the Peloponnese in February 1806. This tour was completed by the end of April when Leake then went on to make his second tour of Northern Greece. This occupied the next six months, after which he returned to England and submitted the diaries of his travels to the Government.

Now with the reputation of being a fully fledged Greek expert, Leake found himself back in the Balkans very shortly. Just at that moment hostilities broke out between the Turks and Britain. Leake was in Salonika at the time and was taken prisoner by the Turks, who had by now allied themselves with the French. He was held for several months. On being released he rapidly

---

[7] Volume 1, p. 80.

returned home and was immediately given a new mission. By late November 1808 he was leaving London for Greece with supplies of ammunition and stores destined for Ali Pasha, an Albanian who was appointed by the Turks to control Albania and Northern Greece, Leake's task being to negotiate with Ali Pasha in order to gain his confidence and ask him to persuade the Turks to move towards some form of reconciliation with Britain.

Leake remained in Greece a further two years and was in Ioannina at the same time that Byron and his companions were being received by Ali Pasha. It is not recorded whether or not the two actually met but it seems highly probable. Leake returned to Britain in 1810, was promoted to the rank of major and awarded, at the age of 33, a handsome pension of £600 per year.

With his military duties now over and the journal of his various Greek journeys handed over to the Foreign Office, Leake appears to have had time to start writing. His first book on his Greek experiences was *Researches in Greece*, which dealt with the then current Greek language; this appeared in 1814, whilst a more substantial work, *The Topography of Athens*, was published by John Murray in 1821. Leake was anxious for the report of his two major Greek journeys to be printed. However, it appears that the move to seek independence for Greece had resulted in a rush of books about that country appearing on the market. Murray advised him to re-work the text to provide more background on the antiquities. This was no mean task and it took Leake nearly fifteen years to deliver the text of his two major works to the publishers: *Travels in the Morea* from Murray in 1830 and *Travels in Northern Greece* from J. Rodwell in 1835 – both works in several volumes!

Leake's final military duty occurred in 1815 when he was recalled to active service. Following the Treaty of Fontainebleau Napoleon had escaped from exile on Elba and the war with

France moved into its final phases. Leake was sent in May 1815 to the headquarters of the Swiss Confederation where he acted as a liaison officer with the Swiss army in Geneva and Lausanne. He reported to the British government on the status of the Swiss army and its defences, wrote a survey of his findings and returned to Britain in January 1816, finally terminating his military service in 1823.

As Peter Greenhalgh so aptly describes, Leake '...when not looking at his watch was a keen observer of the country, its society and customs, and a shrewd judge of character with a good ear for an anecdote. He was also no mean archaeologist, and if he seems to have a blind spot for the wealth of Mani's Byzantine heritage, he went everywhere with a copy of Pausanias and scoured the country for classical remains with a thoroughness that would have done justice to a professional scholar.'[8] Peter Levi, in his translation of Pausanias is even more complimentary about Leake's endeavours: '...but the only writer so far as I know ever to have covered the whole of the ground that Pausanias covered in Greece was the greatest of all Greek travel writers and topographic scholars, Colonel William Leake, who was seconded to the Turkish government to inspect the defences of Greece between 1804 and 1809 ... his *Morea* is required reading for students of Pausanias.'[9]

---

[8] *Deep into Mani, A Journey to the Southern Tip of Greece*, Peter Greenhalgh and Edward Eliopoulos (Faber and Faber, London 1985).
[9] *Guide to Greece, Volume 2: Southern Greece*, Pausanias, (Penguin Books, 1971) p.503.

1

A Brief History of the Mani Prior to Leake's Visit

Before following Leake on his travels in the Mani it is helpful to understand how the Maniots were governed by the occupying Turks. The Peloponnese had been under Turkish rule since the fall of Mistras in 1461, save for two brief periods in the seventeenth and eighteenth centuries (see Chronology). Murray's *Handbook for Travellers in Greece*[1] in its outline of Greek history explains that '…the Greeks were not wholly devoid of landed property, and their Church also, whose hierarchy was sometimes, from matters of policy, rather courted than persecuted by the conquerors, retained part of its ancient possessions. Under Turkish supervision and control all influence was in the hands of the higher clergy and of this landed class; they like the *headman* of the villages in India, regulated the local affairs of the districts in which they resided. By the Turks they were styled *Khoja-bashis* (meaning respected teachers or scribes) and by the Greeks, *Archons* or *Primates*. They adopted many Turkish customs; and the oppression which they exercised over their own countrymen was sometimes more galling than that of the Turkish functionaries.'

The Mani played a pivotal role during the Turkish war with

---

[1] Fifth edition, (London, John Murray, 1884).

13

Russia that ran from 1768 until 1774 during the reign of Catherine the Great. Preparations for a revolt in Greece to overthrow Turkish domination began in July 1762, almost immediately after Catherine came to the throne following the abdication of her husband, Tsar Peter III (Peter the Great's grandson), on 28th June of that year. Peter III was held in the Palace of Ropsha on the outskirts of St Petersburg, but on the 17th July he died in mysterious circumstances. He was widely believed to have been assassinated by Count Alexis Orlov, assisted by a Greek, Georgios Papazolis, then an officer with the Russian artillery. It was Papazolis who gave Catherine the idea of inciting a Greek revolt as part of the Russian plan to seize control of a strategic area of the Balkans from the Turks.

Four years later Papazolis was travelling through Greece disguised as a Turk using a false Turkish name. He finally reached Oitylo where he hoped to land Russian forces, raising Greek aspirations for a revolt with extravagant promises of Russian support. The Mavromikhali family were much more cautious and did their best to discourage him. As they pointed out to Papazolis the Maniot clans were riven by disagreements; although the Maniots were excellent fighters in defence they were quite unsuitable as a disciplined attacking force.

Two years later, in 1768, war between Turkey and Russia had broken out. The Counts Alexis and Theodore Orlov received leave of absence as officers in the Russian army on the ostensible grounds of ill-health. In fact, they were given instructions to lead a Greek revolt. Their first port of call was Venice, to raise money from wealthy Greek merchants there. The Venetian authorities were loth to antagonise the Turks and forbade the recruiting of volunteers by the Orlovs. In January 1769 Theodore Orlov was appointed by Catherine to command the Greek uprising. At the same time she ordered the First Minister of her government to send a letter to Georgakis Mavromikhali giving her 'total support, unsparing compassion, protection and companionship' to free the Greeks from the yoke of the infidel enemies.

The original plan was to send three Russian fleets to Greece. The first fleet of 19 ships left Russia in July 1769 but was woefully ill-equipped and poorly manned, so much so that it was forced to call into an English port for repairs and re-fitting. Six months later, in January 1770, nine remaining ships reached Minorca where Theodore Orlov joined the expedition. Theodore was so anxious to proceed that he immediately left port with only part of this very reduced fleet and sailed directly for the Mani.

The first Russian ship, with Theodore Orlov on board, reached Oitylo bay on 28th February to be greeted by a welcoming fusillade of Maniot gunfire which lasted for 24 hours! The remaining ships arrived the next day and it is reported that 600 Russian soldiers disembarked. It all started well with the Maniot fighters swearing an oath of allegiance to Tsarina Catherine before being put under the command of Russian officers and issued with Russian uniforms which they wore before going into action. This had a very positive effect as the Turks in the two fortresses of Kelefa and Passava fled the Mani at the sight of all these 'Russians'.

The Russian expeditionary force then split in various directions across the southern Peloponnese, gaining Mistras and Navarino and besieging Koroni. Further advances took them to Patras, Nauplio and the outskirts of Tripolis. After this initial success the Turks, who had been totally unprepared to counter this invasion, called on Albanian mercenaries to push back the invaders. Ten thousand Albanians arrived in the Peloponnese. Now the tide turned against the Russian as this augmented force moved south to re-impose Turkish control. Bands of Maniot fighters in several fierce battles put up a brave resistance but were overwhelmed; the

Albanians overran the Mani. This dream of liberating Greece from the Turks was over in less than six months.

Leake describes this insurrection as a 'vain and cruel attempt'. The Turkish response was led by Kapitain Pasha Hassan Seremet, admiral of the Turkish Aegean, sent from Constantinople to quell this insurrection. With him was, rather confusingly, another Hassan who remained in charge once the uprising was quelled. This campaign was explained by Leake, after he had met Hassan Bey in Monemvasia in the following manner: 'Hassan Bey marched from Marathonisi which had been taken by the Pasha, across the *Taygetum* to Kitries, where he shut up several of the Kapitanei in a tower, and forced them to a capitulation. The Greeks, who rose in consequence of Orlov's proceedings, are stated by Hassan Bey to have committed the greatest cruelties against the Turks... The Albanians, who entered the Morea on this occasion numbered, according to Hassan 15,000. They themselves, alarmed at the greater number of their countrymen that were following to share in the plunder, and supported by the Turkish government in their determination to admit no more, stationed parties at the Isthmus, with orders to prevent any more Albanians from entering the peninsula.'

When the insurrection had been quelled, and peace made with Russia, the Albanians, who had committed and were continuing to commit the greatest excesses, were ordered to return home; but repeated firmans having failed to produce obedience to this order, Hassan Bey accompanied the Kapitain Pasha Hassan Seremet in his expedition against them. They were totally defeated and a pyramid of the heads of the captured Albanians was made near Tripolitza. Some survivors joined old colonies of their countrymen at Lalla and Bardhunia, others entered into the service of the Pasha: only a few returned to Albania. Hassan Bey's account of his wars in Mani is very amusing. It seldom happened,

16

he says, that when he wished to destroy a village, he could not find some neighbouring village to assist him in the work, generally under the guidance of a priest, upon condition of the latter having the stones of the ruins for a perquisite. Their own (i.e. the Maniots') civil wars, Hassan says, are seldom very bloody, and months may pass without a single man being killed on either side. The women carry ammunition for their husbands or brothers, and it is a point of honour among the men not to fire at their opponents' womenfolk. To shew the respect in which Hassan Bey's name is held in the Mani, he shews me a poetical effusion which he has just received from thence, and in which he is described as gifted with every possible virtue. 'Poetry and piracy seem to be indigenous plants that will never be eradicated from Greece.'

The result of the Orlov uprising was that the Maniots were forced to submit to a much more rigorous Turkish domination. Up until then, apart from holding garrisons in the fortresses of Keleva and Passava, the Turks as masters of Greece had made little or no attempt to curb Maniot independence. This was due partly to the isolated nature of the Mani; the Turks had not considered it worth the effort needed to restrain the unruly Maniots over such savage terrain. They had not even insisted on the 15 purses as annual tribute. In contrast to the massacre and persecution of the Greeks in other parts of the Peloponnese the Turkish demands of the Maniots were more than surprisingly moderate. The heads of the Maniot clans were required to nominate one of their number as leader, or Bey, and submit this nomination to the Porte in Constantinople for its approval.

Following the Orlov insurrection Hassan Bey was given direct control of the Mani. The Porte in Constantinople transferred to him responsibility for maintenance of law and order and tax collection in the Mani. The Sultan gave Hassan Bey to maintain his galley, the sum of 12,000 piastres per year, 100 cantars of biscuits and 10 cantars of powder.[2] He had held this post for over 30 years. On 28th March a few weeks previously Leake had had the opportunity of personally meeting Hassan Bey when visiting Monemvasia. Hassan Bey's warship (equipped with twelve guns and employing fifteen pairs of oars) was stationed there for the purpose of clearing the Southern Peloponnese coasts of pirates and, more particularly, of preserving the Mani in what Leake describes as its present orderly state. Hassan Bey, besides his role as admiral in charge, was also governor of the fortress of Monemvasia and *voivoda*[3] of the district.

Leake remarks that Hassan Bey is not a little proud of his exploits against the Maniots, claiming not to have left them a single *tratta* to carry out their piratical depredations. Two of these captured Maniot galleys, similar in construction to the Turkish ones, could be seen by Leake lying drawn up on the beach alongside the causeway leading from the mainland to the entrance of Monemvasia. He also affirmed to Leake that he had blown up 18 Maniot castles and destroyed almost as many villages. He then goes on to relate how only a few months earlier, late in 1803, he had captured Gythio. A French brig-of-war had landed at Gythio 90 cantars of powder (in barrels of 400 okes) as well as 40 cantars of shot. Hassan Bey had fired a prodigious amount of shot onto Gythio before landing and capturing this ammunition. Apparently, the French vessel had escaped this bombardment and sailed on to Crete to land further undercover ammunition. There as well the French plans were foiled, however, since the Turkish governor of Chania had seized this illegal cargo.

The current Kapitain Pasha in Leake's time was still Seremet

---

[2] 1 Cantar = 44 okes.
[3] Voivoda = regional governor.

Pasha who had made the Maniots submit to a treaty. Firstly, the Maniots had to agree to being governed by a Bey (whom they would be allowed to choose) but who had to be approved by the Porte. Secondly, they were obliged to pay annual tributes of 30 purses[4] to the Porte and 5 purses to the Kapitain-Pasha. Leake does not specify whether the purses were silver and gold. One presumes the former as a gold purse had sixty times the value of a silver one. Table 1 lists the Maniot Beys from 1766 until the start of the Greek war of independence.

Table 1 The Beys of Mani (1776–1821)[5]

A summary of the Beys of Mani following the failed 'Russian Insurgence' in 1770, when Kapitain Hassan Bey was named governor of the Mani.

	From	To
Zanetos Koutipharis (of Zanata, appointed by Hassoun)	1776	1779
Michael Troupakis (of Kardamyli and Androuvista)	1779	1782 (beheaded)
Zanetbey Grikorakis (of Mavrovouni)	1783	1798
Paneyotis Koumondourakis (of Kitries)	1799	1803
Antonobey Grikorakis (nephew of Zanetbey)	1803	1808
Konstantinos Zervakos Bey (son-in-law of Antonobey)	1808	1810
Thodorosbey Zanetakis (also son-in-law of Antonobey)	1810	1815
Petrobey Mavromichalis (of Tzimova)	1815	1821

John Koutipharis was nominated as the first Bey, but he died three years later of natural causes, and was succeeded by Michael Trubaki (or Mourtzinos) of Kardamyli in 1779. His appointment was contested by certain ambassadors to the Porte, who accused

---

[4] 1 purse of silver = 500 piastres, equivalent in Leake's time to £10. 1 piastre = 5 pence.
[5] *Mani: Travels in the Southern Peloponnese*, Patrick Leigh Fermor, London 1958, p.49.

him of owning a *tratta* (pirate vessel) which had made depredations upon European vessels. Michael Trubaki had not sufficient money to offer bribes (or as Leake diplomatically puts it 'to prevent the effects of the complaint') so the Kapitain-Pasha came to the Mani and took him on board his ship. He was then taken to Mytilene, where he was beheaded in 1782. It was at this point that Ioannis Grikoraki (better known as Tzanet Bey) was appointed for his very energetic 15-year-long reign. On Tzanet Bey's removal Panayiotis Koumoundourakis, a Messenian of Kitries, who had been the one (not unjustly) to accuse him of his alliance with the French, was made Bey. He and Tzanet Bey had been at war for the previous 15 years!

Koumoundourakis's reign lasted seven years until the Turks deposed him. In 1802 he was shipped to Constantinople and subsequently died in the *Bagnio*. The reason for his disgrace and downfall was quite simply piracy! This came about as follows. The brother of the future Bey, Petro Mavromikhali, was returning to the Mani from Livorno, sailing on what Leake describes as an *Imperial* vessel. Also on board were a crew of Maniot seamen, rescued when their ship foundered sailing to Livorno. The Austrian crew were overpowered by the Maniots, who then took command and subsequently sailed the ship back to the Mani. Koumoundourakis's offence was that he had taken a share of the booty (or plunder) from the captured vessel.

In 1798 Tzanet Bey (after his appeal to Napoleon) had arranged with the French to supply him with significant amounts of gunpowder and lead for shot and cannonballs. This material was landed at Gythio but quickly came to the attention of the Turks who brought up their squadron of warships offshore and bombarded the town with a prodigious amount of shot. But Tzanet Bey was determined to withstand this siege. Another member of the Grigoraki clan, Dimetrios, (nephew of Andon

Grigoraki) arrived in Gythio to give him assistance. He was nicknamed the Russian knight (literally the 'Cavaliere from Moscow'). As soon as the Cavaliere saw the situation he persuaded Tzanet Bey that the wisest course of action was to surrender the town to the Turks. This he did, whereupon the Turks forced Tzanet Bey to relinquish his Beydom and banished him to Vakho, his birthplace, 20kms west of Gythio. He died in 1813 at the age of 71.

That Leake's arrival was not entirely unconnected with these events can be surmised by the fact that it had been planned for him to take lodgings in Tzanet Bey's house, which had been taken over by Andon Bey until his new pyrgos[6] was ready for occupation. More evidence of Tzanet Bey's contact with the French is that his eldest son, Petro Bey Zande, had been sent with a letter for Napoleon in 1796. Petro had delivered this to Napoleon in Trieste and then remained in France for three years and only recently returned, was dressed 'à la française' and speaking both French and Italian. Petro was well respected (more so than his father) and lived in Kastania in the Exo or Outer Mani. He was seen as the white hope of the Greek resistance to the Turks.

Having filled in the background of Maniot politics one can now concentrate on Leake's travels in the Mani. It should be borne in mind that he started this, his first tour of the Peloponnese, on 23rd February 1805. In the next five weeks he had covered some 500 kilometres, from Gastouni in the far north west of the Peloponnese, down to Pyrgos and Kipirissia, across to Tripoli, into Arcadia and past Sparta as far as Monemvasia, before retracing his steps to Mistras on 25th March. Thence he travelled on to Gythio and the Mani.

---

[6] Pyrgos – a tower.

21

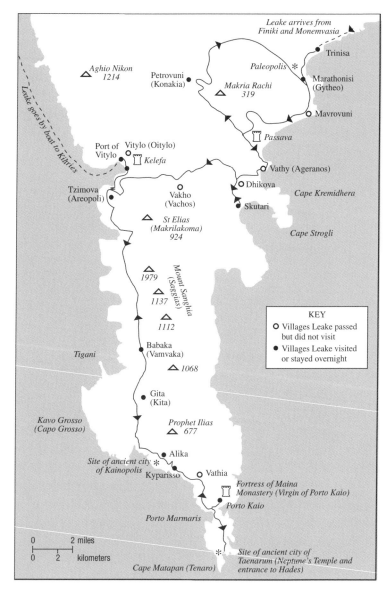

Figure 3   Sketch map showing Leake's route in the Mani

22

2

Laconian Mani (Volume 1, pp. 232–50)

Leake arrived in Gythio on April 3, 1805 at 11.20 a.m. Earlier in the morning he had crossed the Eurotas without dismounting (the waters, neither rapid nor deep, only reached his stirrups). After passing through the village of Limona (consisting solely of mud huts) Leake, unusually for him, stopped for ten minutes to examine a church and to collect a guide. He then struck out for the sea, and crossed a rivulet and rode along the beach until at 8.48 a.m.[1] he reached a rocky outcrop with the ruins of a castle above the shore. This he identified as the boundary of Elos (Laconian territory) with the Mani.

At 09.05 a.m. Leake reached Trinisia which consisted of four houses and a ruined pyrgos (recently destroyed by the Turkish navy under Seremet and Hassan) overlooking the rocky shore and opposite three large rocks in the sea. This site is easily recognised today when taking the road along the coast from Gythio to Skala. The village head, a certain Anagnosti Kritira (Leake does not indicate if he is Greek or Turkish), had been warned by letter from Hassan Bey of Leake's arrival. Kritira had

---

[1] Throughout his text Leake records very precisely the actual time of arrival at any place. He presumably carried on horseback with him both watch and writing materials in order to keep an accurate record of the time for each stage of his travels.

then taken the trouble to bring refreshments from Gythio in order to greet him.

The welcome ceremony lasted a mere twelve minutes! The party was then on the move again at 9.17 along the beach. A further halt of 20 minutes was spent examining the ruins of ancient *Trinasus*. Leake describes the walls as 400–500 yards around and agrees with Pausanias' comment that it was more a fortress than a town.

Leake leaves these ruins at 9.48 a.m. and follows the shoreline until at 10.45 a.m. he encounters a stream draining the marshes behind the coast. This stream is still visible on the Gythio-Skala road. Ten minutes later, passing under cliffs, Leake remarks on a copious stream flowing into a cistern, the outlet a stone conduit which then runs for one-third of a mile to a mill (figure 1). Leake then crosses the valley of *Gythium* leaving some ruins on his right and climbs a bare, rocky hill at the foot of which is Marathonisi (Gythio). The time is now 11.20 a.m.

Gythio and its Recent History

He finds the town consisting of only 100 wretched mud-brick houses. Leake insists that the present town of Gythio was largely built by Tzanet Bey and that much of the stone work came from the extensive earlier Roman settlement. The one building of distinction is the large church with spire and bell tower in the middle of the town. Above the town a new pyrgos was being constructed for Andon Bey (appointed two years before as Bey of Mani) who was making his base in Gythio. In fact, just two hours after Leake's arrival Andon Bey's corvette, which is part of Seremet Bey's Turkish squadron, drops anchor in the harbour and Andon Bey comes ashore, shortly followed by Seremet Bey

Figure 4 Vue de Marathonisi

himself. Leake describes Andon Bey as an unhealthy looking Greek of a weak character, easily made to change his purpose by those around him.

This arrival must have been unexpected as arrangements had been made for Leake to be lodged in the house of Tzanet Bey, which he describes as the best in Gythio. Leake thus had to be re-lodged in the more modest house of Mr W., a Hungarian doctor from Buda who was the resident physician. The doctor is paid six piastres a day to attend the Bey, his family and other persons of Gythio who can afford to contribute to his stipend. Leake describes the house as very simple, having living quarters on the ground floor, properly so called as the floor was bare earth! Above is an upper story divided into two parts by a slender partition. The house had lost part of the roof and one wall, a result of the previously mentioned Turkish naval attack by Seremet and Hassan.

Another incident involving the French and the Maniots had occurred ten days prior to Leake's arrival. A Monsieur P.L. arrived from Hydra on a boat that he had expressly chartered for the purpose. On landing, he enquired for Tzanet Bey, which prompted Andon Bey to search his effects for any relevant papers relating to this visit. Special care was taken to ensure that he had no chance to visit Tzanet Bey. When no incriminating papers were found on him, he was allowed to depart for Koroni. The doctor, this Mr W., who was present when the Frenchman was searched, had spied a *rouleau* of money in his belt which was not discovered by the searchers.

Leake then goes on to describe the five nephews of Andon Bey who were introduced to him and the relationship of various members of the Grigoraki clan whom Leake meets. The aforementioned Grigoraki was the eldest nephew, followed by Constantino Tzigurio from Skutari. Tzigurio made a great impression on Leake: he was tall, hard featured with impressive mustachios whose tips almost touched his shoulders, and armed with a belt containing a dagger plus two pistols of immense length. Leake states that Tzigurio was the greatest hero in the Mani.

Next in age was Katzano Ianiki, also from Skutari, who stood in as commander in Andon Bey's absences. The two younger nephews, Giorgio and Lambro, came from Vathy. Leake was further honoured by the visit of Andon Bey's two sons-in-law, Theodoro Gligoraki of Mavrovouni (close by Gythio) and Constantine Zervakos of Petrovouni. A further visitor was a cousin of Andon Bey, one Dhimitraki also from Mavrovouni. Leake describes these visitors as being civil but rather embarrassed, lacking a natural ease and politeness, which he put down to their (Maniot) upbringing, comparing the Maniot behaviour unfavourably with the more pleasant manners of the other Greeks and the Turks.

Tzanet Bey, though dispossessed of his powers, continued his revolutionary activities and the majority of the Maniots would have welcomed his restoration. Andon Bey held onto power with the support of the Turks and the presence of their naval squadron. Nevertheless, the Maniot kapitanos, though sworn enemies of Andon Bey, obey his orders. The most powerful kapitanos were in the region of Cape Matapan and along the coast from Oitylo to Kardamyli. The kapitanos of Kardamyli had only recently been brought to order by Dimitrios Glikoraki (the Cavaliere), who governed Kitries in Andon Bey's absence and, some said, also in his presence.

The Inhabitants of Gythio and their Trade

The principal inhabitants are Greek and they are agents or family relations of the important Greek families still living in Mistras. Leake encounters P., whose brother he had met at Mistras. P. has lived the last ten years in Gythio; previously he was in Livorno and speaks Italian. His main occupation is lending small sums of money to the peasants at an exorbitant rate of interest. He recovers these advances from the peasants' harvest of vallonea[2] (velanidi), paying them about 13 to 14 piastres[3] per 10 cwt[4] which is brought down to Gythio from the Taygetos.

As the Bey has the monopoly on the export of all the vallonea P. had been forced to sell all his product at a fixed price to Andon Bey. The price for 1805 was fixed at 20 piastres per 10 cwt. So P. only makes a margin of 6 or 7 piastres. However Andon Bey has been forced to pay so much tax to the Porte that he has had to go back to P. for financial assistance! This is arranged by allowing P. to buy back the vallonea at a price of 25 piastres and set the difference of 5 piastres against the debt he owes P.! P. then is free to export the crop at about 35 piastres per 10 cwt. Annually 3 million pounds of vallonea were exported from Greece, and the Maniot valonea is generally one third higher in price in the European market. A greater part of it went to England. This valuable export from the Mani was in the hands of three Greek brothers, one in Ioannina, one in Livorno and the third in Gythio.

As Leake comments, if Andon Bey's financial affairs were not

---

[2] Vallonea are the acorns from the Valonia oak (*Quercus macrolepsis*), these edible acorns are the largest in the Mediterranean and were employed in tanning and making inks; in times of famine they were used as food.

[3] 20 piastres were worth approximately £1 in 1805, which in today's money makes 1 piastre worth approximately £5.

[4] Leake quotes the Greek/Turkish measure of milliaja, 1 milliaja = 10 cwt.

in such a muddle he would have been a rich man making 15 piastres per 10 cwt on a crop that costs him nothing. There is no outlay for cultivation and, with no pests, only August rains (which are rare) can spoil the crop.

The Economy of the Mani

Leake calculated roughly that the annual exports from the Mani had a value of £40,000. Andon Bey holds the monopoly of olive oil and vallonea and fixes the export price of both these products. All other exports carry a duty of 3%, paid to the Bey. As mentioned previously, the Kharatj of Mani, the tax levied on the inhabitants, amounts to a total of 17,500 piastres annually, of which 15,000 piastres goes to the Porte and 2,500 piastres to the Kapitain-Pasha of the Peloponnese. The right to collect customs on imports into the Mani is sold annually to the highest bidder in each port. In Gythio in 1805 it was sold by Andon Bey to a Greek for 2,000 piastres.

In good years the Mani will produce between 8,000 and 10,000 barrels of olive oil (1 barrel contains 48 okes[5]). The majority of the oil is produced on the west coast of the Mani between Oitylo and Kalamata. This oil is reckoned to be of better quality that that of Athens or Salona (Leake presumably means Thessaloniki) and is exported to the Black Sea, Italy and Trieste. In the past the Mani was a large producer of cotton but the yield has recently fallen to a third of the former amount due to civil strife and lack of industry on the part of the peasants. The cotton is sent to the Ionian Islands and the Archipelago (Aegean).

Two thousand okes of silk is produced for export to Mistras,

---

[5] 1 oke = 2.705 lbs = 1.25 kg.

the Islands, Livorno and Barbary. Together with Bardhunia, on the eastern slopes of the Taygetos, the Mani produces 20,000 okes of galls (vallonea). Honey is another major product with two crops per year, one in winter and one in summer. A total of 10,000 okes of honey is sent to Constantinople, Crete and the Islands while the wax goes to Livorno. Leake decribes the form of beehive used by the Maniots with each hive consisting of four slates set upon their edges with other pieces for roof and floor, cemented with plaster. These stand with eight or ten in a row and with two or three storeys. At a distance the structure looks like a wall built of very large stones. A few of these derelict hives can still be found in hidden corners of Mani villages.

A more exotic product were the quails captured around Cape Matapan and, more especially, in Porto Kayio. These birds that migrate from the North African coast to Europe were netted, salted, packed into bags of lamb skins and exported in Leake's time[6] to the Islands and Constantinople. Two shiploads of horse beans were sent annually to Italy.

The Administration of the Mani

The Mani, as Leake found it, is divided into three parts: Outer, Lower and Inner. Outer Mani in the north stretches from the frontier at Kalamata to Kortasia 80 kilometres further south, the peaks of the Taygetos forming a natural boundary on the east. Outer Mani has about 50 towns and villages and is sub-divided into the following four regions: Zanarta, Andruvista, Zygos and Milea.

---

[6] Prior to Turkish rule the Venetians had salted and exported all the quails to Venice.

Zanarta, the most northerly, adjoins Kalamata and stretches as far as Cape Kurtissa; the main village is Stavropighi.

Andruvista, in the foothills of the Taygetos, and Kardamyli by the sea are the chief towns of the bishopric of Andruvista. This boundary lies precisely at the foot of Makryno (Prophet Ilias) the highest summit of the Taygetos. The region of Andruvista continues south along the coast to Zygos and inland to the borders of Milea.

Zygos includes the foothills of the Taygetos from Leftro to Porto Oitylo. The chief towns are Pyrgo in the north, Platsa in the middle and Oitylo in the south. However, as Oitylo is separated from the rest of the Zygos by a projecting mountain ridge, it is independent of the Kapitain of Zygos and is normally considered a separate district. Mani as a whole is divided into seven bishoprics, namely Zarnata, Andruvista, Milea, Zygos, Maini, Kolokythi and Karyopoli.

Milea is inland and straddles the ridges of the Taygetos, Bardhunia forming its eastern boundary. Milea includes the towns of Mikri Kastania, Arakhova, and Garbela.

Leake lists the seven kapitains of the Mani, which Petro Bey had described to him, as follows:

Ghiorgio Kaptaniki of Stavropighi (Zarnata) with 700 houses,
Panaghiota Trupaki of Andruvista with 700 houses,
Khristodhulo Khristea of Leftro (governing both Platsa and adjoining Zygos) with 1000 houses,
Konstantino Nikoraki of Kastania, described as one of the largest villages and situated, claims Leake, midway between Gythio and Kitries.
Ghiorgio Kyvelaki of Milea, with 200 houses.
Anagnosti Venitzanaki, with only 1 village, Kastanitza otherwise

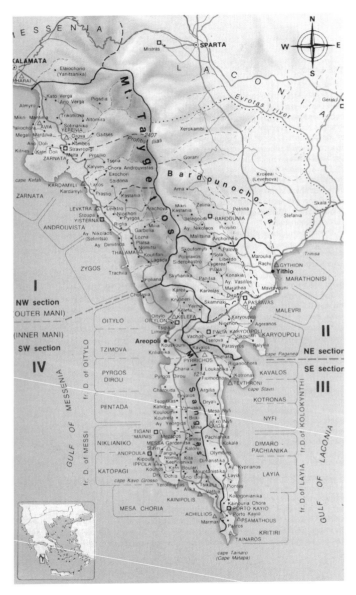

Figure 5   Map showing the various divisions of the Mani

32

known as Mikri Kastania (this is in Bardhunia on the Laconian side of the Taygetos),
Dhimitrio Grigoraki of Mavrovouni without attachment to any villages.

Leake digresses into the geography of Bardhunia and, though he did not visit this region, provides a list of villages with details of those with mixed Greek and Turkish populations. According to Leake Bardhunia was but recently colonised by Albanians; he tentatively dates this to within the eighteenth century. Perhaps this colonisation came to pass as a result of the Albanian soldiery the Turks used to quell the Orlov uprising.

The area was called Bardhunia, Leake explains, after the fortress of the same name. This fortress is of similar importance to the other ones in the Mani, namely Passava, Maini, Kelafa and Zarnata. He ascribes their construction to the 'Byzantine Princes' who erected them for the purpose of keeping these mountain people in order. Leake reckons they were last repaired during the Venetian occupation of the Morea 100 years earlier. The exact location of the castle of Bardhunia is a puzzle. Leake describes it as being near Arna, and a village of this name exists today, but there is no indication of any major ruins nearby. Current maps locate a fortress, called Kastro Zaloimi, seven kilometres to the east of Arna, above the village called today Vasilaki, whose substantial remains indicate that it was most probably of Byzantine origin.

The boundaries of Bardhunia are defined, Leake says, 'by all the southern faces and roots of the great *Tayetum* to within a short distance of the coast above *Trinasia* and *Gythium*'. Leake then lists nearly 20 villages by name, of which only two, Arna and Petrina, can be found on today's maps. All the names are Slav and in several cases these old names have now been abandoned in

33

favour of Hellenised ones. Leake quotes the fortress of Bardhunia as being three to four hours' distant from Kurtzuna and the
same distance from Goranus in the district of Mistras *Vilayeti*.
Leake also mentions a road running along the upper reaches of
the Taygetus linking Goranus to Mistras via Kumusta, Voliana,
Dhipotamus, Sotira, Sokha and Anavryti, the whole route taking
approximately eight hours to travel.

The villages of upper Bardhunia border on the bishopric of
Milea, situated on the western side of the Taygetus. According to
Leake the ownership of these villages swung between the Turks
and the Christians (aided by the Maniots), and even between one
group of Turks and another. In the time of which Leake speaks
control is firmly in Ottoman hands, thanks to the power of Amus
Aga, who keeps affairs tolerably quiet. Arna is the only village
which Leake reports as having a mixed Turk and Greek population. The Turks there occupy five pyrgi and 90 houses while the
Greeks hold only one pyrgos and 30 houses. The next largest
village is Stratza, wholly Turkish, with three pyrgi and 70 houses.
Two other Turkish villages, Kurtzuna (nowadays Kudonisa) and
Tzeria, each have a couple of pyrgi and about 30 to 40 houses.
Leake observes that the Muselmen are sometimes dominant while
at other times the Christians have the upper hand. Nevertheless,
the Muselmen fight one another, just as the Maniots.

The Inner or Mesa Mani consists of the remainder of the
western coastline from Oitylo Bay down to Cape Matapan, its
eastern boundary being the summits of the mountain range.
Leake describes the Inner Mani as a kind of rugged elevated
plain, two to four miles in breadth, lying between mountains and
a range of lofty cliffs which border the coast. The Inner Mani
consists of 35 villages, of which Tzimova (now known as Areopoli), at the northern extremity, is the largest. However, the
inhabitants of Tzimova and its five neighbouring villages are

anxious to be considered separate from the rest of the Inner Mani which was called *Kakavulia*[7] or Land of Evil Counsel. Petro Mavromikhali (or Petro Bey) of Limeni, is governor of Mesa Mani. He is not described as a Kapitain but has more power and influence than the other kapitains in the whole of Mani.

Lower or Kato Mani (also called the sunward side) contains about 45 villages and includes the whole of the eastern coast stretching north from Porto Kaio to the plain of Elos beyond Gythio. The northern extremity includes the confines of Bard-hunia on the eastern side of the Taygetos, the boundary with Exo Mani. Kato Mani's subdivisions are Marathonisi, Skutari, Malevri, Vakho, Kolokythia and Laghia. Kato Mani borders upon Mesa Mani as far as the pass of Karyoploi and upon Exo Mani to the northward of that opening.

Leake lists the total number of towns and villages in the Mani, according to the preceeding estimate, as about 130; previously he had mentioned only 117 villages. Estimates since made of the number of settlements at the time of Leake's visit are given in Table 2. Leake refers to the Maniot poem[8] listing all the villages which total this latter figure. As Leake comments, when he enquires of a native of any particular district, a greater number of names is given than in the poetical catalogue. This is easily accounted for by the dispersed mode of building and partly perhaps by new villages having arisen since the poem was written, which seems to have been at least 10 years earlier.

---

[7] *Kakavulia* is believed to be derived from the Greek word for cooking pot or pail, which in times of conflict the Maniots used as a helmet for protection.

[8] This epic poem, quoted by Leake in both the original Greek as well as in English, was written by a Greek schoolmaster during Tzanet's beydom. It is 314 lines long of which about one third consists of a poetical catalogue of the 117 Maniot villages. Leake made a copy of the text when visiting the Bishop of Mistras.

Table 2 Breakdown of the Population and Fighting Strength in the Mani prior to 1821.

Region	Population	Fighting Men (estimated)	Settlements	Towers
Outer Mani	12,500–14,000	2,800–4,300	58–60	180
Eastern Mani (Sunward side)	6,500–7,500	1,200–2,400	28–30	150
Inner Mani	13,000–15,000	2,000–3,300	90	450
Bardhounia	4,500	2,500	40	50–80

Source: Greek Traditional Architecture: Mani, Yanis Saitas, Melissa, Athens (1990), Pp 28–31.

N.B. Fighting men are defined as being in the service of one of the various Maniot Kapetans.

Maniot Life and Customs

Leake quotes the population in Mani as about 30,000 of which 10,000 are arms bearing (i.e. able bodied males). No Maniot will venture from his village on even the most innocuous errand without being armed with a pistol and dagger in the girdle plus a musket (figure 6). It is reckoned that there are 130 good sized villages in the Mani, and each will consist of 45 to 50 houses. The typical family size is six, and girls generally marry early at 14 years of age. The Mani contributes between 10% to 12% of the total population in the Peloponnese. About 400 Maniot sailors are employed in the fleet of Hydra. One small ship and about 50 coasting vessels form the 'commercial marine' of the Mani.

After the kapitanos, the pappas (priests) are the acknowledged leaders in Maniot feuds, both in council and in the field. Leake comments that the pappas are generally the promoters and the leaders in the strife between the villages or families. In this strife

36

Figure 6   Two armed Maniots

the chief objective is to pull down the adversaries' tower; once achieved, the 'war' is ended. The victim, or victims, are considered conquered and seldom reopen hostilities.

Each person of power and every head of family of any influence owns a pyrgos which is used solely as a means of defence. The ordinary habitation stands at the foot of the tower. The Bey's relations and a few of the *Kapitani* maintain some soldiers in their towers. In general, however, these buildings are uninhabited except in time of alarm. To overturn the pyrgi of the enemy and to slaughter as many of his relations as possible are the objects of every war.

The tower is built with as many loopholes in the different storeys as possible and has battlements at the top. Those owners of the pyrgos who can get a rusty swivel to plant a gun on the top feel even more secure and are not easily subdued. Even the normal house is built with loopholes in the walls. In the poorer villages those who do not have the means to build pyrgi are no more peaceable but quarrel either among themselves or with their neighbours, and endeavour to overturn one another's houses just like their betters! Each pyrgos is equipped with a cistern located under the arch (kamara) closed up with a small wooden door that is kept constantly locked.

Leake compares the Maniots with the Albanians in their manner of fighting. Care is taken not to face one's enemy openly but rather to fire from behind houses, rocks and trees. Owing to the length of their muskets Maniots are forced to rest the barrels before firing. However, the Maniot is an excellent marksman.

It is a case of each man for himself, as no Maniot can depend on the conduct of his neighbour, and there is no sense of discipline. Experience has taught the Maniot that a musket with a long range and good cover is essential for survival. Compared with the Albanians, the Maniots are even more addicted to assassination but do have respect for certain rules, which is not the case in Albania. A Maniot who shows great courage and determination is well respected – Leake calls it obstinacy! In this regard the Maniot women outperform their menfolk.

Leake recounts the story of a woman living in her pyrgos up in the Taygetos who was besieged by a body of Turkish soldiers. She was firing from the windows on one side of the tower while at the rear she sent to safety her children in the company of a female servant. Her ammunition was spent but even so the Turks retreated, frightened that she would blow them up together with her tower if they tried to break in.

Two months before Leake's arrival in the Mani a typical Maniot incident occurred in Vathy (today known as Ageranos). The son of the pappas in the village accidentally killed a boy who was related to another pappas living in Vathy. The latter declared war against his fellow priest in the formal Maniot way of crying out through the village his intentions. The former accused pappas, so warned, went to say mass in his church armed with pistols in his girdle – again a normal Maniot custom. During the service he was obliged to put his pistols behind the iconostasis (altar screen) whilst donning his religious robes. The bereaved pappas arrived during the service with his companions and, as soon as the mass was over, walked up to his enemy and made to fire his pistol. However, the firearm did not strike, whereupon the other pappas rushed behind the iconostasis for his pistols and promptly shot his attacker and one of his companions. Pistols in his hands, he then chased the other attackers from the church. Peace only returned to Vathy after Andon Bey interceded in the quarrel and halted any further bloodshed.

As Leake comments the Maniots will agree to make peace only after blood has been spilt on condition that a suitable exchange of money is agreed. When a feud erupts and a member of a family is killed, a member of the injured family swears revenge for the injury and, until satisfied, refrains from changing his clothes, shaving or eating meat. This considerably hastens the act of revenge! Whilst Leake was staying in Gythio with the doctor W. the Cavaliere's son arrived seeking a remedy for his mother who was suffering from a sore throat. Mr W. recommended a gargle of milk, but the son rejected this with horror! He then applied to Mr W. to be blooded, though in perfect health. This appears, Leake remarks, to be a common practice of the Maniots in the spring.

Gythio and its Environs

Leake describes very carefully the situation of Gythio in respect to the eastern coast of the Mani. At the time of his visit the island of Marathonisi (fennel island) was separate from the mainland.[9] Its classical name was Cranae where Homer described the first union of Helen and Paris. In classical times the mainland adjacent was called Migonium (in celebration of this union) with the hill to the rear named Larysium (known in Leake's time as Kumaro[10]). At the beginning of spring a festival of Bacchus was celebrated, it being asserted that ripe grapes would then be produced.

Water for the town is obtained from two wells. One is situated close to the remains of the classical amphitheatre and is reputed to be the best water in the neighbourhood. Leake did not inspect this well but suspects that it is the well Pausanias describes as the Well of Aesculapius. The more frequently used well, though having water of inferior quality, is situated close to the mill Leake

---

[9] Today Marathonisi is no longer an island but joined to the land by a causeway.
[10] Kumaro is the Greek for the small tree or shrub *Arbutus unedo* (the Strawberry tree), very common throughout the Mani.

passed on his entry to Gythio. This source is near the shore and much more accessible, which explains its use for supplying vessels.

On the afternoon of 7th April Leake walked to Mavrovouni, two miles south of Gythio. The village is on a promontory overlooking Gythio, the gulf of Laconia and the plain of Passava. The plain is well cultivated and on the surrounding hills are pyrgi and small villages (a landscape that survives unchanged today). The village of Mavrovouni is reckoned by Leake to be the largest on the eastern side of the Mani, containing a little over 100 families and four substantial tower houses. Leake affirms that Mavrovouni was also built by Tzanet Bey and that it is alternatively referred to as Tzanetopoli. Besides these tower houses, at the top of the hill is the deserted Tzanet castle. It consists of a central building with a flat roof and battlements. This is surrounded by a courtyard enclosed within a further battlemented wall defended by circular towers. A cistern takes rain water from the flat roofs and various platforms. Leake describes the interior of the central building as 'à la Turque', that is with a large kitchen and apartments for Tzanet Bey and his retainers. Leake was told that at suppertime a bell was rung and all comers would be offered food. The castle had suffered some damage (perhaps from the recent Turkish bombardment) but the principal apartments were little damaged. Leake makes no mention of this but it would appear that the castle had only recently been vacated, possibly as a result of Tzanet Bey's banishment to Vathy.

Leake visits the tower of Theodoro, Andon Bey's son-in-law, is entertained with sweetmeats, cold water, pipes and coffee (in that order). Leake is greatly taken with Theodoro and notes that he is 'the most humanized of his family'. His wife was not there to receive Leake because she had gone to Gythio to visit her father.

41

On his way back to Gythio Leake sees her returning home riding a mule, accompanied by several attendants (figure 7).

Leake carefully describes the topography as revealed in a splendid view of the eastern Mani from Mavrovouni. Looking west, the ridge of the Taygetos stretches south covered by a forest of Valonia oak. It is in this forest that over half the velanidi shipped from the Mani is gathered. The higher mountains rise behind the forest, and extend down to the Gulf of Kotroni (Kolakithia Bay). Taking the range northwards to the summits of the Taygetos the most southerly summit is clearly seen: this is Makryno (i.e. the peak of the Prophet Elias which was in ancient times called Taletum). Below this peak is the isolated mountain village of Pighadia, the home and retreat of the robber Zakharia (known as the 'terror of the Mani').

Looking south, the island of Cerigo (now known as Kythera) is in the far distance and Cape Matapan is just seen though partly hidden by Cape Kremidhara (Leake claims this forms the south side of the bay of Vathy). On the north side of this bay is Cape Petali, from where begins the long sandy bay reaching as far as Mavrovouni. The mountains falling down to Cape Matapan are seen obliquely lying in a north-south direction, as is the rest of the Taygetos.

This southern part of the Mani is entirely separated from the main chain of the Taygetos by hollow, undulating country between Skutari and Oitylo. Here are found the villages of Karyopoli, Vaklio, etc. Leake saw on the heights of the southern range the remnants of the winter snows. The northern boundary of this range is a remarkable cliff called Ai-Elia near the southern side of Porto Oitylo.

Femme de la Maina

Figure 7   Maniot woman

3

Leake Explores Passava (pp. 254–83)

After five days in Gythio Leake sets out on 8th April at 8.10 a.m. for Passava, with Mavrovouni on his left. A slight delay of 20 minutes occurred whilst the owner of the horse Leake was riding had to go back to his house in Mavrovouni for his musket. The way led across the plain of Passava where a further 15 minutes were lost in searching for another horse for one of the servants.

By 9.00 a.m. Leake was crossing the bed of a torrent in the middle of the plain of Passava. He then passed over a hill that separates the two branches of the plain. Descending the west branch he reaches the river Passava, a deep and rapid torrent coming down from the Taygetos, and climbs another low range of hills crowned with watch towers known as '*Katziaouniaxo*'. His guide requests a stop at a pyrgos belonging to a man named Lambro and is refreshed with a cup of wine. Fifteen minutes later the party moves off, descending into a narrow, well-cultivated valley through which a stream, the Turkovrysi, flows whose source is in a pool halfway between Passava and the village of Karvaka.

The Turkovrysi enters the sea between Capa Petali and Vathy. At 10.28 Leake crosses the stream and climbs on foot up to the fortress of Passava, which he finds resembles Mistras's fortress but is only half the size. Passava, its battlemented walls flanked by one or two towers, is in ruins. In the eastern wall near the

45

southern end Leake espies a section of Hellenic wall about 50 feet
in length. It consists of large stones each four feet long and three
feet broad. Leake says that they are not as accurately hewn as 2nd
order walls but better than 1st order.[1] Leake agrees with Pausanias that Passava was the site of the antique city known as 'Las'.

From the summit of Passava Leake can see on the right four
villages: Parakhoro, Karvela, Skamnali and Panitza. These lie in a
line NW and W, the area being known as Malevri and continuing
as far west as Oitylo, including Kelefa, which Leake insists is a
ruined Venetian fortress.[2] Malevri goes as far south as Tzimova
(now Areopoli), Vakho and Skutari. Between SW and S are the
five villages of Karyopoli, Khoriasi, Neokhori, Tzerova and
Parasiro.

Climbing down from the castle Leake finds a herb, which he
had first tasted when dining with the bishop of Mistras on March
24th – it resembles cultivated asparagus in flavour. In Mistra it
was called 'maniatis' as it came from the mountains of the Mani.
Leake uses the Greek word πέτζιγκιαγκον. He now digresses
on 'horta' or wild herbs, and writes that it is the common
occupation for the women of Greece 'to botanize', collecting
these horta in the spring. They form an important part of the diet,
especially during the Lenten fast. The Greek peasants have no
such resource in the summer and during the long fast leading to
the Panaghia on 15th August there is little fresh to eat but
members of the gourd family. The Maniots are renowned in the
rest of Greece for the rigour of their fasting but, sadly, this has
fatal consequences for many womenfolk in the summer. The
Maniots in the summer are too poor to plant such produce as

---

[1] First order ancient Greek walls were roughly hewn polygonal stones only coarsely fitted. Second
order masonry was also polygonal but precisely carved and closely fitted.
[2] Kelefa is Byzantine in origin but enlarged and repaired in turn by Venetians and Turks.

gourds, cucumbers, *badinjans*, water melons and suchlike. Further-more, they do not normally have the means to irrigate such crops. The Maniot peasant's diet during the summer fast consists of salted starfish, olives, goat's cheese and maize bread seasoned with garlic or onion, washed down with some sour wine. The cactus *Opuntia ficus-indica* (prickly pear) is grown around the Mani villages both for its fruit and as a hedging for the cultivated areas. The only other fruits available in the Mani are a few grapes and figs.

Returning to Gythio from Passava Leake takes the route via Paleopoli, the name for the site of the Roman remains behind Gythio, remounting his horse at 11.55 a.m. at the Turkovrysi stream by the ruins of a Turkish bath and arriving at Petrovouni on a rocky height at 12.24 p.m. He then crosses the river Arna (named after the village in Bardhunia at its source). Leake finds ancient remains on the left bank of the Arna. He next enters the gorge of Mount Kumaro and at 1.22 p.m. descends into the valley. The ascent to the pass is difficult, especially on horseback. Some ancient steps are cut into the rock, with 15 perfect steps winding to the right. At the top of the pass are the ruins of a signal tower. Leake leaves the foot of the pass at 1.49 p.m. and reaches Gythio at 2.14 p.m. It is very difficult to trace the route that Leake followed on today's maps.

Next day, April 9th, Andon Bey introduces Leake to one of the leading men of the area who is entrusted with his safety in every part of the Mesa Mani. Leake confusingly calls this the Mesa, or Middle Mani, but on the next page corrects himself, describing it as the Deep Mani or Kakavoulia. He explains that the Maniots of the Deep Mani are notorious for plundering shipwrecked vessels and sailors as well as for their primary activities of robbery and piracy, before announcing his plan to visit Kiparisos (known to the ancients as Taenarus or Kaenopolis) in the Deep Mani.

Leake Leaves for Areopolis

April 10th. Leake leaves Gythio at 8.43 a.m. and 20 minutes later passes by Mavrovouni, reaching the plain of Passava at 10.02 a.m. This is Tzanet Bey's land, described as very fertile with vineyards (which Leake's guide calls a 'fountain of wine') and crops of corn or kolambokki,[3] all irrigated by the river. He then climbs the hills of Petalea, covered with Jerusalem sage and broom in full flower. By 10.35 a.m. Leake has reached the plain of Petalea where he sees the farmers preparing the ground for the cotton crop. He notes that they are all armed with daggers and pistols, remarking that this seems to be the ordinary armour of the cultivator or shepherd, even when there is no suspicion of danger.

Just before 11.00 a.m. Leake crosses the Turkovrysi and arrives at the shoreline. At the end of the beach he climbs Cape Petalea to the village of Ageranos which consists of no more than 20 houses. Leake enters Vathy at 11.19 a.m. and is met by Ghiorghio, one of Andon Bey's many nephews, and taken to his house, a miserable affair! Beside it is Andon Bey's pyrgos (figure 8), which Leake considers much inferior to his pyrgos at Mavrovouni. The Vathy Leake describes is today known as Ageranos, situated over the headland, whilst present day Vathy is on the beach below with one pyrgos and a few buildings. Andon Bey's pyrgos is one of the most handsome in the Mani with battlements around it and quite an impressive entrance. It is now privately owned and there have since been, unfortunately, some rather crude repairs to the original structure using reinforced concrete. One must assume that this pyrgos was considerably enlarged after Leake had seen it.

Ghiorghio then takes Leake to show him some ruins on the

---

[3] Kolambokki is maize.

Figure 8   Andon Bey's Pyrgcs, Ageranos

49

SW side of the cape about fifteen minutes from the village. Leake finds a large semicircular building constructed in the Roman manner with stones and tiles. It is 20 metres in diameter with five windows and almost entirely unspoilt. There is a similar ruin nearby and up the valley more signs of ruined buildings, including the remains of a long subterranean structure that Leake surmises to be a Roman cloaca (sewer). Continuing up this valley Leake notes the villages of Karyopoli, Kafki, Neokhori and Panitza (or Banitza) which he does not visit.

Leake leaves Vathy at 12.27 p.m., crosses a stream flowing down from Karyopoli and passes a rocky height with the ruins of a windmill on it. This is Dhikova which also has vestiges of ancient remains. Peasants have unearthed sepulchres in their fields containing human bones. By 12.45 p.m. Leake has reached the end of the plain and, on rising ground which connects to Cape Kremidhara, he espies Skutari. This is a large village situated on a steep height overlooking the sea within an extensive bay. Out to sea the whole extent of the island of Cerigo (today's Kythera) can be seen.

By 1.20 p.m. Leake enters Skutari and takes lodgings in the pyrgos of Katzano, thanks to an introduction given to him by the Bey. The pyrgos, garrisoned by 15 soldiers whom Katzano pays himself, is constructed in the usual Maniot fashion. The lower storey is occupied by the garrison and in the two rooms of the upper storey (or rather one long room separated by a slight wooden partition) are furnishings for the family. Katzano's family number twenty five; he married when 19 years old, his wife only 14, and they had had 15 children. At one end is the fireplace with kitchen furniture, while at the other is a mattress for a sofa. More mattresses and blankets are piled up in one corner. The rest of the family furniture hangs from the walls or is stowed in wooden boxes ranged around the walls. The floor consists of loose boards. Numerous fleas are to be found in winter and bugs in the summer. These infestations are attributed by Leake to a want of ablution (whether household or human he does not specify).

Ianiki Katzano is described as a 'man of plain modest manner', civil to Leake and ready to answer his questions about his country. Leake notes that such readiness is to be found among all the Maniots with whom he has conversed. He attributes this greater share of candour and veracity to their independence. The falsehood and dissimulation typically found among other Greeks Leake imputes to the fact that they have no other means of defence against their Turkish oppressors, unlike the Maniots who have very largely escaped the worst of the Turkish oppression.

Katzano tells Leake that formerly all the Grigoraki family lived in Skutari until the two brothers, John and Anthony (i.e. Zanim and Andon), the heads of the two houses, fell out. All the many branches of the clan immediately took sides and left Skutari. Currently Katzano and his brother, Tzingurio, are the only two left. Here, as in Khimara which has nearly the same degree of independence as the Mani, the most usual state of hostility between two families is one of non-intercourse and mutual observation (snooping), overt acts of enmity being avoided.

When the two Grigoraki branches were still living in Skutari in this state of mutual snooping, Katzano, then young, was sitting outside his house with his brother. Thirteen members of the other family branch passed by and Katzano and his companions saluted them. When the passing group returned the salute, Katzano and the others, who had been drinking, interpreted this as an insult. Without another word Katzano got up and fired at the passers by. Naturally the fire was returned and both Katzano and his brother were seriously wounded. On hearing these shots, their uncle, Andon, sallied out of his house with his followers, seized eleven of the group and shut them up in a pyrgos. If his

51

nephew's wounds had been fatal, Andon would have had blood for blood and executed the prisoners.

Katzano's wife, when questioned on her skill with a musket, offered (as many other Maniot women would have done) to show Leake what she was capable of. She pointed to a place 150 yards distant and said, 'Set up your hat there, and see if I cannot put a musket ball through it.' Leake replied that he had too much regard for his hat and would take her word for it! She had already received two wounds in battle and affected to consider her husband as no braver than herself.

The son-in-law of Andon Bey's nephew, Lambro (also confusingly called Lambro), arrives that evening at Skutari with a train of friends, and the purpose of his visit is to request Katzano's 'interference'. Lambro lives at Katjaunianika (today's Chaloulianika) which Leake had passed through on the way to Passava Castle. A Kakavouliote,[4] whose brother had been killed by the other Lambro from Chaloulianika, had been thwarted in his attempts to revenge himself like a (Maniot) man of honour, that is to say by murdering Lambro. Leake surmises the Kakavouliote may also have been somewhat fearful that, had he succeeded, he might have met the same fate, owing to Lambro's relationship to Andon Bey. This fellow had, accordingly, resolved to have at least the satisfaction of taking some of Lambro's property. That very day, in sight of Lambro and his friends (who had fired without effect on the Kakavouliote) the man had stolen Lambro's mare and ridden off on her. The purpose of his visit was to seek Katzano's help to intercede on his behalf to have the mare restored and prevent further hostilities. Leake comments that there was every possibility that Katzano would succeed.

Leake concludes that this is a very good example of the

---

[4] Kakavouliote is the term for an inhabitant of the Inner Mani.

influence and authority that the Kapitain Pasha has lately obtained over the Mani, in that his inferiors, appointed to command, are able to check the lawless system of retaliation. This lawlessness is the result of the present uneducated state of the Maniots. Leake believes that the best thing that could happen to the Greeks would be for the Turks to adopt the same system as in other parts of the country, giving the Maniots some form of municipal government, natural to Greece, whilst at the same time keeping overall control. Thus the pernicious effects of 'each man for himself', inherent in the Maniot character, would be avoided.

This move to greater Greek autonomy would also require the Pashas and other Turkish commanding officers to maintain stricter discipline among the Turkish troops when out of their officers' sight. Such a system could well work in the Islands and perhaps even throughout the Peloponnese, but Leake fears that Turkish anarchy, bigotry, greed and cruelty render it impracticable.

Whilst in Skutari Leake is also informed of more ancient ruins lying on the hill above the southern headland, Cape Stavri (now Cape Moundes). They are at a place called Skopa or Skopopoli in the district of Vastas, about two hours' walk from Skutari. The ruins are beside the sea and consist of brick arches similar to those Leake had seen earlier but less well preserved. He conjectures that this may have been Tuethrone, visited by Pausanias. His host, in recounting the details, adds, with a grave face – and all present nod in agreement – that sometimes the sound of a person tossing heaps of gold coins can be heard among these ruins. This site is now the small port of Kotronas, the last safe haven on the eastern side of the Deep Mani until Porto Kaio.

April 11th. Leake leaves Skutari at 12.37 p.m., being delayed until that hour because of the late arrival of mules sent for him from Areopoli in the care of Gika, a member of the Mavromikhali family, who is to guide the party. This is on the express

53

orders of the Bey, or, as Leake puts it, '...to whose care I am recommended by the Bey'. The path strikes north from Skutari, skirting the hill of Aghriloti – this Leake refers to it as a mountain (214 metres high) giving it the name Mount Sanghia – and passing through groves of mulberry trees. The party strikes for Dhikova, passing it at 1.15 p.m., where they follow a small river which they cross several times in a gorge full of large rocks just south of Karioupoli, which Leake describes as a very strong pass. By 1.50 p.m. they are on higher ground with, on their left, the monastery of Panaghia Spiliotissa, pleasantly situated among gardens and cultivated terraces. No trace of this monastery can be found on today's maps. Leake has now reached the main Gythio–Areopoli road and follows its course through a valley full of beehives (as it still is today). As the countryside becomes more barren they approach the village of Vachios, a collection of 30 miserable huts, the birthplace of Tzanet Bey, to where he was banished when the Turks took away his beydom. He died in 1813 at the age of 71. Leake makes no mention at all of meeting Tzanet, possibly at the request of Andon Bey and the Turks.

Leake states that Vachios is situated on the steepest and southernmost slopes of 'Mount Sanghia'. Here Leake has confused the non-existent Sanghia with the peak Kondonaros, 800 metres high. At 3.00 p.m. they enter a narrow pass and, climbing a very rugged road, come into sight of the Bay of Oitylo at 3.30 p.m. as well as the town of Oitylo above the bay. Passing under the precipitous and striking peak of the Prophet Elias that rises above Areopoli, Leake describes the path as extremely rocky and impassable, even for a mule, and observes several wheel tracks of ancient chariots in the stone. They descend and by 4.07 p.m. arrive in Areopoli, a large village situated half a mile inland from the brow of lofty cliffs which form all the southernmost part of the coast on the west side of the Mani.

Leake's guide was Gika Mavromikhali, a stout and active Maniot who that day had ridden from Areopoli to meet Leake at Skutari, then returned on foot, and who now takes Leake to his house. Shortly after his arrival Leake is visited by Petro Mavro- mikhali, commonly called Kyr Petruni. He lives by the sea in Oitylo Bay in the small harbour of Limeni, about 30 minutes' walk from Areopoli. As already explained, Petruni has influence over all of the Mesa Mani but does not assume the title of 'Kapitano'. Leake is also introduced to Poliko Tubaki from Vamvaka, the Kakavuliote chieftain, who is to be Leake's guide through the Deep Mani. He has been ordered by the Bey to escort Leake through the Land of Evil Counsel. Tubaki wastes no time in warning Leake of the possible dangers of the trip by announcing: 'If the Bey had not given such precise orders con- cerning you, how nicely we would have stripped you of all your baggage!'

After this rather savage welcome, Gika's conversation turns to a gentler note, as he comments that the Maniots' only plague is the wind. It destroys the grain crops, this year being a prime example. The eastern side of the Deep Mani is exposed to the Garbino while the Greco and Levante[5] rush through the mountain passes to ravage the western side of the Mani. A fur- ther curse is the lack of rain in April as the grain ripens, drying it up before the ear has any substance.

---

[5] Garbino, Greco and Levante are winds.

4

South from Areopolis (pp. 284–93)

Next day, April 12th, Leake departs with his party at 7.20 a.m. The party consists of the aforementioned Poliko, Gika Mavro-mikhali (his host in Areopoli), his nephew, an unnamed relation of Andon Bey from Skutari and one of Andon Bey's attendants from Gythio in charge of the mules. Wisely, Leake has been advised for this journey to abandon his normal custom of horseback and use a mule as the surer way over the rocky paths of the Inner Mani. Most of the party are coming at his expense; they are armed with 'Albanian' muskets, which consist of barrels manufactured in Northern Italy and mounted in Albania. To complete the entourage is an escort of twelve armed men under the command of Kyr Petruni who accompany the party for a short distance out of Areopoli.

They take a track which strikes due south from Areopoli 0.8 kilometres off the present road, passing mid-way between Omales and Laghokili. By 8.27 a.m. the party is in a deep ravine, having left Areopoli by the Dhikho road. The ravine descends to the coast in a small bay that is the first break in an almost continuous line of cliffs stretching from Oitylo Bay as far as Capo Grosso. This ravine marks the boundary between the sub-district of Areopoli and the Mesa Mani. Passing Kharia (Charia) to the right at 8.50 a.m. the party is in sight of Pyrgos (Dirou) some 15 minutes later.

Leake is advised to skirt Pyrgos as the inhabitants are very hostile towards the English, the reason being that a pirate *tratta* captained by a Cretan with a crew of 25 'sailors', all from Pyrgos, had been captured not very long ago by Captain Donally of the Royal Navy at Delus (today's Delos). The captain had handed his captives over to the Turks who imprisoned them in Constantinople.

The first halt comes two hours after setting out, at Aia Marina (this must be Glezoa, as it is the only church in this area), an old church on the roadside not far from Pyrgos. It is evident that Byzantine churches hold no interest for Leake, as this is one of the very few he mentions in an area where they abound, and then only because it has an inscribed stone in the wall which is obviously much older than the church itself.

The halt lasts a mere ten minutes because by 9.40 a.m. the party is on a stony plain sloping down from Mount Sanghia to the cliffs on the west (this time Leake has got it right, unlike at Skutari). This impressive mountain consists of three peaks, all called Prophet Ilias and between 1,080 and 1,140 metres high. The party is now clearly following the trace of the present main road south into the Deep Mani. By 10.30 a.m. they are abreast of another small bay (either Spathari or Lagadhaki) exposed to the west. After another 30 minutes they arrive at the village of Atja (Axva just south of Paliochora) under a remarkable peaked rock (Prophet Ilias) at 1,137m. Atja is one of a group of five villages known as the Pendadha. These can be identified today as Mandoforos, Triandafilia, Charouda, Nikandhrio and Marmatsouka. Just south east is Babaka (Vamvaka) where the guide, Poliko, comes from. All this region, though stony and with apparently poor soil, is covered with fields of wheat, barley, beans and kidney beans (fasulia). These fields are separated by 'fences' of loose stones piled up as walls. Leake remarks that given more rain and less wind this would be a fertile district.

The road now passes between two parallel walls and its surface consists of bare jagged rocks on which the mules find it difficult to get a secure footing. The next stop is at 11.40 a.m. at a lone house in the fields opposite the northern end of Capo Grosso, anciently known as Cape Thyrides. This is most probably Agios Georgios, as it is currently known, the site lying between the villages of Erimos and Mina. Leake mentions the church of Aia Varvara (Barbara) by the ruined village of Erimos but does not visit it. Midway between the northern cape of this impressive promontory and the house is the small promontory of Tigani[1] with little bays on either side. The eastern bay is the more secure and contains the port of Mezopo, which after Oitylo Bay is the best harbour on the western coast of the Mani.

The promontory of Tigani is not very high and has a flat summit. Leake describes it as surrounded with the remains of an 'Italian' fortification, presumably meaning Venetian. Here Leake is quite wrong as these remains contain a sixth century AD Christian basilica on top of which a Frankish castle was later built using the masonry of the basilica. The promontory is connected to the mainland by a low isthmus or panhandle. Leake correctly describes this situation as the port and Homeric town of *Messa*. He notes that both Pausanias and Strabo mention *Messa*, but only Pausanias precisely locates it at Tigani. Leake also refers to the central and highest part of the plateau of Capo Grosso as the probable location of the ancient site of *Hippola*. Pausanias, when describing Messa, notes that the cliffs of the Capo Grosso abound with wild pigeons, a fact confirmed by Leake's guides.

The party moves on after their hour-long midday halt and, 20 minutes later, at 12.48 p.m. they have reached the villages of Karina and Mina. At 1.14 p.m. they cross the bed of a torrent

---

[1] Tigani is the Greek for frying pan.

flowing down from Mina into the sea three quarters of a mile to
their right next to a pyrgos on the shore near Mezopo. At 2.03
p.m. the party passes between the villages of Nomia (on their
right) and Kita (on their left). Both are situated on a ridge linking
the plateau of Capo Grosso and the mountain. The view from
this ridge allows one to see as far as Areopoli to the north and
Alika to the south.

The peninsular of Capo Grosso is about six miles round,
terminating on the seaward side in high and precipitous cliffs.
The ground rises in great natural steps from Nomia to the centre
of the Capo Grosso. Leake surmises that this high ground is
either bare rock or covered only with a scanty layer of soil, and
therefore cultivated in only a few places. He does not apparently
realise the historic importance of this higher plateau which was
inhabited in Neolithic times.

In Kita, described in the 'poetical' list of villages as 'many
towered', Leake counts no fewer than 22 pyrgi. Kita has between
80 and 100 families whilst the other villages in the region are
generally smaller with fewer than 20 or 30 families. By 3.00 p.m.
the party is now opposite the southern end of Capo Grosso
where there is a bay exposed to the south west. This is today's
Gherolimenas; neither the harbour nor the village existed in
Leake's time. He notes that from this point the aspect of the coast
south to Cape Matapan changes, the lofty cliffs being replaced by
land sloping down from the mountains to the shoreline. The road
that Leake's party follows as a result (though on the same ele-
vation above the sea) is on a steeper slope and much more stony.
It finally becomes nothing more than a terrace of loose round
stones over which it is impossible to advance at more than the
slowest pace.

Here the fields have 'fences' of rock broken into cubical
masses but laid without the help of cement. This rock is a coarse

grained white marble very like that found at Gythio and used in the ancient sites that Leake had earlier visited. By comparison the marble used for building in Sparta was of a much higher quality.

By 3.50 p.m. Leake passes under Alika which is sited at the foot of a mountain. In the middle of the village he finds the rock cut with perpendicular faces for a length of 150 paces, which he surmises indicates that it once formed part of an ancient quarry. Between Kita and Alika the party had encountered trains of over 200 asses, all laden with brushwood from Porto Kaio, and had had to stand aside at each encounter, halting for a minute or so, to let the train pass. This wood was destined for the Easter feast when every home would be roasting its lamb. The Lenten fast is so strictly maintained in the Mani by the Greek Orthodox church that no cooking is attempted while it is in force.

Leake remarks on the contrasting habits of the Kakavuliotes. They would 'make a merit' of hiding behind the wall of a ruined chapel to ambush a member of an offending family: but think it a crime to pass the same ruin (be it ever so insignificant) without crossing themselves seven, or at least, three times.

From Alika they pass over the bed of a torrent and enter the fields of Kyparisso. This was once a considerable village, home to both the Grigoraki and Mavromikhali families. It is now reduced to one pyrgos, a chapel (the Panaghia) and the priest's house. It is 4.20 p.m. and the party which left Areopoli at 7.20 a.m. have taken nine hours to make this trip. Excluding the one hour break, this is quite an impressive time for covering such rough terrain.

The old priest greets Leake with an air of cheerfulness and hospitality, which, the author cynically observes, is due to the fact that the priest has nothing to give and expects to be entertained at the expense of the party. He is dressed only in a jacket and a pair of wide trousers made from coarse Mani flannel or blanketing.

The priest's house offers little hope of supplies to the traveller;

61

however, he points without hesitation to the only fowl he pos-
sesses. Imitating the action of a Pasha ordering an execution he
desires one of the party to 'take off its head'. Leake then hears the
history of the priest. He was originally from Crete, his monastic
name being Macarius. He was a *Kaloiero* (monk) for several years
at the ancient Monastery of Saint Catherine on Mount Sinai, an
experience he says that was infinitely worse than being in *Kakavulia*. He was sent into Egypt to collect charity for the 'convent',
but instead of returning to the Sinai desert with the collected
alms, he was tempted to abscond and came to hide in the Mani.
He has been here for 30 years officiating as the pappas of
Kyparisso.

To obtain pardon for his crime he says daily prayers in a
sepulchre he has built for himself behind the church. After
showing this to Leake, who was not greatly impressed, the pappas
leads him to a small ruined church nearby dedicated to Aia Sotiri
(Saint Saviour). The two door posts intrigue Leake as they are
quadrangular styli decorated top and bottom with mouldings and
classical Greek inscriptions. One of these belonged to the City of
Taenarii in honour of a citizen, the other is dedicated to a certain
Caius Julius Laco (son of Eurycles) from the community of
Eleuthero-Lacones, one of the free cities under the Spartan
League.

Leake presumes on finding these relics that Kyparisso was the
site of Taenarum (or Kaenopolis as it was called in Pausanias's
time). Further, the second inscription appears to indicate that
Taenarum was the principal city of the Eleuthero-Lacones League. Strabo does, in fact, mention a certain Laco who appears to
have been unable to hold onto power after the death of his father
Eurycles.

In front of the chapel Leake finds a similar broken pedestal
inscribed to the honour of another citizen of Taenarum. From

these various remains Leake surmises that this church was built on the site of the temple of Ceres, mentioned by Pausanias. The site, on the summit of a mound roughly one mile in circumference, is bounded to the west and south-west by 40 foot-high perpendicular cliffs with the sea directly below. On the east side of the mound is a valley of cornfields rising in terraces right up the rocky mountainside as far as there is any soil to cultivate. The bed of the torrent in the valley ends to the north in a little inlet to the sea. To the south there is a small harbour where Leake guesses there was a temple to Venus. No sign of any remains can be found there now.

Kyparisso is sited about five miles from the isthmus connecting the peninsular of Cape Matapan to the Mesa Mani. Seawards the hill is of bare rock, inland the slope is partitioned into very small enclosures with walls of slate-like stone, very different from the massive stone walls Leake had seen earlier in the day. Piles of slate had been gathered to clear the land for small enclosures of corn or vines.

Makarios then leads the author through a labyrinth of fences and ruined buildings, accompanied by his son. Leake, rather dryly, comments that this represents another little irregularity in Pappas Makarios' ex-monastic lifestyle. Throughout this area Leake keeps stumbling on antique remains, many Doric and Greek. Two large columns are of the finest red granite of Syene, lying on the ground, carved with dedications to famous Roman emperors, including Marcus Aurelius and Gordian, whilst several smaller columns are still standing in place. It appears to Leake they may have formed part of a large church dating from early Christian times.[2] Then it was no longer Taenarum but had already taken its current name of Kyparisso. There was no room for all the party

---

[2] The remains of the 6th century Byzantine church can still be visited today.

to stay overnight in the pappas' hut, so he reluctantly agreed to let them camp in the church. Liberal as he was, Makarios was shocked that the party should eat a meat supper in the church during the strictest of the Greek fasts. As Leake comments, they were duly punished, for the myriad fleas in the church prevented anyone from getting any sleep! Moreover, the floor space was so restricted that there was only just room enough for them all to lie down.

5

Down to Cape Matapan (pp. 294–310)

April 13th. Leake leaves Kyparisso at 7.50 a.m. for Cape Matapan, following the road to Vathia, which is on a steep hill half a
mile from the sea and one mile in a straight line from Kyparisso.
The road to the Cape quits the Vathia road in a torrent bed near
the sea (at a place now known as Athanasianika).

According to Leake it is this torrent which forms the boundary
between the Inner and Lower Mani. Vathia and its environs
consist of three smaller villages, all included in the Lower Mani
(Athanasianika, Ghoules and Tsi). Leake's companions from the
Mesa Mani do not agree, but claim all on the west side of the
Cape to be in their own division.

By 8.30 a.m. the party is half a mile below Vathia when a band
of armed men from Vathia meet them on the road. Leake's guides
say that Vathia has been divided into two parts for the last 40
years (that is from the 1760s) and reckon that about 100 have
been killed since then as a result of the feud which exists between
the two. After five minutes' discussion Gika and Poliko satisfy the
Vathians of the party's peaceful intentions and they are allowed to
proceed safely. The road follows the top of the cliffs below a very
steep mountainside. The going is difficult as in some sections
they have to clamber over massive rocks that appear to have
fallen off the mountain. Every spot of earth that can be cultivated
is bearing a crop of corn growing in terraces.

By 9.38 a.m. the party has arrived at the point where the road overlooks Marmari Bay and Porto Marmari, a dangerous creek on this steep western-facing coast. They cross the neck of land which separates Marmari from Porto Kaio and forms the isthmus leading to Cape Matapan, leaving the road for Porto Kaio on the left, a route which also leads to the monastery on the northern side of the Bay of Porto Kaio, and turn right to go down to the end of the peninsula. As the road climbs it offers a fine view of the bay and the cultivated terraces around the monastery.

Continuing south-easterly the party arrives at 9.55 a.m. on the summit of a ridge. From this ridge Porto Kaio can be seen to the north, and to the SE is the long narrow inlet of Vathi bay. Everywhere in this direction are terraces of corn whilst on the western side of the peninsula is a higher rocky flank also heavily cultivated. Two small *kalyvia* are on the eastern side of Mount Skourka (315m); these are presumably Mianes and Aghriokambi. The whole area is known as Asomato, after the ruined church near the shore of the small harbour closest to Cape Matapan. By 10.30 a.m. they have arrived at Asomato, now known as Porto Sternes.

The dilapidated church of Asomato had been partly repaired so that the roof only covered the holy table, but the remaining walls were in a state of ruin. Leake finds it very much as it is today. The western end is constructed of irregular Hellenic masonry. The stones, though very large, are not at all quadrangular. At the end of this Hellenic wall by the altar Leake spies a narrow ancient door, concealed from within, having been blocked when the temple was converted into a church. The fact that the orientation is not fully east-west also gives support to its being the site of an ancient Greek temple erected in the honour of Neptune. Leake starts to measure the dimensions of the chapel but his guide cries out *chrima* (shame!) as he enters the sanctuary behind the iconostasis and he has to abandon the project. He could still note that the orientation of the chapel was south-east, unlike the common easterly direction for most Greek churches. In fact, the chapel faces towards the head of the port, a circumstance which convinces Leake that this was the exact site of the celebrated temple of Taenarian Neptune.

Slightly inland from the chapel Leake noted several ancient bottle-shaped cisterns cut into the rock. He finds local women of the *kalyvia* doing their washing in water taken from them. The largest of the cisterns has a mosaic of tiles around the edge, whilst the rock near the cisterns has been levelled in some parts and made perpendicular in others. Leake assumes that these formed part of ancient buildings. He also spies steps cut into the rocks.

North-east of the chapel is a large grotto in the rock, now used by locals as a shelter for their boats when they are pulled out of the water in bad weather. Leake describes this as the place whence Hercules is fabled to have dragged the hound of Hades, *Cerberus*, and confirms Pausanias's observation that this grotto gave no evidence of a subterranean descent to the underworld.

Dubbing the grotto the 'famous entrance to the Infernal Regions' Leake then observed one ancient monument, a large broken stele, on the shore of the creek piously inscribed by a fair Taenarian in honour of her father. A further quarter of a mile south of the inner extremity of this small port there is a rock projecting into the sea. This, the locals maintain, is the real Kavo Matapan, the southernmost point of Greece and all Europe. Leake hypothesises that the word Matapan is of Laco-Doric origin, or perhaps even earlier, being an ancient local form of Metopon. Leake was also most eager to locate the site of the Taenarian quarries where the sumptuous purple marble described by Strabo came from. However, his guides, who were obviously ignorant of the porphyry quarries on the eastern coast of the Mani only a few miles north of Porto Kaio, could give him no information.

The party leaves Asomato at 11.22 a.m., Leake having spent a mere 50 minutes at this site. They take a road to the north lower than the one they arrive by. In ten minutes they are above the inlet containing the harbour of Vathi and in another ten minutes at the junction with the Kyparisso road, taking the fork that strikes out along the ridge of the isthmus. This road continues round the side of the mountain high above the bay of Porto Kaio and leads to the monastery of the Virgin of Porto Kaio where they arrive at 12.27 a.m., one hour after leaving Asomato. In startling contrast to the previous night spent at Kyparisso Leake finds that the monks offer him the most agreeable lodgings he has met with in the Mani!

The monastery is in a spectacular location facing south and overlooking the bay with behind it a spring coming from the mountain above. There are terraces of gardens watered by this spring. In this green and luxuriant spot are olive, carob and orange trees mixed with cypresses. Leake is given a salad for dinner with some of the choicest Maniot honey whilst the rest of the party enjoy bean soup with salted olives. During this meal an old man repeatedly accuses Gika Mavromikhali of having killed his brother. A fine example of Maniot hospitality! On being pressed by Gika the old man admits that the killer may not have been Gika personally but was definitely one of his family. Gika does not contradict this but emphasises that the killing was done in an 'honourable' way in the course of a war between the two families.

He confesses that just sixteen days ago he had destroyed a pyrgos of one of his enemies in Areopolis. Gika also offers 'a crumb of information' telling Leake that in ancient times Porto

Kaio was called *Psamathia*, but when Leake enquires where Gika got this information from the Greek admits he has no idea adding that this name is known only to those who are 'a little tinctured with letters'! Leake accepts that the name was used prior to the arrival of the Franks and Venetians, the latter having called this harbour Porto delle Quaglie. He further comments that the Venetians, and subsequently the Turks, have been greatly responsible for destroying any vestiges of antiquity here in the Mani as in the rest of Greece.

On the Greek Islands and the southern coasts many Italian words have been adopted into the dialect, whilst in the same manner Turkish words have found their way into the northern and continental dialect. Greek sailors, more than any other class of the population, are familiar with the Italian language.

Leake describes Porto Kaio (figure 9) as a beautiful circular harbour with a narrow entrance and a fine sandy bottom. It has a good depth of water for large ships, a sandy shoal midway between the entrance and the shore beneath the monastery being the only underwater obstacle. At the harbour entrance are the remains of a battery erected by a Major Lambro, an insurgent with the Russians, when Porto Kaio was his stronghold in 1773.

Beyond the ravine in which the monastery has its garden the mountain slopes into the sea. On its summit stand the ruins of a square fortress which Leake considers more respectable than Passava. Leake quotes Coronelli (a mediaeval Venetian traveller) who identified this as the famous fortress of Maina.[1] In the 13th century Maina consisted of a town as well, according to contemporary reports by Pachymer and Nicephorus Gregoras. The latter lists it as one of the three main fortresses of the Southern

---

[1] Inspection reveals that the monastery appears to have been built on the site of the abandoned Fortress of Maina.

69

Figure 9   Porto Kaio

Peloponnese, along with Mistras and Monemvasia, and in Leake's time Maina was still nominally one of the suffragan dioceses of the bishopric of Monemvasia. It was the Italians who first used the word Maina, calling the whole Taygetic peninsular the Braccio di Maina. The fortress of Maina is the boundary for the district of Laghia of Kato Mani or the sunward side. Laghia is the largest and most populous village between Porto Kaio and Skutari on the east coast of the Mani. Near Laghia is Vatas, the chief place of the bishopric of Kolokythi.

Leake and his party leave the monastery at 3.00 p.m. and in just under two hours have passed Kyparisso on the left and by 5.00 p.m. reached Alika. Here Leake lodges in a hut belonging to a friend of Politiko. He obviously did not relish another night with the fleas in Kyparisso!

At 6.30 a.m. on April 14th Leake leaves Alika and at 7.35 a.m. passes between the villages of Ano and Kato Borali (Boulari), and by 8.00 a.m. the party is alongside Nomia and Kita. By 8.35 a.m. they cross the torrent of Mezapo and a halt is called at the solitary hut where they had stopped two days earlier.

Their route now takes them off the direct road and passes through the villages of the Pendadha, then turning right to reach Babaka (Vamvaka) where they halt. It is 10.15 a.m. and Leake dines in the house of his guide, Politiko Tubaki, who has a pyrgos nearby. They are on the road again at 11.00 a.m., leaving Atza (Akia) above them on the right. By 11.25 a.m. they pass through Palkhora and regain the original road taken on the outward trip, arriving in Areopolis at 2.20 p.m.

So ends Leake's trip to the Land of Evil Counsel. He notes that it all went well without any loss or accident, except for a double barrelled pistol of his which had vanished mysteriously. This was on the 12th when they had halted at the solitary house at midday. Leake's suspicions that it had been taken by one of his

71

companions were aroused because, on the return trip, a most suspicious show was made of specifically halting at exactly this spot to search for his missing pistol.

Leake was greatly struck by the misery of the Kakavuliotes. When he asked of his servants what were the commonest articles of provision the reply was: 'Where are we to find oil, vinegar, or wine or bread?', as if such things were luxuries in which the Kakavuliotes never indulged. The scarcity Leake finds during his visit, undoubtedly at that time very pressing, was the consequence of the insufficient harvest of the previous year (1804). To these occasional dearths may perhaps be chiefly ascribed the habitual penury and avarice of the people. Leake's Tzimova companions say that even when the Kakavuliotes had numerous *trattas* (doubling as fishing boats and pirate vessels) in the Archipelago (i.e. the Aegean), and brought home a great deal of plunder, they continued to live in the same miserable manner.

The chief instrument of household furniture in the Deep Mani is the hand-mill in which the *kolambokki* is ground. This is the employment of the women at night, who generally accompany the work with a song of lamentation of some deceased relative who has been killed, perhaps by a hostile family. It is their custom to continue these songs during the whole period of mourning whilst the men allow their beards to grow. This hand-mill is a lineal descendant of the ancient Greek hand-mill just as the songs, which accompany the grinding, are descended directly from *odai epimilioi*.

Except on the great feasts, none but the richest of the Kakavuliotes kill mutton or poultry: they sometimes indulge in an old ox no longer fit for the plough, or a sheep or fowl already at the point of death. Cheese, garlic and maize bread are the principal food; as their district produces none, wine and oil are seldom used.

Even a boy of fifteen has a wrinkled, weather-worn appearance, but diseases are rare. The Maniots live to a great age and their chief evil is a population in disproportion to the natural resources of the country. In its soil and other aspects it (the Deep Mani) resembles many of the islands, such as Kefalonia, Tzerigo, Naxia, Zia, etc. where as in the Mani, all the produce, though excellent of its kind, is seldom plentiful. The villages have in or near them cisterns used to capture rainwater, the prime source of water. The (prickly pear) cacti are very commonly grown around the villages for the sake of their fruit and these, with a few figs and grapes and some common esculent[2] vegetables, are the only horticultural products of Mani.

However, Leake's Kakavuliote companions, who are some of the *first* (sic) characters on the Greek western coast, do not complain: on the contrary, they boast of the sweetness of their mutton, that they send their corn (in good years) to Cerigo, that they occasionally supply the Morea with cattle, and that when the seasons favour them they want for nothing from abroad but wine and cheese. This may be true with regard to the western coasts of the Mani taken as a whole, but there seems to be a great difference between the country to the south and that to the north of Port Oitylo. The latter produces some wine, and a considerable quantity of oil. It is not subject to the drought which destroys the hope of cultivation in the Outer Mani (sic)[3] nor to those gales (which both by sea and land) are the most mischievous in the immediate vicinity of Capes Matapan and Malea.

[2] Esculent = edible.
[3] Leake has here confused the Inner and Outer Mani.

73

6

Leake Leaves Areopolis for Kitries (pp. 311–24)

On his return to Areopolis Leake is lodged once again in the house, or as he describes it, the 'cottage' of Gika Mavromikhali. To make room for the visitor all the females of the household are sent to Gika's pyrgos. As night falls the 50 sheep and twelve oxen are driven into the yard; the Maniots never feel secure enough to leave their cattle out in the fields at night.

Leake explains that, not so many years previously, a Frenchman came to Areopolis, it is thought fleeing from justice, and set up as a doctor. His method of curing patients, or rather those who believed in him, was to give them a pinch from his snuff box. Over the course of several years he obtained a reputation among the Maniots for predicting the future. Unfortunately, he did not predict his own fate. One day, returning by sea from Koroni, some Kakavuliotes lay in wait for him and murdered him for the sake of only a few piastres.

Next morning, April 15th, Leake walked down from Areopolis to Limeni, the port, a distance of two miles. The last mile is a very steep descent and Leake comments that the road is only fit for a Maniot and his mule. He then spends the day at the house of Kyr Petro Mavromikhali beside the sea. Limeni, he tells us, consists of five or six magazines[1] and two pyrgi.

---

[1] Magazine – This has the customary meaning of a storage place for arms, ammunition and other provisions for use in war. (OED).

North of Kyr Petro's pyrgos is a small monastery with a little garden.

Oitylo Bay extends to the north of Limeni. On a hill above the north-east corner of the bay is the ruined fortress of Kelefa. Leake appears to have forgotten that he had previously described it as a Byzantine fortress, for he now notes that tradition has it that it is of Venetian construction and that the Turks repaired and enlarged it. Nevertheless, Leake then adds that Kelefa and Zarnata existed before the Venetian conquest of 1685 and were only taken over by the Turks in 1715.

On the brow of the next steep hill is the town of Oitylo (Vitylo) which has up to 250 houses. It is separated from Kelefa by a steep ravine, the sides of which are green with corn. As the Oitylites were in conflict with Andon Bey, Leake felt it was not prudent to go there but comments that Mr Morrit (of Rokeby) had visited the town in 1795. Leake refers to the whole bay of Oitylo as Porto Oitylo and remarks that it is a bad harbour as it is fully exposed to the western winds.

He then recounts the story of the emigration of fifty families from Oitylo to Corsica in 1655. He repeats the story of Napoleon's so-called Maniot origins – his ancestors were supposedly one of the 35 emigrant families. Their name was *Kalomegas*, which can be very roughly translated as *Buonaparte*. The Tzimosites[2] (hating the neighbouring Oityliotes), like Leake, disbelieve this story of Napoleon's origins. Instead, Leake suggests this was an Italian name from Corsica, pre-dating the arrival of the emigrants.

Petro Mavromikhali, or Kyr Petruni, as he is commonly called, is described by Leake as the grandest Maniot he has yet seen: a smart and genteel looking man of 30 to 40 years old and dressed

---

[2] The inhabitants of Areopolis.

76

in green velvet. He does not take the title of kapitain but holds the position of deputy governor of Mesa Mani. In fact, Leake adds, this gives him more power and influence than any of the neighbouring kapitains. Kyr Petruni recounts the story of how his father 'rescued' an English ship in a most resolute and brave manner in 1792 (i.e. thirteen years previously). The vessel belonged to a London company, Smith and St Barbe, and was commanded by a Captain Brown. It had been driven into the Gulf of Messenia by a gale which, when it subsided, left the vessel near the coast by Pyrgos (Dirou). It was in grave danger as there was a tremendous sea setting on the shore. The crew had given themselves up for lost and were making no effort to save the ship. Kyr Petruni's father put off from Oitylo Bay with a small boat to give assistance and was able to pilot the English ship into Limeni. As it arrived all the local Maniots gathered, both by land and sea, in preparation for plundering it. But Kyr Petruni's father, along with the members of the Mavromikhali clan, kept watch to protect the vessel. Captain Brown and his ship remained at Limeni for 19 days before safely setting sail again.

Kyr Petruni's aunt, his father's sister, is the wife of Andon Bey. Following Leake's visit Andon Bey fell into disgrace with the Turks in 1807 because he had not been very assiduous in halting the anti-Turkish activities of his cousin, the deposed Tzanet Bey. Kapitain-Pasha Hassan had bombarded Gythio for a second time with much greater force, as he had described to Leake during their meeting at Monemvasia, and did considerable damage to the houses and towers of the Grigorakis clan. Andon Bey hung onto his position but resigned discreetly three years after Leake's visit in favour of his son-in-law, Konstantinos Zervakos, who had good relations with the Pasha at Tripolis. This did not please the Maniots, especially the Grigorakis family, who drove him back to the Pasha. In the same year, 1810, the assembled heads of the

Maniot clans met in Gythio and elected another Grigorakis, one Theodore Zanetakis, as the new Bey. His uncle was, of course, Tzanet ex-Bey! Theodoro Bey Zanetakis ruled until 1815 when he was deposed and replaced by the last and greatest of the Maniot Beys, Kyr Petruni, a position he held until the Greek 'revolution'.[3]

Leake reports that Andon Bey has done his utmost to assist the Turkish government (i.e. Hassan Bey) in destroying the *trattas* and pirate boats of the Maniots, and in reducing them to submission. All the best part of the Mani – viz. Zanarta, Andruvista, Milea, Kastania – however, are against him and more inclined to his enemy Tzanet (the ex-Bey) and to his son Peter, the Bey-Zaade, who is their hero. Khristea, captain of Zygos, is considered neutral, having married a Mavromikhali, being personally a friend of Hassan Bey and carefully cultivated by Kyr Petruni. The latter was the chief supporter of Andon Bey's interest on the western shore (i.e. the Outer Mani). Khristea therefore adds no strength to the party of Tzanet, though obliged to live on good terms with that party on account of his position in the midst of them.

On the eastern coast (of the Mani), between Skutari and Porto Kaio, Andon Bey has many enemies; his power, as a Turkish lieutenant, is disagreeable to the Maniots in general, though they are too weak at sea to dispute it: their family quarrels are a great assistance to the Turks. These quarrels result in families often unpredictably changing sides. As a result the Maniots have a proverb relating to their politics: *Maniatika Miniatika* (monthly Maniots!).

On the next morning, April 16th, Leake sails from Limeni in a little *Kaïk* belonging to Kyr Petruni. There is a brisk Levanter (east wind) blowing down between Oitylo and Kelefa, but as soon

---

[3] Greenhalgh and Eliopoulis, *Deep into Mani*, p. 32.

as they reach the entrance to the bay and the open sea the breeze dies and they are in a dead calm. However, there is a great swell from the south which, together with the lack of wind, makes sailing more difficult. The sailors tell Leake that this is normally a sign that a strong on-shore southerly wind will start to blow. In the relative calm the *kaik* is rowed for seven miles under steep cliffs (Leake makes no mention of passing by Trahila) until they are abreast of Aios Dhimitri. This consists of a pyrgos and a village on the water's edge. Above is the town of Platsa, the chief place of the area of Zygos. On the road to Oitylo are Langahda and Poliana (today also known as Aghios Nikon).

Three miles beyond Aios Dhimitiri is Leftro, with a pyrgos and church; this is the residence of Kapitain Khristea. Between these two places the mountain side is covered with olive groves while above is a green looking glen where there is the village of Iznia, belonging to Milea. Above Leftro is the town of Pyrgos. Leake had planned to stop off at Leftro, which was the only place in the Outer Mani, thanks to the stable state of the parties and family alliances there, that was safe enough for his reception. However, as the expected sirocco had freshened, and with a heavy sea running, it was not possible to land and they were obliged to steer directly to Cape Kurtissa.

The shoreline gave way from high cliffs to regular fertile slopes rising up to the range of Taygetos (figure 10). The Mani peak of Saint Elias or Makryum (Prophet Elias) appears close to the coast halfway between Leftro and Skardhamula (Kardamyli). The latter is four to five miles from Leftro and has an island opposite it on which there is a monastery. Beyond Kardamyli a deep ravine descends almost directly from the peaks of Prophet Elias. The olive plantations in this region are very fine.

It is five miles from Kardamyli to Cape Kurtissa along a steep rocky coast. The *kaik* ships some water, being heavily laden and

Figure 10 View of the Taygetos

low-masted, and the situation becomes quite dangerous as the following wind leaves the sails flapping. The Maniots are good sailors, as Leake encouragingly remarks, and with cautious steering they arrive safely under the lee of Cape Kurtissa where the harbour of Kitries is situated, lying at the bottom of a bight one and a half miles east of the Cape. It is 12.30 p.m. when they arrive and find the frigate of Seremet Bey (the Kapitain Pasha) anchored with a corvette in the roads. It is estimated to take ten hours by land from Oitylo to Kitries which is about 30 miles, but parts are so rugged that it would take anyone but a Maniot twelve hours. By footpath Kitries is three and a half hours north from Kardamyli, and Leftro one and a half hours to the south of Kardamyli.

On landing Leake refuses the offer of accommodation by Cavaliere Dhimitrio Gligoraki in the house of the Bey, preferring to stay in one of the magazines by the seaside. The Bey's pyrgos and its adjoining buildings are large and agreeably situated on a height above the sea. The hills around Kitries are covered with terraces of wheat, which is now in ear and already beginning to look yellow at the bottom of the stalk. Rain is needed if the wheat is not to be spoiled. Sowing of the corn is done at the time of the first rains of autumn, either September or October, but in the higher villages at the foot of the Taygetos where snow is on the ground all winter the crop sown in September is not reaped until the following August. In the more fertile parts of the Mani a yield of ten parts of crop to one of seed is obtained but this falls to three or four parts to one for the higher ground. In contrast to the Mani, in the best lands in Messenia the sowing is delayed until November or even December and, without irrigation, a yield of twenty parts to one of seed is harvested.

Leake finds that, apart from the Bey's pyrgos and houses. there are only five or six magazines in Kitries. In one of these he notes a Turk keeping shop for the Greeks. This notable reversal of roles could only have happened in the Mani where the Turkish presence is so rare. The Cavaliere Gligoraki, whom Leake finds to be a sensible, quick and conversable character, tells Leake, in the course of their conversation, of his stay in St. Petersburg. There he encountered the British ambassador who, apparently, spoke Greek. The ambassador warmly invited the Cavaliere to visit England but the Empress (Catherine the Great), on hearing of this invitation, told the ambassador to 'shut up'!

The Bey's pyrgos was built by Tzanet Koutipharis, the first Bey, and was the residence of the Bey of Mani until Tzanet Bey built his pyrgos at Mavrovouni. Andon Bey intends to make Marathonisi (Gythio) his residence. The land between Kitries and Kardamyli is called Zanarta which extends to the highest ridges of the Taygetos. At a distance of one and a half hours from the sea stand the ruins of the fortress of Zanarta. Leake, quoting Coronelli, reports that in 1685 it was taken by the Venetians from the Turks who then held there a garrison of 600 men and 51 pieces of cannon. Strangely, Leake omits to mention that, more recently, when Zanarta was held by the Maniots, the Turks besieged it without success and only managed to gain possession by negotiations with Tzanet Kutifari. The Maniots were allowed to leave peacefully with their cannon. They then settled themselves near Milea in the village of Kivelia and fortified the neighbouring peak by dragging their cannons rescued from Zanarta to the very top.

For a period from 1771 to 1780 Kitries served as the main port for the southern Morea, loading European vessels, including those from London, with vallonea, vermilion, oil, figs and other local products. Kitries had the great advantage of being the safest harbour to the west of Cape Matapan. But Leake does not add that another important advantage for Kitries, as opposed to mooring in Kalamata at the head of the Gulf, was that better winds could be obtained from Cape Kurtissa, so avoiding the risk of vessels being becalmed.

On April 17th at 7.05 a.m. Leake leaves Kitries by land for Kalamata, proceeding along the summit of the cliffs overhanging the sea beach (figure 11). At 7.43 a.m. he crosses the ravine of the Vyrou gorge and at 8.10 a.m. reaches what he calls Palea Mandinia, which is now known as Mikri Mandinia. Palea Mikri Mandinia is actually two kilometres inland and consists of nothing but a church with the remains of some Hellenic buildings. Leake states that the two villages of Mikri and Meghali Mandinia are a mile east of Palea Mandinia and together consist of about 100 houses. In fact, the latter is Meghali Mantinia and Leake appears to have got his topography in a muddle. What he refers to as Palia Mandinia was really Paliochora Avias. Leake ponders on how the Hellenic name of Mantineia came to be used, for he is certain that this is the site of Abiea (Avia). Little did he know that he was right! His confusion is quite understandable. He passes some fine fields of wheat where women are clearing weeds. When asked what they are doing they answer *laconically* that they are *botanizing*, that is gathering horta.

At 8.25 a.m., after resting by the church, Leake and his companions descend to the beach and pass under a steep cliff covered with myrtle and ivy. Thirty minutes after, they reach a mill situated on a stream strongly impregnated with salt. This place is called Armyro (nowadays Almiro), after the salt river. Opposite this is the anchorage used as the port for Kalamata in times when ships cannot safely stay in the roadstead nearer the town. They take a five-minute halt and continue along a stony beach under a large mountain. At 10.00 a.m. they arrive on a sandy beach in the south-eastern angle of the great Messenian plain. At 10.15 a.m. they enter olive plantations with Selitza on the right but out of sight above unstable cliffs. Large masses of

Figure 11 View of Doli above Kitries

84

rock break off at times, an occurrence which the Zarnatiotes believe prophesies the fall of some great Maniot kapitain.

Leake observes that all the olive trees are young, the older trees having been destroyed in the course of the wars between the Maniots and the Turks. This destruction of olive trees is one of the greatest calamities to which the inhabitants of Greece can be exposed. Nothing of a similar nature is found in more northern countries. As Leake sadly observes, the olive which has provided food and profit for centuries, thanks to its very slow growth, can be destroyed in a moment.

At 10.26 a.m. they cross a brook. Then, ten minutes later, they reach a pyrgos belonging to the *Kavaleraki,* as the son of Dhimitro Gligoraki is called. All the ground is covered with wild lavender until they reach the gardens of Kalamata, (figure 12) which are fenced with prickly pear. Unfortunately, the fences and the gardens are in a state of ruin owing to the frequent battles in this frontier zone of the Mani. Leake enters Kalamata at 10.45 a.m., nearly three and a half hours after leaving Kitries.

Figure 12   View of Kalamata

7

Leake in Kalamata (pp. 326–51)

The first thing which strikes Leake on entering the town is the ruined mansion of Benahki that had been destroyed over 30 years earlier by the Turks in reprisal for the heads of the Greek families supporting the insurrection on the arrival of the Russian invasion. Benahki's son became Russian consul in Corfu but is still in receipt of the rents from his considerable estate in Kalamata that are collected by his sister who lives in a pyrgo in the town.

Leake is housed in the house of Kir Elias Tanzi whose brother, Dhimitrio, is the *hodji-bashi*[1] of Kalamata. On this visit Leake does not meet Dhimitrio as he is absent in Tripolitza to attend a meeting, summoned by the Pasha, of all the *hodji-bashas* of the Peloponnese. They are discussing how to raise troops to support Turkish reinforcements which are expected shortly.

April 18th, the next day, is the Holy Thursday before Easter. Leake is awakened two hours before dawn by a young sub-deacon knocking on the doors of all the houses. He calls out, 'Christians, come to church!' The Lenten fast is very gradually relaxed. Oil is permitted on the Thursday, but on Good Friday it is forbidden even to set the table for dinner. At 7.30 p.m. the church services begin and continue until 11.00 p.m., during which twelve masses

---

[1] *Hodji-bashi* is Turkish for respected citizens who have made the pilgrimage, Moslems to Mecca or Christians to Jerusalem.

are said and an equal number of readings from the Gospels describing the sufferings of Christ prior to His crucifixion, which the Greeks believe took place at midnight on Thursday. Just before the service, Leake felt a slight earth tremor, which he considered very appropriate on this special occasion, the first tremor he had encountered on his travels in the Peloponnese.

On April 19th an important Turkish official, Mahmud Aga, arrives in Kalamata on a mission from the Pasha in Tripolitza to make enquiries about some robbers in the vicinity which were a source of concern to the Turkish authorities.

The next morning, Saturday April 20th, the ceremony of the Entombment is held two hours before dawn. All the population of Kalamata are gathered in the dark streets, scrambling to light their candles from the pappas' candle (figure 13). Then a procession forms, consisting mainly of women, which makes its way to the church. Leake comments that Kalamata is the only town in the Peloponnese where this Christian ceremony is generally carried out in the open, otherwise it takes place only inside the church or in monastery precincts out of sight of the Turks. Obviously, in remote villages the procession takes place unhindered by the Turkish authorities.

Easter Sunday, called by the Greeks *Lambri,* is a day of modest celebrations[2]. When two acquaintances first meet on Easter Sunday the general custom is for one to say, 'Christ hath risen!', to which the other replies, 'Truly He hath risen!' All morning is occupied in visiting and drinking coffee. At about 11.00 a.m. dinner takes place, after which it is not unusual to sing the words of salutation given above or something else applicable to the day.

---

[2] Leake, on page 351, calls this April 20th. He is mistaken, however, as he had correctly stated that Good Friday was on April 19th. Leake leaves Kalamata the next day which he accurately gives as April 22nd.

Figure 13   Archevêque Grec

The population of Kalamata consists of 400 families, of whom only six are Turkish. The government of the town is controlled by the leading Greeks. The *voivoda*[3] can be readily removed in case of complaints. The resident *voivoda* is only responsible for revenue collection. The *mukata*[4] *of Kazasi* is generally given by the Porte to one of his favourites in Constantinople for a period of twelve to eighteen months, who then sells it on to another Turk for four to six months. It is the latter who then appoints the resident *voivoda*.

In like manner the *kadi* (or *judge*) is a deputy appointed by a principal in Constantinople who has purchased the *kadalik*. Law and order is maintained in Kalamata and its environs by an Albanian *boluk-bashi*[5] with 40 men under his command, who are responsible for apprehending robbers, etc. This band is in the control of the Greek *archon* (magistrate).

Trade and Manufacture in Kalamata

A fair or market is held in Kalamata every Sunday when maize, wheat, barley, cheese, butter and skins are traded for manufactured goods coming from Europe or Turkey. This produce is gathered from a wide distance including Arcadia, Tripolitza, Karitena and elsewhere. Kalamata is an important market too for cattle and all kinds of livestock as well as olive oil, figs, raw cotton and leather produced in the Messenian plain and the nearer parts of the Mani.

It is also a manufacturing centre for silk handkerchiefs (exported to the Levant), and a silk gauze (or muslin) used as

---

[3] Governor.
[4] *Mukata* is the 'farming out' of public revenues.
[5] *Boluk-bashi* is a mercenary under Turkish control.

mosquito nets in Constantinople, Greece and the western parts of Asia Minor. This gauze sells for 13 *paras* per yard. The raw silk used in the manufacture of these two products amounts to 1,500 okes (1840.5kg), the finished articles being sold at sixty times the value of the raw silk.

The third most important manufacture is tanned leather boots and slippers; the hides are tanned with vallonea and coloured red, black and yellow. The leather requires five months' soaking to complete the tanning and an equal quantity of lentisk (*skinos*) leaves are added to the vallonea. The dyes used for the colouring are a closely guarded secret.

Kalamata's principal exports consist of :

1. Raw silk. About 7000 okes (8590 kg), valued at 180,000 piastres (or £900,000 in today's terms), are exported to Turin, Smyrna, Chios, Skodra and Ioannina. In the latter two places the silk is made into lace for Albanian dresses.

2. Figs. These come locally from Andrusa and Nisi (Messini) and nearly two million *tzapelis* are exported. Leake explains that a *tzapelis* is a small basket weighing two pounds. Half of these figs are sent to Trieste, the rest go to Greece and Smyrna. The Kalamata figs are surpassed only by those from Smyrna.

3. Olive oil. This comes entirely from the vicinity of Kalamata and, in a good year, 6000 barrels are exported. The oil can fetch 30 to 38 piastres per barrel (equivalent today to £150–£190), but in the year of Leake's visit the price had risen to 40 to 48 piastres (£200–£240). All of the oil remained in Greece and cost the consumer, for example, in Ionannina 84 piastres per barrel (about £2.60 per litre today).

The Surroundings of Kalamata

The Messenian plain and the foothills of the Taygetos are covered with figs, vines and mulberry trees. This presents as rich a cultivation as can well be imagined. Leake notes that the fertility of the plain, one of the most favoured and fertile districts of the Peloponnese, was a fatal gift of nature to its ancient inhabitants. The Laconian neighbours were tempted from their more impoverished soils around Sparta and gradually encroached on the western slopes of the Taygetos. After a gallant resistance of 80 years in the eighth century BC the Messenians were subjected by the greater numbers of Laconians to a most cruel servitude which lasted three centuries.

Leake comments that on the seaward side of Kalamata the lack of drainage may render the air less healthy than it was in classical times, and that a native of northern Europe would differ in opinion from an Athenian as to the clemency of the summer heat. However, Leake does not doubt that, generally speaking, Kalamata and the Messenian plain offer a climate that is salubrious as well as delightful.

The town of Kalamata is situated a mile inland from the sea on the left bank of a torrent from the Taygetos, the river Nethonas, and in front of a hill crowned by a ruined castle. This torrent, which can at times be as much as a hundred yards wide, flows below a steep cliff on top of which are the remains of the (Frankish) castle walls. To the west of the torrent is a small suburb of Kalamata with mills and gardens situated alongside an artificial channel which diverts water from the river.

The ancient Greeks could not have failed to see the advantages of the castle hill, on the banks of a river, with the mountains close at hand but within a short distance of the sea. This site in classical times was called *Pharae* and was reputed to have been founded by

Hermes. After the Trojan wars *Pharae* was the residence of Ortilochus, and Homer recounts how Telemachus rested overnight here on his journey from Pylos to Sparta. Homer indicates that *Pharae* was approximately midway between Pylos and Sparta and that Telemachus took two days each way on his outward and return journeys.

Kalamata's importance as a port is emphasised by Leake since it not only served the district of Andrusa, Londari and even Mistras but was an important *entrepôt* for commodities from the interior of the Peloponnese and all its southern coasts. However, it is a safe anchorage only in summer months. From October onwards ships retired for safety to Armyro on the Paralia Verga under the lee of the Taygetos. But an even surer anchorage is Kitries, the best harbour in the Gulf of Messenia. Cape Kurtisa gives protection from the prevailing southerly gales and is without danger from any other winds save those of the rarer north and north-westerlies. Leake comments that a large fleet might anchor at Kitries and that Messenia has the resources to supply an army better than any other part of the Peloponnese.

Before the French revolution the port was chiefly frequented by French vessels carrying grain, morocco leather, raw silk and cotton to Marseilles. With the outbreak of the Napoleonic wars the only vessels coming to Kalamata were from the Greek islands, Albania and Sclavonia (Croatia).

The Raising of Silkworms and Manufacture of Silk

Almost every house in Kalamata is provided with a chamber for rearing silkworms. The eggs are purchased by the householder and the price varies according to the crop of the preceding year. The year of Leake's visit it was five piastres for a measure of eight *drams*, but in more plentiful years the price could drop to two piastres.

The eggs are wrapped in a cloth and the worms (*maudlia*) hatch at the end of April or the beginning of May. Once hatched mulberry leaves are placed on them. The worms then mount upon the leaves which are put in round shallow baskets. In this state the worms are called *miga*, and each worm is given each day fresh small leaves. As the worm grows, so does the size of the collected mulberry leaves. At the end of 15 days the worm sleeps for two days and sheds its skin, when it is called *portokuli*, and in this state it eats for twelve days with fresh leaves each morning. The worm has a second sleep of two days and again sheds its skin; at this stage it becomes *dhefteraki*.

The worm is then moved out of its basket and put onto a frame of reeds tied together, about twelve to fourteen feet long and five to six feet broad. This is called a *kalamoti*. The *kalamotes* are placed one above the other at intervals of eight to ten inches, making a stack as high as the chamber permits. In Asia Minor the worms are kept in special huts in the fields where the mulberry trees grow, but in Kalamata they are kept in the private houses. The *dhefteraki* now eats for a further ten days and sheds its skin once again to become a *tritaki*. The worm is quite sizeable now and its appetite has increased accordingly, so it gets leaves three times a day, at morning, noon and night. This period lasts eight days after which the *tetraki* sleeps for three days and once more loses its skin. In its last and largest state the worm is called *megales* or great. Once again the worms get leaves three times a day but cease eating on the eighth day when they begin to climb upwards.

Branches or *khladia* are placed on the *kalamotes* for the worms to climb upon and it is from these branches that the silk is spun. The branches are taken from the lentisk tree. On a single branch as many as four worms will form a group, which is called *kukulia*.

At the end of fifteen days the *kukulia* are placed in the sun which, as it is now late June and at its solstice, kills the chrysalis by its heat. Some of the *kukulia* are reserved to make the eggs for the next year and soon after laying their eggs the moths, or *nefteres*, eat their way out of the cocoon.

This whole process, in particular the appetite of the worms, is totally dependent on the state of the weather. If May and June are hot it proceeds more rapidly and the worms eat more leaves, but if it is rainy and cooler their appetite diminishes and their growth is slowed down. The worms are so delicate that the sound of thunder or even a pistol shot can sometimes kill them.

On the Tuesday after Easter, April 22nd, Leake continues his travels in Messenia, leaving Kalamata after a stay of five days and heading in the direction of Andrussa, Itome and Pylos, Methoni and Koroni.

8

Leake Returns to Kalamata (pp. 448–76)

By May 2nd Leake has reached Koroni and from there he sails back to Kalamata, arriving in only four hours thanks to a brisk breeze (*imbat*[1]). The *kaike*, he remarks, most greatly resembled the boat Ulysses built on the island of Calypso; the only difference being that Leake's boat has two masts rather than a single one. He also remarks that the construction of the gunwales with vine branches is exactly as Homer described. Leake finds a greater difference between the temperature of Koroni and Kalamata, and remarks that the latter place is one of the hottest situations in the Peloponnese. At Koroni the *imbat* is fresh and blows towards the mouth of the Messenian Gulf. In Kalamata in the middle of the summer the *maestrale* blows with great force in the afternoon and is much less refreshing than at Methoni. Leake remarks that it has come across the heated mountains and plains from the coast of Navarino before reaching Kalamata. Leake stays the next few days with Kyr Elias, who explains that one of his ancestors came from the Medici family in Florence. Elias' forbear was wrecked off Oitylo and lived there for many years taking the family name of Iatrianos, according to Leake's host a Greek translation of Medici! It was still a leading family in the town and commanded 205 muskets. Kyr Elias is related to the

---

[1] Turkish for the cool sea breeze prevailing in the summer months.

Iatrianos family but does not bear its name. As Leake comments, this is the reverse of the story of the Buonapartes of Corsica coming from Oitylo and with the family name Kalomeros, and perhaps has no better foundation.

Leake plans to continue his travels on 5th May through the Taygetos mountains. He wishes to examine the pass linking Laconia to Messenia, describing it as the ordinary communication between the two. He wishes to reach Mistras by the mountain road through Kutzova, known today as the Lagharda pass. Leake's map shows a village marked Kutzova with, in brackets, the word Thalame. There is no place of this name on present-day maps. The village of Artemisia is on the road through the pass and is probably where Leake was aiming for.

He realises that this route may be difficult on account of robbers. Two months previously robbers had come down from the mountains to the surroundings of Kalamata and committed some depredations. Kyr Elias Tanzi was ready to arrange for one of the mountain villages friendly with the robbers to supply mules and an escort for Leake. Unfortunately, however, only three days previously Captain George Kolokotroni himself, with a large body of followers, had appeared in the gardens around the rear of Kalamata and carried away as hostages five or six persons. The 40 Albanian soldiers, lately sent by the Pasha in Tripoli to keep order in the region, sallied forth and near the Monastery of St Elias encountered Kolokotroni and his band and wounded a couple of them. But Kolokotroni escaped with his hostages and took refuge in Kutzova.

Leake's janissary, Amus by name, with the help of his friend Captain Andonaski of Longastra (probably Logastra) proposed to conduct Leake through the mountains. The Captain's plan was to provide Leake with one or two of his sons as security, but this plan met with problems. The Primates of Kalamata raised objections to this plan by stating that if Leake succeeded in going through the mountains safely, the Pasha would consider their recent representations concerning the danger of the robbers in the selfsame mountains to be false.

Leake is in no doubt that the robbers would undertake, in return for a stipulated sum of money, to conduct him safely through the mountains. However, his host in Kalamata, the *hodji-bashi* Dhimitrio Tanzi (figure 14), was terribly alarmed at this proposal and told Leake that he would certainly lose his head if he (Leake) did in fact reach Sparta safely! Diplomatically, therefore, Leake abandons his plan, realising that the robbers are in control of all the summits of the Taygetos as far as the *Lycoeum*. They were close to his path across the Makryplai the day he had crossed from Sparta, as he had been informed by the *dervendji*. It seems the band had retired to Bardhunia where they were well received by Amus Aga.

Leake also has fresh news of recent events in the Mani. Since his visit Seremet Bey, the Turkish Admiral, has extracted from the people of Oitylo a fine of five piastres (60 pence) per house as well as demanding hostages against their future good behaviour. It appears that they had neglected to obey his mandates regarding the tributes they were obliged to pay. Likewise Tzanet Bey had been forced to give the Admiral similar securities and surrender his son George. Also hostage is his son Petro Bey-Zaade. Furthermore, Captain Khristea had had to give his son as hostage together with his famous cannon which he had used to batter down his enemies' towers! The Admiral too has had his misfortunes. His corvette was driven ashore in Oitylo Bay during a gale on 23rd April. Although its masts were cut away, this was not sufficient to save it from being driven ashore, and it is now being repaired.

Leake attended that Sunday morning, May 5th, the Kalamata

Figure 14   Archonte Grec

fair, which since it coincided with the feast day of St George was not so well attended. On St George's day all those who can afford it kill one of their best lambs and pass the day in feasting and idleness. For this reason the market was unusually empty. In Constantinople the lambs are not killed before the feast day, but the Moreites (*sic*) boast that they keep Easter in a superior style to those from Constantinople. Leake takes his final leave of Kalamata at 12.05 p.m. that day, setting off in the direction of Andrussa.

Glossary

Agoi	Vettura or four wheeled carriage for hire.
Agoyates	Coachman.
Archones	Magistrates.
Basha (Bashaw)	Variation of Pasha, applied to a grandee or haughty imperious man.
Bedaat	Tax.
Boluk bashi or basha-bazouk	Literally 'wrong headed', a mercenary or irregular Turkish soldier with a notorious reputation for pillage and brutality.
Dhekatia	Tithes, one seventh of harvest or product.
Hodji (Hajji)	An individual who made the pilgrimage or hajj.
Firman (Firhman)	Oriental sovereign's edict, grant or permit.
Kalyvia	Settlement or village.
Kintal (Cantar)	Measure of weight, equivalent to 119lb (54kg)
Kazasi	Court or region of justice, subordinate to a governate e.g. to the Morea

Kharatj	Annual capitation tax paid by Greeks, known as 'to karti', since if they left their own districts they had to carry a written receipt to prove they had paid the tax, otherwise it would be imposed again.
Khoja (Khwaja)	A scribe or teacher in a Turkish school.
Kolambokki	Corn or maize.
Konak	Rest quarters at end of day's march
Liva	Governate, i.e. the Morea.
Malaya	Tenant.
Malikhiane	A 'farm' for life, i.e. the right to collect the tax or revenue due from an activity yielding profit.
Milliaji	Measure of weight, equivalent to 10cwt.
Modhia	A group of uninhabited islands in the Ionian sea east of Ithica.
Mukata	'Farming out' of collection of public revenues.
Oke	Unit of weight = 2.705 lb.
Spahi	Member of Turkish irregular cavalry.
Tjiftlik	A Turkish-owned domain or estate.
Vilayetia	Civil district or commune.
Voivoda	Regional governor.

Bibliography

Bowen, Sir George, *A Handbook for Travellers in Greece*, 5th Edn, (John Murray, 1884)

Brewer, David, *The Flame of Freedom*, (John Murray, 2001)

Brewer, David, *Greece, the Hidden Centuries*, (I B Tauris, 2010)

Charles-Roux, François, *L'Angleterre et l'Expédition Française en Egypte*, (Royal Egyptian Geographic Society, Cairo, 1925)

Greenhalgh, Peter, and Eliopoulos, Edward, *Deep into the Mani*, (Faber and Faber, 1985)

Leigh Fermor, Sir Patrick, *Mani: Travels in the Southern Peloponnese*, (John Murray, 1958)

Marsden, J. H., *A Brief Memoir of the Life and Writings of the Late Lt Col William Martin Leake*, (1864)

Pausanias, *Guide to Greece* (2 volumes), translated by Peter Levi, (Penguin, 1971)

Playfair, Sir Robert Lambert, *Handbook to the Mediterranean*, 3rd Edn, (John Murray, 1890)

Saitis, Yannis, *Greek Traditional Architecture, Mani*, (Melissa Books, Athens, 1990)

St Clair, William, *That Greece Might Still Be Free*, 2nd Edn, (Openbook Publishers, Cambridge, 2008)

Stephanopoli, Dimo and Nicolo, *Voyages en Grèce Pendant les Années 1797 et 1798*, rédigé par un professeur de la Prytanée, (Guilleminet, Paris, 1800)

Wagstaff, J. M., *Actes du Colloque, 4-7 Novembre 1993 Limeni, Aeropoli*, (Institut de Recherches NéoHelléniques, F N R S, Athens, 1996)

My Life
(With a Nod to
Billy Joel)

*Growing up in Brighton in the 1960s and 70s with a hair
lip and wearing bikini bottoms*

Stuart Owen

Warning: Contains some words that might not offend!

Table of Contents

Thanks

Special thanks to David and all the editing team at Global for maintaining a significant level of professionalism and very kindly laughing at my crap jokes, whilst having to deal with an absolute comma retard of a client! Now this is all over, you can get the urgent therapy that you so desperately need!

Dedication

To the Love Of My Life, Di, for putting up with me for so many years; to Charlie, Georgina and Lewis, for being such fabulous kids; to Megan, for producing my gorgeous Granddaughter, Ava; and to Fi, for being a great sister, thank you x

Intro

As I approached my 60th birthday, I thought about all the things I'd achieved and experienced throughout those years. The people I've met, some famous, some not; the places I've been to; the health issues I've experienced since birth and more recently (both mental and physical); music; my fascination with BRA's; women; kids, etc. I know very little about my parent's lives as they never wrote anything down, and I wanted to provide my children and their children with a detailed background of the things I've done so they know more about me. Friends, too, and the important role they've played in my life. Some of it may appear to be a bit self-indulgent, but I wanted to cover everything, warts and all, so much so that my story may appeal to people I don't know and resonate with others.

Throughout my life, I've always tried to make people laugh, whether it be through a gag or pretending to trip over the pavement or whatever. Seeing and/or hearing someone laugh at something you've said or done is such a great feeling as, without getting too morose, there's plenty of sadness in the world. To offset that even for a second, well, where's the harm? Unless you're a cyclist!

I hope you laugh at least once, enjoy it, and thank you for reading it.

Start

I've always been a fat bastard! I once weighed over 20 stone as an adult, partly due to eating 22 fist-sized profiteroles at one sitting for a bet – and was astonished to learn many years later that I was diabetic! I was a plump youth and a fat baby. In fact, I took so long coming out, they shaved my Mum twice!

I eventually made my first worldly appearance at 4:15 pm on April 2nd, 1964, in Buckingham Road Maternity Hospital in Brighton. The hospital was a cold-looking Victorian building that closed for maternity purposes in 1970, presumably because they couldn't be arsed to erect a blue plaque noting my significant arrival six years earlier!

It wasn't just the exterior of the building that was cold. Even at that young age, I remember it being a bit drafty on the inside too, although that was probably more to do with the hair lip (and cleft palate) that HE decided I should be born with. For shits and giggles like! Operations to repair the lip and palate took place during my first few months and were conducted by Dr Crosland. According to Mum, he did a really good job, and it was only later in life that I realised how shit it looked. As, presumably, did any girl to whom I took a fancy, hence my lack of teenage success (and plenty of teenage angst) in that department.

Mum desperately wanted me to be a girl, and as far as I could tell, I wasn't, which was a disappointment for her. There can be no other explanation for the ridiculous clobber she made me wear! Frilly bikini bottoms, a white furry hat that was tied under my chin, and a purple coat. Hideous stuff. The problem was Mum shopped for clothes at M&S, expensive stuff that kids in posher environments might wear but which no other child in Coldean was wearing. This caused me significant problems further down the line.

Our home was a 3-bed, semi-detached house in Coldean ('28PR') on the northern outskirts of the town, with access to Wild Park at the top of the road and a pathway into Stanmer Park at the bottom. Unsurprisingly, those crazy dudes in the planning department back in the 1930's decided to call it Park Road! It was situated on a steep hill, and it's austere, slightly dark design clearly inspired Alfred Hitchcock to shoot the distant shots of the house in Psycho. It remained the family home for 60 years.

Family Entertainment

Dad was Rupert John Owen – he hated being called 'Rupert' – named after his father- so he was always known as 'John'. Apart from when he completed his full name for inclusion into the Brighton Phone Directory. And proceeded to receive phone calls at all hours from cheeky youths in a phone box, who, having stumbled upon his name and number during a random search of the phone book, proceeded to sing 'Rupert The Bear' down the line. Which did not amuse him! I can only remember two things making Dad laugh – The Two Ronnies, and Terry and June –(Dad was the spitting image of Terry Scott)- so a bunch of pissed up, pizza-faced scrotes singing 'Rupert The Bear' down the phone line wasn't going to raise too much of a smile. And it didn't!

Dad was born on Boxing Day, 1920, in Wellfield Road, Streatham, but was, as I've only recently discovered, a genuine bastard! His mother, Lizzie, had married William Owen in 1900 and they had a few kids. William died during the First World War, and Lizzie decided to marry his brother (my Dad's Dad) as you do! Only the marriage didn't take place until November 1921, by which time Dad was 11 months old. Scandalous! Not a lot is known about his early life, other than he spent some time in High Wycombe from where his father's side of the family originated, hence his love of

Wycombe Wanderers, who he watched play Hayes in the FA Amateur Cup Final at Highbury in 1931 (Wycombe won 1-0 in front of a crowd of 32,489), and who he continued to follow from a distance until he died. Together with some of his siblings, he used to follow the drey cart from the nearby Youngs brewery in Wandsworth, collecting up the horseshit in bags and selling it to the gentry for their gardens as a means of earning money to put food on the table.

Dad joined the RAF in the Second World War and saw service in North Africa. Again, not a lot is known about his actual involvement, although I think he was invalided out with pneumonia and sent home. A bit dull, really!

At some point during the 1950's, he started working as a heating and fitting engineer and met (and married) Helen, a nurse who provided massage services as a top-up to her main income. He'd already bought 28PR, and she moved in. The marriage didn't last long, and he divorced her for adultery after a couple of years. Presumably, the 'friendly, professional massages' she provided were just a bit <u>too</u> friendly!

Working for a local firm, Benham's, he also started helping out at the Boys Brigade at St Andrew's church in Moulsecoomb, where he met Mum. As far as I know, she wasn't actually in the Boys Brigade – it was her local church!

Dad's best mate at Benham's was a huge bloke, Alec Bell, who had dark, bushy eyebrows and who only had to look at you to scare the shit out of you! It later transpired that he had been in the SAS, so the shit scary look wasn't all that surprising. He had a lovely petite wife called Trisha, and a year or so after I was born, they had a son, Scott. Given the relative closeness of Dad and Alec, Mum and

Trisha spent some of our early years with their new boys playing together (usually with Scott wearing boy's clothes and me wearing that fucking bikini!).

It's almost certain that Dad contracted asbestosis whilst working at Benham's. He talked with pride at how he had helped rip out the old kitchen at The Metropole Hotel on Brighton seafront and installed a new one. This type of work wasn't uncommon for him and involved asbestos dust and particles being present. No protective clothing or masks in those days. Dad didn't have many friends, but he got on well with Alec. Our families grew apart over the years but were re-acquainted when I took Mum to Trisha's funeral in 2019, about which Alec and Scott were delighted. Sadly, Alec died the following year during Covid, and Scott arranged for his funeral to be shown on Zoom, like so many of those at that time, as the restrictions meant that people couldn't attend in person. Scott came to Mum's funeral two years later, and it was great to restore our friendship.

Joyce Winifred Hicks was born on 24th March, 1931, at Brighton General Hospital. She hated the 'Winifred' bit, so it was never used. Except to wind her up! She had an older brother, Paul, and an older sister, Bet. Home was in Baden Road, Brighton, where she lived until she married Dad on 8th June, 1963, and moved into 28PR.

Mum attended Coombe Road School, close to her home, and eventually won a scholarship to Varndean Girls School in the town. Paul had attended Varndean Boys many years before and was incredibly intelligent. Mum idolized him all his life, and her determination to achieve academic success much later in her own life was, in part, inspired by him. Her first job was working on the Post Office switchboard before she progressed to working for the Foreign and Commonwealth Office and was responsible for the

'Cyprus desk' during the 1950's crisis when it got a bit lively! She attended St Andrew's church from a very young age and joined the Youth Fellowship at the church. Through this, she travelled to the likes of Austria and Switzerland with a very close-knit group of friends.

Neither Mum nor Dad ever really commented on exactly how they met, suffice to say it would have involved St Andrew's church in some way. They courted in the late '50s/early '60s and, in 1962, by now engaged, went on holiday to Guernsey. Accompanied by their respective mothers as chaperones! (Both fathers had long since passed away).

They say opposites attract, and that was never truer than with Mum and Dad. She was a Telegraph-reading, Tory voter who spoke in a posh voice, and he was a Mirror-reading Labour voter with a South London accent who despised women in power (and, as he got older, women in general). He detested Margaret Thatcher, not necessarily due to her politics, but because she was an extremely influential and powerful woman.

I suspect that what probably brought them together was that he was on the rebound, and she was the spinster of the parish. He was 42 when they married; she was 32. Their body clocks were ticking.

Yellow Submarine

Music has always played a big part in my life. My initial bedroom was the box room at the front of our house, and my earliest musical memory is of a couple of blokes walking past our house one night on their way home from the pub at the bottom of our road (the notorious Hiker's Rest), whistling Yellow Submarine, which would date it around 1968.

The next 'popular' tune I can recall was when I attended a party in 1971 and Middle Of The Road's 'Chirpy Chirpy Cheep Cheep' was playing on the radio. When I say it was the best song I'd heard up to that date, it will give you an idea of how crap Mum and Dad's record collection was!

Tug Boat Annie

Also in 1968, another racket turned up in 28PR. My sister, Fiona, was born on 4th June. I'd been told that Mum was going to have a baby and I was going to have a brother or sister. I think my preference was for a sister so I could hand down my dreadful clobber! Anyway, cousin Janet (one of Uncle Paul's daughters) was charged with looking after me while Mum went into hospital. After a while, Mum and Dad arrived home with my sister and, as a sweetener for no longer being an only child/spoilt bastard, gave me Tug Boat Annie. TBA was a huge, blue plastic boat (with two white sideboats), which I was supposed to play with in the bath. The trouble was it took up most of the bath! It was massive! The reason I smelt so badly for many of my formative years was because I couldn't get to the fucking soap! As an attempt to placate this spoilt bastard, TBA was a bit shit!

Twisting My Melons, Man

Life was a bit different now with a younger sister in tow. She used to cry a lot, had a permanently runny nose and was a bit girly. Mum was naturally delighted, and I made it my lifetime's ambition to make my sister's life hell. You can blame Tug Boat Fucking Annie for that! She really didn't deserve me as a brother. She was blonde, pretty and cute, almost the complete opposite of me (although I was blonde). Unfortunately, she looked up to me and would do most things I told her to which, for my part, involved getting her in as much trouble as possible. We were shopping with Mum one day in M&S –(there's a shock)- which had counters with clothes laid out on them and wooden drawers underneath. I persuaded Fi to climb into one such drawer to play hide and seek, which she duly did. I closed the wooden door behind her and wandered off. Mum finished browsing and enquired as to where my sister was. With my honed, perfected, innocent look, I told her I didn't have a clue and that she must have got lost, whereupon Mum went frantic, demanding that a call be put out on the shop tannoy and was searching every aisle for her. After a while, when Mum wasn't looking, I very kindly opened the wooden door so Fi could emerge, blinking in the bright daylight, and I announced to Mum that I'd found her. Fi got a bollocking and I was, temporarily, in the good books for finding her.

Fi also started to play the piano and was quite good, unlike her violin playing, which was shit! She attended Margaret Hardy school in Patcham which involved Mum having to drive her there each day. Some of her friends who lived nearby and attended the same school used to call at our house to catch a lift. I'd answer the door, and they would ask for Fiona. I'd tell them that I was really sorry, but my sister had been hit by a bus the night before, whereupon mascara-streaked tears would stream down their faces—served them right for poncing a lift from Mum!

Fi was very brainy and attended 6th Form College in Dyke Road, Brighton, before going on to Teacher Training College in Bognor. There, she met several friends for life including Keely Allaway, who was skinny and fit and came from Kent, and Darren, Keely's future husband, who was an accomplished musician playing in bands gigging around Brighton.

As she got older and achieved a great deal, initially as a teacher and then as a Deputy Head, I became really proud of her. She had a very close relationship with Mum, who was a constant source of advice when Fi's marriage to her husband, Nick, was crumbling and also when her young sons, Harry and Fraser, were growing up. Having obtained her divorce from Nick, Fi sold the family home in Braintree and moved with her boys to Colchester, close to her new partner, Ian, who Mum adored and who was nicknamed 'The Saint' as he could do no wrong in her eyes. She was a rock when Mum passed away, and whilst she still has plenty of 'blonde' moments, I love her to bits. However, I still refer to her as 'Melons' on account of her unfeasibly large tits when she grew up!

Piano Man

At around the age of 5, I started to play the piano. I can't fully recall exactly how it happened, but I may have first tinkled the ivories of a piano at one of Dad's sisters, Aunty Micky's place in Polegate, and shown a bit of promise. Aunty Micky was the first lesbian I ever met. She lived with a German lady, Celia, in a 2-bed bungalow which had a main bedroom for those two and a spare room for guests. Micky had two short, failed marriages behind her (no kids), and whilst I'm not convinced it was a physical relationship, they certainly shared the main bedroom and slept together. They frequently attended shows at the nearby Congress Theatre in Eastbourne and the subsequent after-show parties, where they met the likes of Danny La Rue and Russ Conway. Micky and Celia would often host large parties at their bungalow, to which Dad would drive us all. I would often be asked to entertain them, either by telling jokes or by playing the piano. They usually had their local Catholic priest present at these parties, which would ramp up the risqué-ness of my gags. So, I guess those were my first real public performances.

My piano playing improved to the extent that I passed the practical exams from Grades 1-6 fairly easily. Unfortunately, for me to be able to go beyond Grade 6 and reach the maximum of Grade 8, I had to pass theory exams, at which I was hopeless. Whilst I could read sheet music, my preference was to memorise the sounds and where the relevant notes were on the keyboard and to play that way. Studying theory in books and taking exams wasn't for me and I was stuck at Grade 6 forever. Like I really gave a shit!

Apart from the impromptu sessions entertaining Aunty Micky's guests, I recall playing a solo recital at Brighton's Royal Pavilion when I was around 9. I think the piece was by Schubert, and I wasn't nervous or fazed at all. I'd got the bug for public performances.

Parklife

Fiona and I initially had a reasonably happy childhood. Money was always tight, so Dad grew vegetables in our back garden, which Mum cooked. We didn't have exotic holidays abroad; most of our holidays were spent in caravans or bungalows in various parts of Dorset, a breathtakingly scenic part of the country. Whilst these trips were discussed in advance, they weren't actually booked until the night before we were due to set off. It later transpired that Mum had a phobia about travelling. She suffered terribly from post-natal depression after Fi was born and wasn't remotely interested in the fact that TBA had capsized and nearly drowned me in the bath! The first signs of strain in her relationship with Dad started to appear as he showed her no sympathy, neither did her Mum, and she only received any kind of support from her sister, Aunty Bet. She was in a very dark place for a long time and oblivious to my strange gurgling noises emanating from the bathroom!

On Sundays, we would all go to St Andrew's church in the morning, and usually to Stanmer Park in the afternoon, where Dad would kick a ball around with me for all of 10 minutes before he gave up, gasping for air. And would then light up a cigarette! He was 43 when I was born and was never really in a fit state to play any sport with me. He occasionally took me swimming at St Luke's school swimming pool in the Queens Park area of the town. The Victorian baths stank of disinfectant, and the water was always freezing, but the coloured, tiled walls were impressive and very much a period piece. He also took me to have cricket coaching sessions at the County Ground in Hove when I was a bit older. Roger Marshall was the pro cricketer who was given the hopeless task of perfecting my forward defensive batting stroke—poor bloke. I couldn't bat to save my life, but I could bowl a bit and delivered figures of 2 overs, one maiden, two runs, and five wickets in an inter-house game at my secondary school, which elevated me to the school team. I only played once as the match overran; Mum and Fi had come to collect me, and as I was going to be late for my paper round, I just walked off, much to the chagrin of my Sports Master. I wasn't selected again. What could have been ......!

Neither Fiona nor I were allowed to have bikes at all because we 'lived on a hill'. This was the absurd reason given whenever I pleaded for a Chopper or a Chipper bike as all the other kids on the estate were tearing around on them, including Ross, who only lived three doors up on the same hill as us! No, it was too dangerous and so we had to make do with arty farty stuff, which I resented and probably explains my lack of interest in basket weaving!

Leaving On a Jet Plane

Our Sunday jaunts into Stanmer Park would occasionally involve Grandma Hicks (Mum's Mum) joining us. Grandma Owen died in 1967 before Fi was born, and I only have very vague memories of her. Grandma Hicks was quite a formidable woman who always seemed old, and I don't recall her ever smiling much. She moved out of the Baden Road house and into Aunty Bet's house in The Avenue and died on 5th December 1975. The date is permanently etched into my memory as it was the day before Brighton played Hereford in a top-of-the-table Division 3 clash at The Goldstone Ground, and Dad had promised that we could go. Grandma's untimely passing, together with Mum's uncontrollable blubbing, meant that for once, Dad had to do the right thing and support his wife, and our attendance at the epic 4-2 win could not take place. Of course, I didn't see it like that and threw a massive tantrum and never forgave Grandma. I doubt she cared, to be honest!

I'm not saying that Auntie Bet and Uncle Paul were desperate to get away from Mum, but they both emigrated to Australia! Bet and her husband, Dick, moved to Perth in December 1976, and Paul and his wife, Gladys, departed a few years later.

Bet was a very kind lady, always jolly and would often give Fiona and me sweets whenever we visited (which we weren't allowed to have at home). Her adult daughters, Sue and Joy, had emigrated to Australia some years before, so when her Mum ruined Brighton v Hereford for me by dying, it made sense for her and Dick to move there too.

Their local church was a Baptist church in Moulsecoomb Way, and they put on a leaving do for Bet and Dick, which involved a young girl playing an acoustic guitar and singing Peter, Paul, and Mary's 'Leaving on a Jet Plane'. It was lovely but not as nice as the mushroom vol-au-vents from the buffet!

Several of Uncle Paul's adult children had also emigrated to Australia in the '60s and '70s, and he had a house built in Scotts Head, north of Sydney, right on the Pacific coast which could be accessed 200 yards from his home. It was absolutely idyllic, and I fell in love with the place when I first visited it in 1994.

Friends Will Be Friends Part 1

Ross, Cliff, and Steve were my only friends growing up as we all lived in close proximity to one another. Ross, Cliff, and I lived in Park Road and Steve lived in a bungalow in Ridge View at the top of our road (and he is the main 'Steve' in this story). Funnily enough, 'Bungalow' was my nickname at school – because I had nothing upstairs! Age-wise, there were exactly three months between Cliff and myself, and Steve was 18 months younger. Ross, on the other hand, was four years older than me, but the four of us used to go over the Wild Park, accessed via a twitten at the top of Park Close, and kick a ball around or play cricket. Ross was a genuinely funny bloke, incredibly bright and sporty and came runner-up on The Krypton Factor on TV in 1992. He had a dark side to him though, and when bowling to each of us, would hurl beamers towards our heads with a sadistic look on his face. God knows what would have happened if the ball had actually connected with any part of us. My crap forward defensive stroke was certainly not required there! He was ultra-competitive and would never lose at anything. Games of Subbuteo in his conservatory would continue way beyond the 90-minute mark until he had scored an equalizer or winner to ensure his unbeaten record remained intact.

Ross managed a Youth Hostel in Bala, North Wales, and together with another friend, Barry, I stayed there in May 1985, where we intended to watch the European Cup Final between Liverpool and Juventus at the Heysel Stadium in Brussels. Unfortunately, a combination of hooliganism and shite Belgian stadium construction put paid to that!

I always thought the four of us were quite close –(well, Cliff, Steve, and I were due to our being of a similar age)- and I know that Steve, as the youngest, was often the butt of Ross' pranks which Cliff and I went along with, but I never considered it as bullying until Steve recently opened up about it and how it had affected him. I was mortified as Steve is one of the kindest, most gentle blokes you could ever wish to meet (unless you're an irritating drummer!), but, looking back on it, he was probably right and knows how incredibly sorry and embarrassed I am about it now. Having said that, nothing could have been as bad as Ross throwing a cricket stump at me and the pointy bit lodging in my leg!

In addition to Ross' escapades on The Krypton Factor, Cliff successfully climbed Mount Everest in 2002, coinciding with the 50th anniversary of Sir Edmund Hilary conquering it for the first time. An incredible achievement, and he followed it up by climbing the highest peaks in the other six continents. Oh, and he still runs marathons at 60! Being the determined little bugger that he is, Steve wouldn't be left out, and after leaving the band I was in at the time (Nothing From Nowhere) in 1985, formed his own Rockabilly band (The Midniters), released a couple of albums and supported The Stray Cats on their UK tour, culminating in playing in front of 4,000 fans at Hammersmith Odeon. It wasn't my musical genre, but he was bloody good at it and I was incredibly proud when he played that gig. After a 38-year hiatus, he and I collaborated on The Last Time in 2023 – more about that later.

We Don't Need No Education

My first school was Coldean Infants, towards the northern end of the estate. I don't think I particularly liked it, and my only memory is of Miss Williamson, a strict old battleaxe of whom everyone was shit scared. She had a small closet/room inside her classroom and went in there one day. No doubt egged on by my classmates, I followed her in and for the benefit of my audience, exclaimed, 'Ooh Miss Williamson, what a lovely room you have here and what a lovely colour of paint on the walls'. Unlike my classmates, she was not amused. Mum was summoned, and I vowed never to do anything like that again. I started lying at a very early age!

After the Infants school, I attended Coldean Junior School in an adjacent building on the same site. My only recollections from here are that an outside swimming pool was being built and that I was bullied. I can't fully remember how the bullying came about, and I thought I was getting on fine with the other boys but apparently not! I'm convinced that looking different, both facially and in my god-awful M&S clothes, made me a bit of a soft target. Most of the other boys were far more streetwise than I was, and all knew each other from the various parts of the estate. There was only Cliff and me from our area who were in the same age group. Anyway, I got a bit of a pummeling during a couple of lunch times, one of which Mum witnessed as she had dropped off my forgotten packed lunch. She immediately contacted the headmaster who assured her it would be investigated, and the culprits duly punished. I remember some of the boys being forced to come round to our house with their parents to apologise, but I don't think it solved the problem, and fairly soon afterwards I moved on to Patcham Middle School, over the hill from Coldean in, funnily enough, Patcham!

I loved Patcham School for many reasons. The children there were nicer than those at Coldean, and I fitted in. One girl in my class, Carina Stone, had moved there from Coldean when her parents moved house. She was part Swedish (on her Mum's side), and I'd spent time at her house in Coldean, looking at pictures of Pippa Longstocking, a Swedish cartoon character, that she had on her bedroom wall. (Behave – we were only about 6 or 7!). Anyway, she was a (pretty) welcome face, and I soon made other friends, particularly Phil Abbott, a Derby County supporter, who had moved down to the area as his father, a vicar, had taken up a post at a nearby church. Phil and I hit it off immediately and would spend alternate weekends at each other's houses, kicking a ball around in the garden or a local park before heading into his house to watch World of Sport with Dickie Davies or Grandstand with Frank Bough at mine, watching the football results come in. He was a nice lad, very tall with a northern accent which he never lost. The teachers at Patcham were also really nice – except for Mr Welsh – more about him later!

BRA Heaven

By far and away the best bit about going to school in Patcham was the bus ride there. I had to catch the 13 or 15 bus – (both went there)- from the stop at the bottom of our road. They went up Coldean Lane and eventually to Ladies Mile Road in Patcham, where my school was located. Next to my school was Margaret Hardy School for Girls, a secondary school for girls aged 11-16, a number of whom were already on the top deck of the 13/15 bus by the time I caught it, smoking, swearing and fit. Very fit! I was 2-3 years younger than them, but despite my freakish looks, they kind of took me under their wings and let me sit and smoke with them. I ponced theirs as I didn't dare buy my own, but they didn't mind. They wore lipstick and eyeliner. And BRAs! Fuck! I was in heaven on the way to school, and they all caught the same bus as me on the way home. Could life as a 10/11-year-old get any better? Mum and Dad were quite pleased that I enjoyed going to school each day but never knew the reason why. I've got those dickheads at Coldean school to thank for enforcing the move to BRA heaven!

A Star Is Born

Mr Welsh was northern, but unlike Phil Abbott, he was a northern twat. I always seemed to do my best schoolwork for female teachers (I can't think why!). Mr Welsh was not only my English teacher but my form tutor too, so I saw him every day. I couldn't stand him, and I don't think he liked me much as he was always bollocking me for no apparent reason in his lessons. However, Mr Welsh was heavily involved in casting and producing the school plays, and much to my amazement, he cast me in a significant role in the 1975 Christmas play where I played the main policeman, acting and singing 'A Policeman's Lot Is Not A Happy One' from Gilbert & Sullivan's 'Pirates of Penzance'. Welsh and I got on like a house on fire during rehearsals and the actual production over two nights – and went back to hating each other afterwards!

The Summer play in 1976, my final year at Patcham, was 'The Park Keeper' and Welsh cast me in the main role of Herbert Pringle, Park Keeper. This was a far more substantial role than I'd had in the Christmas play, as I was required to be on stage acting and singing in most of the scenes. Again, Welsh and I got on well in rehearsals, which were considerably more detailed due to the amount of my involvement in the whole play, and over two nights in June, it went really well. As with my piano recital at the Royal Pavilion several years earlier, there were no nerves, and I felt completely at home on the stage in front of an audience that included a very proud Mum, Dad and Fi.

'A Star Is Born', starring Kris Kristoffersen and a fellow thespian with facial issues, Barbra Streisand, was one of the big hit films of 1976, so could it be an omen for my future career? Could it fuck!

Gary Glitter

At this point, it's probably worth mentioning the influence that Gary Glitter had on my life at the time. (No, not in that way – sake!). In 1973, Mum and Dad took Fi and me to Pontins in Camber Sands for a few days break. One of the highlights was the kids talent show, usually held around 6 pm each evening, when the parents could drop their kids off at the entertainment centre and clear off for a couple of hours. I dread to think what ours got up to! Actually, Mum probably did the Telegraph crossword, and Dad read that day's Daily Mirror. Volunteers would be sought from the kids to go up on stage, do a bit of dancing and miming in a sort of talent contest, and win a prize. You'll not be surprised to learn that I did indeed volunteer and joined five other boys and girls on stage, where I danced and mimed my way through a GG number. I recall grabbing my crutch from time to time, so it was probably 'Do You Wanna Touch Me?'. I impressed the judges enough to go through to the final with one other boy and a girl and had to dance to Cozy Powell's 'Dance With The Devil', which was a bastard of an instrumental to dance to! I gave it my best Pans People shot and, lo and behold, was voted the overall winner. Mum and Dad had returned to the venue before the end and enquired of Fiona where I was; she pointed to the stage, and their jaws dropped when they saw me cavorting around.

I think they were more approving of my Park Keeper role a few years later!

Love at First Sight

12th February, 1972. The most important date in my life so far. The occasion was Brighton v Walsall at the old Goldstone Ground. Dad had acquired tickets in the West Stand for my first-ever game. We lost 2-1 - (Eddie Spearitt scored our goal, and their winner was miles offside)- but I didn't care. I was hooked. He took me to several more games that season, a successful one for us as we were promoted in second place behind Aston Villa. He would park 100 yards away from the ground in Old Shoreham Road, and I would walk excitedly towards the cathedral of hope, a buzz inside as I saw the floodlights, the smell of the programmes, the entrance to the East Terrace on Goldstone Lane, the climb up the steep bank until I reached the top and, there before me, was this vast green ocean of a stage with some perfectly marked out white lines. And some brown bits. In fact, quite a lot of brown bits! But I didn't care. This was my team for life. For better or worse (often much worse). For richer or poorer (certainly poorer, the amount I've spent on them over the years). In sickness and in health (we've certainly experienced the former). Til death do us part (hmm, a bit morbid, but it's been touch and go for both of us from time to time). The roar of the crowd as the men in blue and white stripes did something useful. The smell of pipe and cigar smoke wafting across the terrace. The sound of a rattle being whirled and the occasional noise from a transistor radio nearby informing me that, on my 13th birthday, at exactly the same second that Peter Ward was brought down for a penalty by a Mansfield clogger, Red Rum crossed the winning line in The Grand National. With the greatest of respect to Dickie Davies, I had my World of Sport right here.

Lovely Day

During the next few years, on every other Saturday, I would awaken excitedly, anticipating another afternoon at my new 'church'. Brian Withers would call at our house, and either he or Dad would drive to the ground. Brian lived with his wife and daughter in The Roundway, higher up on the Coldean estate, and to the best of my knowledge, wasn't related to Bill. There was a fairly obvious reason for that! Dad didn't have many friends, and I don't know how or where he met Brian, but they would go for an occasional drink in the Hikers (until Dad was banned from drinking by Mum and his doctor – who were one and the same person half the time!). Brian was a nice bloke but didn't have a sense of humour. It could be absolutely pissing it down outside when I answered the door to him, and the conversation would go:-

Me: 'Hello, Uncle Brian, lovely day.'

Him: 'Er, not really, Stuart, it's pissing down'.

Even at that young age, I was trying out new material.

Procession

Our game against Aston Villa in the 1971/72 season was my first experience of crowd trouble. There were a number of arrests, and on the following Monday, my photo appeared in The Evening Argus for the first time alongside a photo of some Villa fans being nicked by the Police ('OB'). The game was played on the weekend of Palm Sunday, which as any church-going worshipper knows, is the weekend before Easter, something that my current priest, Pat Saward, neglected to mention in his programme notes! Anyway, I was chosen (by whom, I've no idea) to play Jesus riding a donkey through the rough streets of Coldean - (which even Beirut declined to be twinned with!)- with various choirboys accompanying me decked out in choristers robes and carrying palm leaves. An older woman, who worked at the chemist's on the estate, walked by my side, presumably to prevent me from falling off (or, more likely, preventing me from digging my heels into the donkey to make it go faster!). The poor donkey had a permanent look on its face that said, 'Get this fat bastard off me; I want to go back to Blackpool'. A photographer from The Argus was on hand to capture my first public appearance to date – the crutch-grabbing GG episode hadn't yet occurred- and so there it was, in the Monday edition next to the photo of the nicked Villa fans. It wasn't great for my street cred, but I'd take any publicity I could!

Scum

On 17th August, 1974, Dad took me to my first game against the scum (Crystal Palace). I didn't realise they were scum at the time, but I soon found out. He parked in the usual place, and we walked down Old Shoreham Road, turning left into Goldstone Lane. There, slouching against the wall, were four long-haired blokes wearing hideous flares who looked like they could have been in Mud. (I never did find out who Les Gray supported so he could have been one of them!). My blue and white scarf was tied around one wrist, and my other hand held Dad's quite tightly. 'Brighton wankers', Les Gray called out. I felt Dad's hand grip mine tighter and suspected he wanted to chin Les but couldn't because I was with him. There I was, a naïve 10-year-old with a Dad who grew up in scum territory (Streatham), and we were being called wankers by Mud. They became scum to me that day and have been ever since. We won the game 1-0 thanks to Ian Mellor. The violence made the Villa game look like a kids tea party, and the result was all the more pleasing as they had been relegated from Division 2 the previous season. Their Billy Big Bollocks attitude was epitomised by their Fedora-wearing, cigar-smoking manager, Malcolm Allison, who was better at shagging Fiona Richmond in the players bath than he was managing a football team. You never forget your first match against the scum (as my two sons are all too painfully aware!).

News of the World

I'd had several operations when I was a baby and was missing hospital food and craving the attention that only fit nurses can provide, so I decided to have three more aged 8 (tonsils removed), 9 (circumcision) and 11 (tooth removed from my nose). See, I told you I was a freak! Although the operation to repair the cleft palate had initially been a success, as I grew older, it opened up again and a tooth from my upper jaw started moving up into my nose, which if not removed, would have caused that nostril to become blocked.

The circumcision was fun. I wasn't losing a small part of me for any religious reasons – I'd never even heard of Maccabi Tel Aviv at that point! - but because of frequent infections in that area (I still couldn't reach the soap because of Tug Boat Fucking Annie!), so I was admitted to the children's ward of the Royal Alexandra Hospital in Dyke Road, where I met a couple of 'celebrities'.

Firstly, Princess Alexandra herself, who visited the hospital before I'd had my op. Telegraph-reading Mum was beside herself with excitement, grabbed me from my hospital bed and rushed me to where the Princess was surrounded by a sycophantic, flag-waving crowd. I got up close to the Princess and smiled at her. She smiled back and royal protocol probably prevented her from telling me how much she'd enjoyed my GG impression earlier that year.

The second 'celebrity' was in the next hospital bed to me and went by the name of Russell Bishop. He also lived in Coldean and was very much the runt of the litter. His older brothers were David (who seemed to be permanently in Borstal when we were growing up), Alec, a couple of years older than me who I always got on well with, and Micky, who was part of the Hikers mob who used to terrify home fans whenever the Albion were in town. All as hard as nails – except Russell.

On Thursday, 9th October, 1986, I'd finished taking part in football training for the Amex FC team I was involved with at Brighton Boys Club on Eastern Road and caught a bus home to 28PR, travelling north along Lewes Road. There was a thick fog through which I could only just make out the streetlights until we approached Wild Park, where there were many more lights straining to shine in the gloom. They were all moving, some slowly, some more quickly, like loads of glow worms in the dark. I didn't think much of it and arrived home. The following morning, on the radio and TV, there were reports that two young girls from North Moulsecoomb had gone missing the previous day and despite the efforts of the police and many locals, hadn't been found. Upon returning home from work later that day, I watched the local news which showed that members of the public had again joined the police when they resumed their search. Among those interviewed at the scene was Bishop. (His appearance was mirrored several years later by Ian Huntley, who murdered two young girls in Soham and who pretended to search for them. He even had the same noncey, wispy moustache as Bishop).

The girls' bodies were found on 10th October, hidden in a makeshift den in the park. Bishop was immediately the main suspect, arrested and tried at Lewes Crown Court. He was acquitted due to the efforts of his barrister, Ralph Haeems, who listed the Krays as previous clients. Haeems convinced the jury that there had been a series of blunders in the prosecution's case, namely the potential for cross-contamination of a blue Pinto sweatshirt that Bishop had been wearing on the evening in question and this, together with the retraction of his girlfriend's statement that Bishop did indeed own the Pinto sweatshirt, resulted in him being acquitted. The sight of him and his family swigging champagne and protesting his innocence in the following Sunday's News Of The World (for which he was paid £15k) was nauseating.

Three years later, Bishop was found guilty of the kidnapping and attempted murder of a 7-year-old girl in Whitehawk. Thankfully, she survived, and he was finally banged up. He was never released as he was subsequently found guilty of murdering the Wild Park girls and died in a prison hospital in 2022.

What's with Terry?

Another notorious Coldean resident was Terry Boyle, who was a proper villain. One of the notorious Brighton knocker boys, his 'work' enabled him to buy the detached house on the corner of Park Road and Rushlake Road in the 70's. He proceeded to install an outdoor swimming pool, the only one in Coldean. I never saw much of him when I was growing up as he was either inside or, er, inside, but his attractive wife, Georgie, lived in the house with their son, Terry Junior, and daughter, Michaela, who Fi played with on occasions. As a means of earning pocket money, I started washing neighbours' cars for a quid or two. Georgie very generously gave me a fiver even though I never cleaned anywhere near the boot for fear of what might be in there! They split up many years later, and at the age of 73, Terry was back inside, having been found guilty of running a cannabis farm in North Chailey. He died in May 2020.

Murder on the Footpath

8 years before the Wild Park murders, there was another murder in the vicinity, this time at the bottom of the road on the footpath leading to Stanmer Park. Margaret Frame, a cleaner at nearby Falmer school, was one night walking home from work along the path. Each evening, she would, upon leaving the entrance to the woods, either catch a bus from the bus stop at the bottom of my road or walk through the Coldean estate until she reached her home in Saunders Hill, towards the north of the estate. (Ironically, if walking, her journey usually took her past Bishop's house in Coldean Lane). On this occasion, she never arrived at the bus stop nor at her home. She had been raped and strangled on the lower path, and her body was covered in the autumnal leaves. Despite a huge police/public search, her body wasn't initially found. The killer returned to the scene after several days and dragged her naked body across a field to an upper path in the woods, where it was discovered a few days later. No one was ever charged with her murder, which remains unsolved to this day.

Winfield Plimsolls

I left Patcham Middle School in July 1976, and after one of the hottest summers on record, attended Dorothy Stringer High School in Loder Road. It was a hell of a trek from 28PR, and in the early days, Mum usually gave me a lift. Initially, my schooling went quite well, and I was placed in the 3rd highest class on account of some tests I'd done at Patcham, where I'd presumably shown a bit of promise. My form tutor, Miss Jenkins, was young, reasonably attractive, and also taught me history, which I loved.

The most notorious teacher in the school was Mr Hickman, who taught RE and was a fucking sadist! He dished out corporal punishment like it was going out of fashion, and my arse copped it more than once. In fairness, on one particular occasion, it was entirely my fault. It was April 1st, the time for pranks and similar merriment. I mentioned to some of my classmates what I was planning, and they thought I was off my nut. During one of Miss Jenkins' history lessons, I asked if I could go to the toilet, and my request was granted. As I left the room, I could see my classmates shaking their heads in despair. I pegged it up to Hickman's room, which was in a separate block. I knocked on his door, and panting profusely, told him that Miss Jenkins wanted to see him urgently. I then ran back to her history class and was in my usual seat when

Hickman turned up. Miss Jenkins obviously denied knowing anything about asking him to see her, at which point I shouted out, 'April Fool'. Hickman looked at me calmly but terrifyingly. Fuck! He hasn't got a sense of humour! I think I had 'Winfield' imprinted firmly on each buttock by the time he had finished administering my (admittedly deserved) punishment during the next break. My classmates enjoyed it though.

Soon after I joined Stringer, it merged with its sister school, an Annex located in Moulsecoomb, and all the pupils from there transferred to the Loder Road site. One such pupil was Neil Cornford. He was a very good footballer and massively into the Albion, so we hit it off immediately. We also shared a complete lack of interest in Biology, which was taught by an older lady, Mrs Booth, who was from Chesterfield and who loved nothing more than talking about Chesterfield FC. Our Monday Biology 'lesson' consisted of Neil or I asking her how they had got on the previous weekend, which she was more than happy to recall minute by minute, while Neil and I sat at the back playing hangman and taking no further notice in her or her subject. Fuck knows how we managed to have five kids between us! Our paths would continue to cross throughout our lives.

1977

In 1977, my life changed forever with the phenomenon otherwise known as Punk. Although I'd always had an interest in chart music, and actually once liked a Supertramp record, when the punk scene came along, I'd never heard anything like it. (Yes, I know it really started the year before, but '77 was the year punk records flooded the market). Buzzcocks, The Clash, the Pistols, The Damned. The sound, the anger and the energy were simply amazing. The two fingers up to the music and general establishments, coupled with the 'do it yourself' mantra, really appealed, and I was completely hooked. Steve obtained the first Stranglers album, 'Rattus Norvegicus', and we sat listening to every track on repeat for hour upon hour at his place. The same for The Clash's first album, Buzzcocks, etc. There was absolutely no chance of me buying any of these masterpieces just yet, let alone playing them at my house. The first record I'd ever been allowed to buy was Bohemian Rhapsody, and that was on the strict proviso that I bought Cliff Richard's 'Miss You Nights' the following week. I shit you not! Mum and Dad's musical tastes ranged from Nina & Frederik, a Danish-Dutch duo who looked like continental swingers, to Eartha Kitt. To be fair, Eartha could bang out a decent tune or two, but Orgasm Addict, she certainly wasn't. At least, as far as I knew!

At school, another Steve came into my life. Steve Johnson lived in Eldred Avenue in Westdene. His parents had split up, and Steve was allowed to run amok doing whatever he wanted, which, naturally, involved the punk scene. He took himself off to gigs in London and would regale me with tales of the night before at school the next day. He also dyed his hair green, which looked really cool. I tried to do the same thing, liberally plastering my hair with Mum's green food dye. Unfortunately, I went out in the rain, the dye ran down my face, and I looked a bigger twat than usual!

My other abiding memory of Steve is that he was quite vocal about hating four-eyed, ginger-haired mods and got in a fight with, funnily enough, a four-eyed, ginger-haired mod!

Topper Headon

In a vain attempt to steer me away from the evils of punk, it was decided that my musical talent should extend to a second instrument. It had long been recognised that I was too thick (or, more accurately, too disinterested) to obtain my Grade 1 theory certificate for the piano, and, thus, the Holy Grail of Grade 8 practical for that instrument was never going to be achieved. I'd had a dabble in the school orchestra, led by Miss Cowl, where in addition to playing the piano, I'd had a thrash about on the Timpani, which I quite enjoyed. Could my next instrument possibly be the drums? This idea was quickly dismissed by the realisation that there was nowhere to set up a drum kit at home, and even the odd bash on a snare drum would negatively impact Mum's concentration levels when trying to do the Telegraph crossword. So, I was never going to be the next Topper Headon (probably for the best, considering the way he turned out!).

Miss Cowl was a very short, rotund spinster of the parish who was pleasant enough (if a bit scary at times). She had an embarrassing, almost girly fixation on Richard Durrant, a lad who was a year older than me and who played the acoustic guitar. She would visibly melt and go weak at the knees when he played in her presence. All a bit unprofessional in my eyes but she clearly got off on it! To be fair to Richard, he was incredibly talented and went on to have a fantastic career as a guitarist, playing in the band Sky and touring all over the world.

So, Miss Cowl obviously had an eye for talent – would she cast one of them in my direction? I could only hope – sort of.

Cliff Michelmore

Between them, Mum and Miss Cowl decided that my next instrument to learn should be – not the electric or acoustic guitar – not the drums – not the saxophone – but the cello. The fucking cello! That big old bastard that I virtually had to straddle between my legs which emitted very low farty noises when I first attempted to play it. I was allowed to borrow one from the school orchestra and took it home to practice. It sounded awful but was marginally better than Fi's attempts to play the violin, which caused every dog in the neighbourhood to howl until she stopped!

I was assigned a cello teacher who looked like a cross between Cliff Michelmore and someone who should have been on a register. And I'm not talking about a school register! He had a greasy comb-over that even Bobby Charlton would have baulked at! He gave me the creeps, particularly when, during my first lesson, he told me to practice using the bow without actually having a bow in my hand. Try it. See what I mean?

Apart from dodgy hand movements, the worst thing about learning the cello was that my lessons were held during the morning break in a room next to the tuck shop. Both the practice room and the tuck shop were situated on a walkway and had windows that looked out over some of the playing fields. Students entering the tuck shop for their Curly Wurly's or Monster Munch would then leave the shop and eat them whilst looking in through the windows of the adjacent room, which was the practice room. Which had me in it, trying to perfect the art of playing this monstrosity! As word got around, a crowd quickly gathered, but not in a good way. Leering faces, gobbing bits of Monster Munch at the window, flicking the V's and making wanker signs at me. To be fair, I was giving the latter back, only I had a bow in my hand while I was doing it, which negated any kind of retort I was attempting!

This public ridicule wasn't in the script for my musical world domination and, unsurprisingly, caused me to hate the instrument even more. I did manage to successfully obtain Grades 1 and 2 in cello exams before sacking it off. I don't think Miss Cowl even noticed, as she was still infatuated with Richard bloody Durrant!

Dennis Waterman

Girls were plentiful at my school and by now, most of them were wearing BRA's. Phwoah! I was still painfully shy (except when on stage) and would blush profusely whenever I spoke to them or, more particularly, if they spoke to me. When I was still at Patcham, at the end of year summer disco and still fresh from my Oscar-winning role as Herbert Pringle, I'd had a dance with Julie Blazey and carefully remembered not to do my GG impression in front of her! We seemed to get on okay, and after ringing the house phone and (presumably) stifling any giggles about my Dad being called Rupert, she caught the bus over from Patcham one summer's day and rocked up at 28PR. With her large, ginger-haired friend, Susan Duplock as her 'minder'. I made them both a glass of Ribena but, with my nervous fumble, spilt some down Julie's new white top. First impressions, eh?! (No, I'm not talking about 'shut that door' or 'just like that'. Not those sorts of impressions). Her interest visibly waned, although she did suggest that she, Dennis Waterman, and I go for a walk in the Wild Park. Maybe she had a thing for Park Keepers!

Too Shy

Back at Stringer, one girl I particularly liked was Jane Naylor. She seemed to blush a lot whenever I spoke to her, which I thought was a good sign. So I proceeded to get a mate to ask her if she'd go out with me. Imagine my amazement when the answer came back as 'yes'. Wow, I've cracked it. Piece of piss, this dating lark! And I then did absolutely nothing about it! We'd still smile and blush at each other in whichever lesson we were in, but I was too shy and, I guess, fearful of rejection – despite her previous affirmative- to actually ask her out on a date. This went on for months until she started going out with Russell Hill. He was a good-looking lad, to be fair, and whilst I was outwardly heartbroken, a voice inside my head said, 'It's your own fault, you daft twat'!

Porn

My lack of success, self-inflicted I know, led me to do what all like-minded 13-year-old boys did. I discovered porn. Well, sort of. The twitten at the top of Park Close led to Wild Park, and, in order to get to the park, you had to go through a wooded area that was relatively flat. Judging by the amount of cigarette butts and empty beer bottles, it was clearly a place where people sat and smoked and drank. And looked through porno mags, the pages of which they then proceeded to rip up and throw around. The wind also helped to disperse the material. Occasionally, on my way to a kickabout in the park, I'd come across some of the discarded pieces of the mag. (Not literally - sake!). Unfortunately, the discarder, combined with the wind, had done a great job of ensuring that no two pieces of the same photo were in close proximity to one another. They'd be a tit here, a few pubes there, even a partial picture of IT! But nothing that you could reassemble as one complete photo and, er, enjoy. Some boys were known to spend hours crawling around on their hands and knees, covered in mud, trying to find the missing pieces of the photo. Well, one boy in particular. It was almost as frustrating as not being able to ask Jane Naylor out properly!

Billy Joel

The local radio station in the 70's was Radio Brighton, which was situated in Marlborough Place, opposite the entrance to The Dome. Each Sunday morning, they ran a competition whereby you could ring in and win a prize if you correctly identified a song from its musical intro. It was hosted by Neil Coppendale, and one particular Sunday, I thought I'd give it a go. I listened to Radio One a lot in those days and had a decent knowledge of current and older songs. With Mum, Dad and Fi listening excitedly on a transistor radio in an upstairs bedroom, I rang the station and explained that I wanted to be a contestant on the show. The receptionist took my name, age and address and told me I'd be the second contestant. Dad had it in his head that he'd previously given Neil some lettuces that he'd grown in our garden, and all I could hear from upstairs was Dad shouting, 'Tell Neil I'll drop some lettuces off to him'. 'He doesn't want your poxy lettuces', I replied, 'and I need to concentrate'. Through the phone line, I could hear that the first contestant was struggling to identify his intro, which was probably something god-awful by Yes, and when the first vocals kicked in, his time was up. Neil commiserated with him and then introduced me as 'Stuart, aged 15 from Coldean'. 'Tell him about the lettuces' was being shouted out from upstairs. Neil asked if I was ready, and I confirmed that I was. No more than two notes of the song had been played when I shouted out 'Billy Joel – My Life', which Neil confirmed was indeed correct. There was a cheer and applause from upstairs, followed by 'lettuces'. Neil congratulated me on my win and told me to visit the station the following day to collect my choice of LP.

I was buzzing when I went to school the next day and told my mates what had happened. 'Which LP are you going to get?' they asked, 'Clash, Buzzcocks, The Jam?'. 'I don't know', I replied, 'but it's bound to be something good'. I wasn't particularly attentive in my lessons that day – studying had long since gone out of the window to be replaced by the punk scene- and it was a rare day in that I'd actually bothered to turn up. Mum and Fi collected me from school and drove me down to the Radio Brighton studios. Parking in central Brighton in those days was a doddle. Sadly, over the years, the anti-car brigade on virtually every council has treated the motorist as a cash cow who dare not emit any exhaust-fume damage to the lungs of the dungaree-wearing artist reciting poetry on a street corner! So, we were able to park outside the studios and go in. I explained to the receptionist who I was and why I was there, and after checking her notes, she told me to accompany her to another part of the reception where I could choose my prize. There were 3 LP's, of which I could only choose one. These were: -

James Last's Greatest Hits

James Galway's Greatest Hits

Brian & Michael – Matchstick Men and Matchstick Cats and Dogs.

My heart sank. 'Is this it?', I asked, more out of hope than expectation. 'Yes', she replied, 'choose which one you'd like'. It wasn't much of a choice! A German orchestra conductor, an Irish Flutist and a couple of dodgy-looking blokes singing about a niche northern artist. 'The matchstick one', I mumbled but couldn't bear to look at it as she put it into a bag and handed it to me. There was virtual silence in the car on the way home, interspersed with Mum occasionally extolling the virtues of Messrs. Last and Galway.

I dreaded going to school the next day, and early on, my dread was vindicated. A number of mates gathered around and asked me what I'd got. 'The Clash? The Jam? Buzzcocks?'. 'Er, no,' I replied, 'Brian and Michael's Matchstick Men and Matchstick Cats and Dogs', at which point they all pissed themselves laughing and ran off shouting out 'loser' and 'wanker'. All except one. Steve Krol was a tall, quiet lad whose hairstyle would be replicated some years later by Neil Tennant of The Pet Shop Boys. 'I quite like that one', said Steve, 'can I buy it from you?'. I caught my jaw as it hurtled towards the ground and said, 'Of course, Steve, how much do you want to buy it for?'. '3 quid ok?', he asked. 'Done', I said, and he well and truly had been. The exchange of currency and the result of my hard-earned first radio appearance took place the following day, much to my relief. It could have been worse, I suppose, it could have been something by Nina & Frederik!

Charlton Heston

Money had always been tight at home, and things were starting to get even tighter. Dad had left Benham's, dazzled by the potentially huge salary and bright lights as a Sales Rep for Hilti, a Lichenstein company that provided tools for the construction industry, a subject that Dad knew very little about. He was initially away for a few days at a time attending training courses in northern hotels, and when he returned, would need to be out on the road for long hours each day trying to persuade builders and the like to buy his stuff. The problem was that Dad couldn't sell lettuce to Neil Coppendale, let alone a drill bit to Bob the Builder, and he would regularly receive phone calls late into the evening from his Sales Director bemoaning his lack of success. Dad was now in his late 50's and couldn't cope with the pressure his new job was causing. So, he took it out on us. Shouting, swearing, and slamming doors became the norm. Visits to the Hikers would result in him coming back pissed, and on one occasion, so drunk that he passed out on Christmas Day at home and missed the whole day. He couldn't handle his beer in any quantity, couldn't deal with the pressure, and lost four jobs in one year alone (1978).

To try to help pay the bills, Mum set up her own business, Owen County Catering, in which she started out providing food and drinks at wedding receptions, which were usually held in Stanmer House. She had a team of local women who would each be assigned a particular food item to cook and prepare (Maureen on mushroom vol-au-vents, Ann on gateaux, etc.). These ladies would also attend the event dressed in green, black and purple outfits, which Mum had designed, and would wait on the guests. Dad and I would run the drinks side of things as wine waiters. Mum would buy some of the food items and drinks from Cash and Carry in Davigdor Road, Hove. The problem was, neither Mum nor Dad had a clue about wine, and she would always come back with cheap German stuff (Niersteiner and Liebfraumilch), which tasted like paint stripper and which the poor saps we served had to pretend to enjoy as there was nothing else.

Her business branched out into other events. She provided catering for receptions held by The Mayor, working lunches at TSB Trustcard and other banks, and after-show parties at The Theatre Royal, where she got to meet some of the stars. She was a big fan of Christopher Biggins but less keen on Charlton Heston, who spat out a piece of her quiche and asked for crackers. She brought home the spat-out quiche bearing his teeth marks and it took pride of place on our breakfast bar in the kitchen until it began to stink and had to be thrown out. The Foods Standards Agency wasn't a regular visitor in those days!

As a way of helping Dad earn an income that didn't involve selling lettuces or drill bits, Mum bought a hot dog van. After looking around Sussex for a suitable pitch, they found one in a layby on the A27 near Selmeston. It was the perfect place for lorry drivers travelling to the port of Newhaven from Folkestone/Dover (and vice versa), for sales reps in need of a cuppa and a bacon butty at 10 am, and for casual drivers out on day trips. He started to build up a regular and profitable business and seemed to enjoy it. He would start the noisy diesel van up at 5 am in all weathers so as to be in his layby for an hour later and thus provide hungry truckers with breakfasts. Mum paid for the van to attend other events such as antique fairs on Lancing Beach Green, and the biggest earner of all, Bonfire Night in Lewes, where the prices were marked up, resulting in huge profits. Unfortunately, as the reliability of the van started to fade, so did Dad, and he found the early start too much to continue doing, so the van was sold. Perhaps his internal ticking time bomb was starting to diffuse!

The Headmaster Ritual

My rapidly declining interest in anything academic was borne out by my lack of any real attendance at school during my last two years there. I'd go in for registration and then bunk off around Steve Johnson's house, listening to records and reading the NME, or a few of us would head to Paula Sergison's house in Hollingdean. I quite fancied Paula, but it was in no way reciprocated, even though she had braces on her teeth! I'd then head back to school and register for the afternoon enrolment before heading out of the school grounds to somewhere else. With my love of performing and being on stage, I only really wanted to be in a punk band, and nothing else mattered.

One day, during my final year there, I noticed the Headmaster, Mr Hoddell, and the Deputy Head, Mr Shepherd, were watching me from a window in Hoddell's first-floor office. I gave it a few minutes and when they'd averted their gaze, set off on my afternoon jaunt to anywhere that wasn't school. A few days later, Mum received a letter informing her that I'd been playing truant and inviting her (and me) to a meeting with Hoddell. She went nuclear! I eventually told her what had been going on, how I hated school and studying, and how things had gone downhill since I won that Brian & Michael LP. I don't think she bought it. (She didn't, Steve Krol did for £3!).

The meeting with Hoddell went as expected. 'Disappointed', 'waste of talent', blah blah blah. There were only a few months to go until I had to sit my 'O' Levels. At the start of my penultimate year, I had been scheduled to take 9 'O' Level subjects, but my lack of attendance or any coursework meant that these were now down to three. English Language, English Literature and Economic History. Oh, and the less meaningful CSE in Maths. I duly paid lip service as to how hard I would revise for these, but my heart wasn't in it, and I only read a few bits to keep everyone happy. I did turn up for the exams but really didn't give a toss about the outcome as I'd already got a job lined up.

Queen

In December 1979, something magical happened. I was allowed to go to my first-ever gig. Cliff had been a huge Queen fan from early on and regularly played bits of their first five albums whenever I went around to his house. He'd managed to get tickets for their concert at the Brighton Centre, and off we went. Although their music wasn't remotely close to the punk scene or ethos that I was immersed in, they were absolutely fantastic. The light show was amazing, and Freddie was one of the greatest frontmen I've ever seen. I went to a further two concerts of theirs over the years, both with Cliff, culminating in their performance at the Milton Keynes Bowl in 1982, where Fat Alan from Grange Hill walked past me as I sat on a grass bank, and where Julian Cope threatened to steal the show with his magnificent Teardrop Explodes.

Losing My Religion

St Andrew's church set up a youth club in the late 70's which was held in the crypt every Friday evening. It was run by a young, married couple, Pam and Alec, who were quite churchy. Most of the kids there were around my age and lived nearby in Moulsecoomb or Bevendean. It was a place where you could buy soft drinks and sweets and bring your own records to play on the record player. Smoking wasn't initially permitted inside the crypt, so I had to go outside the main church doors if I wanted a puff. Pam and Alec were very pleasant but insisted on introducing something biblical at the end of the evening, which rather spoilt it somewhat, particularly as I was rapidly becoming an atheist.

Mum and Dad had taken Fi and me to St Andrew's since we were born, and their fellow parishioners had always taken an interest in us. They were generally nice, kind, intelligent people, and Mum and Dad classed them as friends (Mum in particular, as she'd grown up with a lot of them). I'd been confirmed at 14, which involved reading a book with various religious stuff in it, answering some questions and being presented with a certificate, which was nice! But, shortly afterwards, I started to have serious doubts about the whole thing.

I'm sure there was a robed bloke in Roman times who went around saying this and that, patting people on the head, that sort of thing, and people used to gather to hear what he had to say. His reputation as a before/during/after dinner speaker grew as did his crowds. He probably had a sideline as a hot cross bun salesman, so he had a vested interest in perpetuating the Easter myth. After the Romans decided he was too much of a nuisance and bumped him off, a number of those closest to him decided to write about him and presented it as fact, when in reality, it was a series of fictional stories designed to give people hope that good things could happen to them. Utter bollocks really! If people want to have faith and believe in something, that's absolutely fine, and they should be allowed to get on with it unless it results in conflict, which it does. Frequently! But it's no longer for me.

I hadn't been back to St Andrew's for many years until I accompanied Mum to the first Sunday service after Dad died in 1991. The usual crowd was there, as pleasant as always, and genuinely pleased to see me. As I mentioned previously, lovely, intelligent people. And then the service started. I'd forgotten how bad it was. All these bright people (Mum included) turned into sheep, repeating this and that as if they had been programmed to do it, whilst the vicar told them what to say from a large book in front of him. He couldn't even be arsed to turn the pages himself, delegating it to a robed bloke (probably on minimum wage) to do it for him. It was a horrific sight and completely vindicated my newfound atheism.

Jane Warner's Tampons

After attending the youth club on a Friday evening, the following day, I worked doing a Saturday job in Boots on London Road. The job entailed punching the cost of items into a till, which totaled the amount due, and putting the customers' cash payment into the till drawers, giving the customer any required change (no credit or debit card payments for those types of transactions in those days). Probably the most famous customer I served was Jane Warner, a local model, who used to get her tits out – (sadly, not in Boots)- and have them photographed to appear on Page 3 of The Sun. She bought several items, including makeup and tampons. Which was nice!

Boots had a record department that sold all the chart singles and albums, and as a staff member, I got a 15% discount, so I would spend some of my weekly wage buying records, which I then took to play at the youth club. Punk had died down by now and had been replaced by New Wave groups like The Jam, The Undertones, Boomtown Rats, etc. I'd put the record on the turntable and pogo around pretending to be Bruce Foxton or Micky Bradley until I lost control of my pogo and nudged the record player, causing the record to jump and bear an eternal scratch for my transgression.

Hypnotised

There was an even mix of boys and girls at the youth club, and one, a girl named Carol, was quite nice. She had slightly 'home and away' eyes but was a fucking oil painting compared to me! We got chatting, and after the club finished one evening, made our way to Debbie Williams' house nearby. I made sure I sat next to Carol on the sofa and asked Debbie to put The Undertones 'Hypnotised' LP I'd brought with me onto her record player. As Feargal Sharkey bemoaned that he'd 'Never Kissed A Girl Before', I did just that with Carol, getting a warm glowing feeling, together with another feeling which I managed to adjust with my GG impression!

I walked her home, which was a few doors along from Debbie's on Colbourne Avenue, where Carol told me that her Dad was really strict and I wouldn't be allowed in. Never mind. We had another peck, and she went indoors, agreeing to meet again at the following Friday's youth club, which we duly did and had a proper full-on snogging session. I walked her home again and as she went to Falmer school, arranged to meet her during her lunch break the following Wednesday. (No Feargal, not Wednesday Week!). We met by a tree at the top of a hill that looked down over some football pitches (where my Amex FC Saturday team would play their home games many years later). We had a cuddle and a snog, and at one point, I could make out the strapline of the BRA she was wearing under her school shirt. Phwoah! She had to go back to school, and I wandered home with a stupid grin on my face. And that was that! All because of Paula Cox.

The Lotus Eaters

Paula was small, blonde, pretty and worked on the other till at Boots alongside me, so I'd got to know her quite well and fancied her. She lived in Peacehaven, which involved catching two buses to get there, and I went over there one Sunday afternoon. The Lotus Eaters 'If I Had You' was playing on the radio in her bedroom – was this a sign, perhaps? Not really. We chatted and went for a walk, and I caught my buses back home. Cowardly, via Debbie Williams, I broke up with Carol and was going to throw in my lot with Paula. Only her parents moved to Newbury shortly afterwards taking Paula and her sister, Ruth, with them. And that was that. Again! It wouldn't be the last time I backed the wrong horse!

Man in the Corner Shop

Prior to the job in Boots, I'd done a paper round via the newsagents at the bottom of our road. The round itself had seen a higher than usual turnover of paperboys over the years but, keen to impress, I was happy to take on anything. I soon found out why my predecessors hadn't lasted long. The round incorporated the roads of Newick, Chailey, Ringmer and Barcombe, all named after quaint Sussex villages, but there was nothing remotely quaint about this place. Constantly vying with Whitehawk to be the toughest place in Brighton, the North Moulsecoomb estate commenced being built in 1925 and consisted almost solely of council houses. It was situated on the other side of the A27 from Coldean, which was considered posh by comparison.

I collected my first round from the newsagent and set off past the Hikers Rest, under the tunnel above which the A27 traffic roared, and out the other side – into Beirut! The place was an absolute dump – literally. There were more discarded sofas, white goods, and tyres in the gardens than there were blades of grass! I delivered the first papers in my bag to houses in Barcombe Road without any trouble. So far, so good. The next road in the round was Newick. I didn't immediately sense anything that would give this piano-playing 'posh' boy any concern, and I successfully delivered another couple of papers. I noticed three lads hanging around the gate of one of the houses, but I didn't say anything and continued on my way. Then, THWACK! One of them had crept up behind me and punched me in the back of the head before running off laughing with the others. Being the consummate professional I am, I bravely soldiered on and completed my round. 'Fine' was my reply when Mum and Dad asked how I got on, but my head was pounding. This continued for the first week or so, but I was determined to see it through, mug that I was. And then, one evening, the chief protagonist came up alongside me and instead of punching me, started chatting about racing pigeons he kept in his back garden. Weird! I made a comment about my bird being fitter than his birds, and he laughed. And, thereafter, the physical stuff completely ceased. I'd learnt that coming up with the odd one-liner could get me out of all sorts of tricky situations. And that laughter is less painful than being twatted!

You Little Thief

I'm surprised that the newsagent gave me a paper round as I'd previously nicked loads of sweets from his shop. Whether it was a cry for help or attention seeking or, more likely, that I was a naughty sod, I don't know, but I went through a phase (which lasted several years) of taking things without paying for them. Dad would send me down the road to buy his cigarettes, and when the shop assistant's back was turned to find the cigs in the cabinet, a packet of Opal Fruits or Rolo's would find their way into my pocket. This went on for some time until, whilst in mid-nick of a Yorkie bar, she turned round suddenly and caught me. Mum and Dad were told, and I obviously promised not to do it again. Until a few years later, when I was in a shop in Churchill Square with Mum and Fi. Churchill Square was a 60's concrete monstrosity for which someone probably won the 'Most Shit Looking Shopping Centre Design Anywhere In The World Including Beirut' award! Mum was in the queue to pay for her shopping, and very bored, I spotted a row of model cars in boxes on a shelf. I didn't collect model cars, wasn't remotely interested in them, and had no need for them, but seconds later, one of them was in my pocket. Unseen, I walked out of the shop, returned home, and put it in a drawer, where it remained unopened until I chucked it out years later.

My main bout of thieving occurred when I attended Brighton Technical College in Pelham Street for a few months at the end of 1980. Nearby was a second hand record shop, which was run by a couple of permanently stoned hippies, and which contained old and rare singles across all types of genres with a heavy emphasis on Punk and New Wave. I had a brown card folder, slightly bigger than A4 size, in which I kept all the papers for my course at the college. These pages made excellent 'dividers' when I slipped in various singles from the shop whilst the owners were distracted by someone extolling the virtues of the first Yes LP. I reckon that half of my singles collection was acquired this way, and my thieving only stopped when one of the owners sobered up enough to realise that his stock was rapidly diminishing, which seemed to coincide with whenever I was in his shop, and thereafter, he watched me like a hawk. I did hand over £25 cash for The Factory Sampler EP, so I felt I was actually giving them something back, which was kind of me!

House of fun

Steve's house was the place to be of an evening. His Mum, Brenda, had Steve and his sister, Tanya, when she was quite young, so when she split up with Steve's Dad, she decided to find the life and times she never had whilst she was constrained by bringing up two young kids. Consequently, she would go out to pubs and clubs virtually every evening, leaving the house available to Steve, Tanya and whoever they wished to invite around, which was always myself and plenty of others. It was like a continuation of the youth club without the churchy bit! Tanya used to have her friends round, mostly female, and they all wore BRA's! The evenings would pass by in a haze of drink/drugs and the odd fumble here and there, but, from my point of view, nothing remotely romantic as I was still too shy and self-conscious to ask any of the girls out on a date. Mum and Dad often wondered aloud why I couldn't have these 'gatherings' at our house as we had a record player and a Nina & Frederik record, and I didn't have the heart to shatter their blissful unawareness as to what actually went on at Steve's.

Working for the Yankee Dollar

On June 27th, 1980, I officially left Stringer although, apart from sitting four exams, I hadn't been there for ages. On July 1st, I started working full-time in the mailroom at American Express. It was one of three jobs I'd been offered: an agricultural merchant in Patcham (who went bust two years later), a firm of Solicitors, Burt Brill and Edwards in the Old Steine, and Amex. Mum was desperate for me to take the Solicitor's (office boy) job as it would clearly lead to an outstanding career in law and the Amex one was obviously a dead-end job out of which I'd never make a career. I chose Amex, partly to piss her off but mainly because my interview with the Manager, Rod Clarke, consisted of him asking me whether or not I liked football, and if so, which team I supported. I answered in the affirmative/Brighton and got the job. I had a feeling I was going to enjoy it far more than wearing a wig or trying to sell bags of compost!

The mailroom was a whole new world. Located in the bowels of Amex House, which was Amex's European Headquarters, a building known by the locals as 'The Wedding Cake' on account of its award-winning unique design, which opened in 1977. It was known as 'Asbestos House' by its employees due to the amount of deadly dust that was used in its construction. Despite the obvious health hazards, I stayed for the best part of 25 years.

The mailroom contained numerous characters, some of whom have remained friends for life. The whole ethos, whether intended or not, was to have fun while you worked. The management team was Rod, Mick Green (Assistant Manager), a scum fan but a nice bloke otherwise, and Steve Brooks, the Supervisor, who was about 4ft 6 tall and the same dimensions wide. He was incredibly stocky and took great delight in grabbing your head in a vice-like grip and rubbing your face in his armpits, which stank!

The other key characters were Barry Hambrook, Kev Brimley, Paul Picton and Gary Overington, a Ramones fan who I hit it off with on account of our musical tastes, whereas all the others were into crappy soul and disco. Many other characters came and went over the years, but Barry, Kev and Paul, in particular, helped with my first experiences of going out, clubbing and getting pissed. The weekend would start on a Thursday and finish on the following Monday or Tuesday, usually with me throwing up at regular intervals and usually at home, where Mum and Dad didn't have a clue how to deal with me. As I was their first child and they were that much older than other first-time parents, they couldn't cope with this new life I'd found, and I quickly became an alcoholic (in their eyes).

Most of the mail boys were into football and, in particular, watching the Albion, and Barry, Kev, and I would attend most home games watching from the North Stand. Barry lived over the hill from me in Hollingbury, so after the game, we would catch the same bus home on which someone would have a transistor radio blurting out Sports Report at 5 pm, and James Alexander Gordon would read out that day's results from all 4 English divisions.

Rod and his younger brother, Rory, had attended many away games in the 70's and often met lots of home fans! They continued to organise private coaches and minibuses during the 80's as well, and Barry, Kev and I would usually join them to far-flung places across the country. These jaunts always involved copious amounts of alcohol, the odd punch up and, on one occasion, a stripper. None of this ever got back to Mum and Dad.

I'd only been working in the mailroom for six weeks or so when disaster struck. I received my 'O' level results, and to everyone's amazement, bearing in mind my complete lack of studying or revising, I'd passed all 3. Oh, and I'd achieved Grade 1 in CSE Maths, which was the equivalent of passing an 'O' level. Fuck! Mum was naturally delighted and insisted that I now had to go on to further education and enrolled me at Brighton Technical College on a B-Tec in Business Studies. I really didn't want to go as I'd quickly made friends in the mailroom, enjoyed going out and getting pissed with them and was quite enjoying my salary of £192 per month. But she was incredibly forceful, and I had no choice if I wanted to continue living at 28PR. I said a tearful goodbye to the mailboys and started college in September 1980. The blokes on my course were friendly enough and diverse in their musical tastes, and I even played a couple of games of football for the college team, but my heart wasn't really in it at all. I'd usually have Wednesday afternoons off from college and would pop back into the mailroom to see the boys and do a bit of unpaid work just to keep in contact with them. After Christmas, I was completely broke and decided I wanted to return to work. Rod told me I could start again in February 1981, and that's what I did. Mum was unimpressed, but I was back, working for the Yankee dollar. And the threatened eviction never materialised!

Shortly after my return to the mailroom, a new bloke arrived. His name was Mark Nye, and he'd been an apprentice at the Albion when Alan Mullery was Manager. He regaled us with tales of life as an apprentice, one of which involved Mark pissing in Mullery's shampoo bottle prior to the latter taking a shower. It's not known exactly why Mark wasn't awarded a professional contract, but this may have contributed to it. In view of Rod's strict recruitment criteria, I doubt he even met Mark before giving him the job!

Mark and Paul were as thick as thieves when it came to pulling the girls and would frequently try to outdo each other, usually involving very attractive women and usually with some degree of success. Rumour had it that, written in lipstick on every mirror of the ladies' toilets in every Brighton pub, were the words 'I've shagged Mark Nye'! Barry and Kev also had a periodic dabble but were much more selective. I still couldn't get a shag even if my life depended on it. Our nights out would follow a familiar pattern. Meet in The Druids Head in The Lanes at 8 pm (Kev would always be half an hour late), then on to various pubs until it was time to hit a club. All the others were into their crappy soul/disco music, which I detested, so occasionally, I'd see if I could entice them to go somewhere different: -

Me: 'Can we go somewhere where they'll play Killing Joke or The Cure?'

Them: 'No'.

Me: 'Righto, Alexander O'fucking Neal, it is then'!

I would then miserably enter the dreaded nightclub with them where, in addition to the shit music, I'd have to put up with shit beer. They were all lager boys, so were quite happy with Fosters or Heineken – absolute gnat's piss. I preferred bitter but was lucky if I got a watered-down pint of John Smiths.

Move Closer

Another lowlight of these evenings in the club was my inability to chat up and pull a girl. This usually resulted in a 'Move Closer' moment at 01:55 hours. Clubs in those days closed at 2 am, and five minutes before the end, the lights would dim, and the DJ would play a slowy designed to bring successfully pulled couples together to have a last dance and engage in a bit of tonsil tennis. For me, it would involve identifying a rare, unpulled girl, grabbing hold of her and shuffling/stumbling around to Move Closer by Phyllis Nelson, which required minimal effort and, on occasion, I managed to get my arms all the way round the large lass who was taking part in this charade with me. And then, mercifully, it would be over. The house lights would come back on, the large lass would waddle off to the chip shop, and I'd make my way home alone. Again.

This lack of female companionship was really starting to get me down, almost solely because of the way I looked. It probably didn't help that I frequently listened to Joy Division's two albums, the second of which, Closer, was probably the longest suicide note in history. Black clouds were gathering, and I could 'feel it closing in' as Ian Curtis once sang.

The Call Up

A few notable things happened when I reached the age of 18. On my birthday, the boys took me to a local pub at lunchtime and proceeded to ply me with alcohol. Barry was charged with looking after me, and we ended up on Brighton Beach, where we met a stoned (older) couple from Shepherds Bush. The woman appeared to be interested in me, and I think the bloke took a shine to Barry, but I was too pissed to do anything about it and after I'd sobered up a bit, Barry took me back to work.

That evening, the family went out for a meal in the Eaton Garden restaurant in Hove with Uncle Paul and Gladys, who were over from Australia, seeing family. Also that evening, Argentina decided to invade The Falklands.

Shortly afterwards, I received an official-looking letter in the post. My very limited experience of foreign travel at that point extended to a day trip to Dieppe when I was at school, where we set off loads of firecrackers and scared the shit out of the locals. I looked up where The Falklands were on a map and decided they were a bit further away than Dieppe was.

Excitedly, I opened the letter to discover that I'd been summonsed. Not to serve Queen and country in a far-flung corner of the planet but to attend jury service at Brighton County Court in

Edward Street, a short banger's throw from the side entrance to the mailroom. I attended at the date and time shown on the summons and was sworn in to serve on the jury. I was licking my lips at the prospect of the case being about the smashing of a Scandinavian porn ring and was positively salivating at the thought of sitting through weeks and weeks of detailed evidence. Sadly, all I got was a domestic, which was all over in a couple of days. I was gutted. I wouldn't even have had to get my knees muddy!

Song for whoever

The job in the mailroom was a great means of me getting around the whole building and gaining an understanding of who was who and what role they played in the organisation. There were several Amex buildings dotted around Sussex and one was opposite Amex House at 154 Edward Street. The mailroom at 154 was unsupervised, so after being dropped off there with my sackload of mail to deliver to the departments located there, I'd have a couple of hours to kill before the van came back to collect me and take me back to Amex House. Instead of reading a paper or magazine, I started to write songs. Reading them back recently, I could see how influenced I'd been by other writers, particularly Ian Curtis. My writing mostly consisted of feeling rejection and my inability to meet and form a relationship with a member of the opposite sex. I was becoming more convinced that my deteriorating facial looks were a major cause of this.

Not all my songs were about my despondency. There was a long epic about the fall of the Roman Empire, 'Caesar's Dream', which not many 18–19-year-olds were writing about at the time. There was also the cheery subject about the aftermath of a nuclear war in *Protein* as follows: -

Protein

Their only happiness comes in cans

Charlie's left with swollen glands

Acrobats dangling in mid-air

The Viet Cong lies in despair

Ex boy about town now has no hair

Glistening red where once was fair

The beauty queen is full of scabs

She walks around with slimy crabs

Clinging to her legs, and finds

Justice exists not in mankind

If you had a button, would it help

To increase your personal wealth

Or would it inflict anger and pain

In the shower of atomic rain

Umbrellas proved to be no match

The chickens can no longer hatch

Their eggs, and so we lose another source

Of protein in this holocaust.

Cheery, huh?

The opening lines to another one went as follows:-

I'm going back to the womb

I came out too soon

From a far-off moon

To a world of gloom.

Ian Curtis had a lot to answer for!

Although they may have been a bit morbid, my lyrics seemed to me to actually mean something but, despite my best efforts, I couldn't persuade The Samaritans to use them in an advertising campaign. Unlike The Real Thing, whose lyrics were a godsend to the Scandinavian Tourist Board with their 1970's hit 'Can't Get By Without You';

'Cause I love you

Girl, I need you

And I can't get by without you, Norway!

B&B's in Oslo were probably sold out for months on the back of that!

The Bitterest Pill

Despite my deepening malaise, I started going to a lot of gigs, usually with Steve, Cliff or Barry. New Order, The Stranglers, The Clash, Echo & The Bunnymen, The Cure, etc. Probably the most iconic one (with the worst ever sound system) I went to was The Jam's last ever gig at The Brighton Centre, with Barry and Cliff. The band was at the peak of their powers, and although I preferred a lot of their older stuff, I was glad I was there. Together with virtually my entire year at Stringer, I'd caught a bus up to Virgin Records on Queens Road to buy Going Underground on the day it came out. Everything they released at that time went straight to Number 1, and they could do no wrong. Paul Weller was an astonishingly good songwriter for one so young and clearly wanted to go off and do his thing post-Jam, which was fair enough given the number of classics he'd written, but I always thought he was a bit of a tosser for refusing to ever reform even for a one-off gig, the proceeds of which would have set up Bruce Foxton and Rick Buckler for life. He may have fallen out with the other two and couldn't bear to be in rehearsals or on stage with them, but John Lydon put aside his animosity with the other Pistols to play a couple of comeback gigs (although he needed the money to plough into the musical love of his life, Public Image Limited). But Weller wasn't having it. So much for Champagne Socialism!

Perfect Day

T he 1982/83 season was memorable for Brighton fans. We were crap in the league and were deservedly relegated. The FA Cup, however, was a different story, and we reached the Final for, so far, the only time in our history. The 5th round tie saw us travel to Liverpool, who hadn't lost at home for what seemed like 400 years. Barry, Kev and I went up on one of the many coaches that left Sussex early on a Sunday morning and witnessed a miracle as we won 2-1 to stun the football world. Matches on a Sunday were extremely rare in those days. Both Liverpool and Everton had been drawn at home in the 5th round, but both couldn't play in the city on the same day, so a coin was tossed which Everton won, and they chose to play their game on Saturday. This was handy for me as I had an appointment at the Queen Victoria Hospital in East Grinstead on Saturday and would have had to miss the Liverpool game if they'd won the toss.

After defeating Norwich 1-0 in a drab quarter-final at The Goldstone, we were drawn against Sheffield Wednesday at Arsenal's old ground, Highbury, in the semi-final. Although Wednesday were in the division below us, that didn't count for much, so impending was our relegation.

On a baking hot April Saturday, Barry and I joined the exodus of thousands of Albion fans leaving Sussex for North London. Our tickets were in the Clock End, where we had the perfect view of

Jimmy Case thundering in one of his trademark rockets to put us 1-0 up. Wednesday equalised down our end in the second half before the late Michael Robinson stabbed in what proved to be the winner up the other end, and there was bedlam in the away end. I walked out with the surreal feeling that my little club, Brighton, would be playing in the Cup Final.

Barry and I caught the train back to Brighton and headed for The Cannon, a bar in a seafront hotel, where he had arranged to meet a friend. Time passed, and there was no sign of him, so we decided to leave. As we headed for the door, who should walk in but the entire first team squad, all very pissed, who proceeded to buy drinks for us (Champagne in Steve Foster's case) for the rest of the evening. The perfect end to the perfect day.

Norman 'Tosser' Whiteside

And so off to Wembley. Our Cup Final wasn't my first visit. The previous season, Rod had obtained tickets for the League Cup Final between Spurs and Liverpool and put on one of his notorious coaches. As I thought there was more chance of me dumping in the late Queen's handbag than there was of ever seeing the Albion play there, I agreed to go. I can't remember anything about the game or the score, but I do remember turning round at one point and seeing one of Rod's mates pissing on the terrace behind me.

The FA Cup Final tickets had to be obtained in person from the club shop on Newtown Road at the ground. Barry and I queued for hours but eventually reached the front where I bought 2, one for me and one for Dad. 11 years after he took me to my first ever game, I was kind of repaying him for that, and I also bought his seat next to me on Rory's coach. It turned out to be the last Brighton game I attended with him, which makes it even more memorable.

The game itself was a thriller. Gordon Smith put us 1-0 up; Norman 'Tosser' Whiteside then crippled our right back, Chris Ramsey, and while we were readjusting, United equalised. They then went in front, and all the fans of the odds-on favourites were looking forward to the open-top bus parade around the mean streets of Surrey the following day. Only Gary Stevens hadn't read the script and lashed in a late equaliser to take the game into extra time. And then 'And Smith Must Score' – so he didn't. And that was that.

The replay was held at Wembley the following Thursday. I went, but Dad didn't. We lost 4-0 and it was a huge anti-climax after the first game. And the residents of Weybridge got to see the open-top bus after all!

Meat is Murder

In the 1970's, there was a sitcom on BBC1 called The Good Life, in which a couple who lived in stockbroker belt Surrey gave up their well-paid city jobs to become entirely self-sufficient. Their next-door neighbours were an extremely rich, very posh couple. Having failed the screen test to play the posh woman, Mum decided that we should live like The Good Life and proceeded to fill the back garden with chickens and ducks. Dad was ordered to build fox-proof pens over a large section of the garden, and amazingly, considering he was generally crap at DIY, did a really good job. He also built sturdy houses in which the birds could lay their eggs. Occasionally, Mum would borrow a cockerel who would come in and sire a few chicks but made a bloody racket while he was there.

Having just seen my beloved Brighton lose in the FA Cup Final, my head was all over the place, so much so that I did what I suspect most fellow fans did. I went veggie!

Shortly after the Final replay, I was eating Sunday lunch at home, which consisted of Roast Chicken. I looked up the garden and could see our free-range birds running around without a care in the world. I looked at the dead bird on my plate, pushed it away, and to this day, have never eaten meat again. Mum and Fi thought it was a good idea to follow suit; Dad, being a typical meat and two veg bloke – (that's not an intended euphemism)- was less keen but didn't really have much choice. We started to explore alternatives which, at that time, weren't as vast as they are now, and I continued eating fish until the 90's when supermarkets slowly began to introduce veggie alternatives. I've never preached to my carnivorous friends as I believe it's everyone's right to choose what they eat, and all 3 of my kids have been brought up eating meat, although I did once draw up a list of people I'd like to kill, and Bernard Matthews was very close to the top!

Jimmy Jimmy

After a couple of years in the mailroom. It was time to move on. I absolutely loved the place and the people in it, but it wasn't much of a career. I obtained a job in an admin department where the Supervisor was Jenny Jones. This was very close to The Clash's 'Janie Jones,' so I knew we'd get on well. It was in this department that I began to use a computer for the first time. Made by Raytheon, it had crunching, clunking keys, not too dissimilar to the noise made by my till in Boots, and (thankfully) Jane Warner's tampons weren't lying around! Soon after I joined this department, another young bloke rocked up. James Betts was a couple of years younger than me but was a very good-looking lad, and we struck up an immediate friendship (even though he supported Leeds!). His Dad, Ken, was an ex-copper and had a responsible role elsewhere in Amex and his sister, Caroline, also worked there. It was quite a family-oriented company, and I think I sussed the reason for this.

I'm convinced that, around this time, someone high up in the company, possibly in New York or, more probably, Utah, decided it would be great to create an American Express family. St John's school, situated behind Amex House, was bought and converted into a Social Club with 2 bars, full-sized snooker and pool tables, dart boards, video juke boxes, a quiet lounge that randomly contained suits of armour and a dance floor. Oh, and cheap, very heavily subsidised beer. The perfect location and environment for all Amex House employees to leave work at 5 pm each day and head over to the club on their way home. In this way, lots of future Mr and Mrs Amex could meet and have future Amex children, a scenario that happened on numerous occasions. The man from Utah was spot on!

Myself, James, the mailboys and dozens of others frequently took advantage of this great cheap night out, and James and I became friendly with a girl of a similar age who worked in the next department to us, Caroline Pratt. In addition to going over to the club after work, the three of us would often visit The Thurlow pub opposite the Law Courts for a few pints and games of darts at lunchtime. Thankfully, she was a fellow Brighton fan and not keen on that dirty northern lot!

Also, around this time, Amex started accepting youngsters, usually aged 16-18, on a Youth Training Scheme. Although legally, they weren't supposed to drink, this didn't stop them from heading over to the Social Club every Friday after work. There were some attractive females among them, and being the good-looking bloke he was, James went through them like a hot knife through butter! Invariably, once he'd dumped them, I'd try to console them with a comforting arm around the shoulder and occasional snog, but when they'd sobered up, they'd run a mile. I couldn't really blame them.

Dave Jackson

One of the benefits of the Social Club was that I could sign up to 3 guests per visit. On one occasion, I took Ross and his friend Neil up there to play snooker and have a few drinks. I signed them into the visitor's book, and they had to do likewise. Ross wrote his name and signed but Neil wrote his name as 'Dave Jackson'. 'Why Dave Jackson?', Ross asked him. 'Everyone knows a Dave Jackson', replied Neil. I liked the name so much that I used it as my pseudonym thereafter. For instance, if I was on a work call with an irate customer who asked for my name as they intended to report me, I would reply 'Dave Jackson'. 'Right, Mr Jackson', the customer would say, 'I'm going to get you sacked'. 'I don't think you are, you tosser', I would think to myself, and naturally, nothing ever came of it.

The Queen Vic

etween 1984 and 1986, I was a regular visitor to the Queen Victoria Hospital in East Grinstead. The hospital, and in particular, the McIndoe Burns Unit, gained fame during the Second World War for treating badly burned and disfigured servicemen with pioneering plastic surgery. By the early 80's, my face had become a huge issue for me, severely denting my confidence and leaving me in a very dark place at times. As my body grew through my teens, my nose flattened out of shape and my lower jaw had grown way beyond the upper jaw and noticeably jutted out. The hair lip was still there but I accepted nothing could be done about that (although, shortly before I started writing this book, I grew a beard and moustache as, even at 60, I still can't bear to look at photos of me taken from a certain angle showing the hair lip. And it's not because Carly Simon once sang a song about me!). I was so conscious of how I looked, I had to sit on the left side of a bus up against the window so that only the slightly better right side of my face was visible to other passengers or someone sitting next to me. Similarly, if chatting to someone at work or in a pub, I would tilt the left side of my face away from them. Frequently, in a queue in a supermarket, I would see a young child looking at me followed by them saying 'Daddy, why does that man look funny?' It was horrendous and I make no apology for seeking help to overcome it.

Facial disfigurations are some of the hardest things to come to terms with. The hair lip, a 'port wine stain' birth mark, even a large mole or warts are all something immediately visible when meeting someone for the first time and unfortunately, judgement on 'looks' plays a big part in whether or not you fancy that person. (Fellow sufferers reading this will almost certainly know what I'm on about and the damage that can be gleaned from the other person's initial expression or, indeed, the little girl in the supermarket with her natural question; it causes a huge loss of self-esteem and a huge amount of unhappiness).

I greatly admire the actor, Tom Burke, who played the lead role in the TV series 'Strike', and who has had a great career on TV and stage. He too was born with a hair lip but that hasn't put him off regularly performing in public. He's obviously had luckier breaks than I did! Or a better agent!

After several consultations during the previous couple of years, I had the first of 3 operations in 1984 when a piece of bone was removed from my hip and inserted into my cleft palate, which had opened up as I grew, and which had caused the tooth to grow through the roof of my mouth and into my nose where it was removed when I was 11. The operation was a success but one of my lungs collapsed (probably because I hadn't had a smoke for 12 hours!), so I was rigged up to this and that until it recovered.

The second operation, the following year, was much more complex and involved my lower jaw being broken on both sides and set back so it was aligned with the upper jaw. A metal plate was also inserted into the left-hand side of my upper cheek and remains there to this day. Both jaws were then wired together for 3 months. I could only 'eat' liquidised food which, to be fair to Mum, she managed to come up with varied and 'tasty' dishes, but I lost loads of weight –

something I wasn't used to. Once the grotesque swelling had gone down and the wires were removed, it looked very different, and I felt a bit better in myself.

The third and final operation took place in 1986 and involved my nose being reset and realigned with the rest of my face. It too was successful, and my self-confidence started to return. As, thankfully, did my weight!

Whip It

The Social Club was available to hire for private functions, and for my 21st birthday, Mum did just that, putting on one of her memorable buffets in the process. All the mailboys and friends from other Amex departments, plus external friends, were invited. Rod Clarke, in his infinite wisdom, decided to hire a Whippagram, who rocked up in bondage gear (mostly removed) and proceeded to whip my sorry arse to the amusement of everyone present. Except one. Churchgoing, God-worshipping Mum was utterly appalled; it apparently 'ruined the evening' – I was too pissed to really notice- and she spent the whole of the following Monday on the phone and writing letters to all and sundry expressing her disgust. Which was more embarrassing for me than the public flogging!

My actual 21st birthday was on a Tuesday, and the Albion had a league fixture at scum that evening. Barry very kindly offered to drive me up there and came to collect me from 28PR. The problem was that Mum and Dad had got it into their heads that we'd all go out for a nice family meal with Fi and couldn't understand why I would prefer to go to the arse end of South London instead. The atmosphere in our house became terse and very unpleasant as Barry's arrival time approached and was positively toxic by the time I ran out slamming the front door behind me.

The game itself was a 1-1 draw and notable for three things; Caroline had arranged for my birthday details to be read out over the tannoy before the game; Gerry Ryan had his leg broken in a horror challenge from scum's Henry Hughton; and I spent most of the game dislodging sections of the crumbling terrace with my Doc Martens before lobbing bits at the scum fans below. And then returned home to a reception frostier than Ice Station Zebra!

Friday Night, Saturday Morning

Whilst I was working in Janie Jones' department, a bloke came in one day to collect internal memos for the department where he worked. He had John Lennon style glasses and tousled hair, not dissimilar to that of Ian McCulloch in Echo & The Bunnymen. His name was Les Bell. We got chatting and he mentioned that he was a bass player in a band who were urgently seeking a keyboard player as they had their first gig coming up shortly. I told him that I'd played the piano to a decent standard when I was younger but hadn't touched it for a few years. He invited me down to their next rehearsal at Grapevine Studios in Vine Street the following Saturday. I also advised him that I didn't have my own keyboard and was buggered if I was lugging the piano down from 28PR, and he said I'd be able to borrow a synthesizer from another musician who rehearsed there. His band was called The Embankments, and they played covers by The Specials, The Beat and Funboy Three, none of whom were my preferred genre, and apart from their big hits, not much of which I'd heard.

I turned up at Grapevine at the agreed time and was met by Les, who introduced me to the other members of the band. Mark Annetts, the singer, who looked and sounded like the late, great Terry Hall, Hugh Barker, a quite posh guitarist, and Martin Wilson, the drummer, who was only 15 and who still attended Stanley Deason school on Wilson Avenue in Whitehawk, which was where the venue of the first gig was to be in less than two weeks. They were all pleasant enough and ran through their existing set of covers, which included 'Save It For Later' and 'Jeanette' by The Beat, 'Our Lips Are Sealed' by Funboy Three, and 'Friday Night, Saturday Morning' by The Specials. With that last song in particular, I could see why they urgently needed a keyboard player, and it remains the favourite song I have ever played live.

Les had indeed borrowed a Casio synth and suggested some chords I could play in each song. We had a few goes; it was a bit chaotic at first, but I slowly started to get the hang of it and wrote the chords/notes down and where they fitted into each song. I then went back home and practiced these chords/notes 'hearing' where they should be played and met the band again for rehearsal the following Saturday. My practice had paid off, and we were good to go for the inaugural gig at the school the following Friday. I took the day off work, collected the borrowed keyboard from Grapevine and headed up to the school. We set up the instruments and equipment on what seemed to be a tiny stage in the school hall and awaited the arrival of the audience, which comprised around 50 kids from the top year (the same year that our drummer, Martin, was still in). The set went quite well, considering my limited practice sessions with the band and the whole gig was videoed by someone in the audience. I never did see it or find out what became of it. No matter. I was back on stage, the adrenalin was pumping, and I loved every second of it.

We continued meeting and rehearsing at Grapevine every Saturday lunchtime, and if the Albion were at home that day, I'd head off to watch the game afterwards. We were getting much tighter with our sound and introduced a few new songs, including the theme from The Munsters, with which we began to start our live set. We then obtained our first gig in front of an adult audience at The Kensington, a pub on the corner of Kensington Gardens, for which we received the princely sum of £35 to be split amongst the five of us. I had to pay £2 each time I borrowed the keyboard, so after buying a few beers, I was out of pocket. This gig was the first and last time I had a drink before we played. I was struggling to remember the chords/notes, and whilst the other band members thought it was ok, I wasn't happy with my performance. The crowd was around 30 in number, made up of friends and pub locals, and they seemed to enjoy it. We were up and running – or were we?

A few rehearsals later, Hugh dropped the bombshell that he was leaving. He'd been accepted for a place at Cambridge University, which was too far for him to come down for rehearsals and gigs. I immediately suggested Steve to Les as, although he hadn't yet been in a band, he could definitely play a bit. Les told me to invite Steve down to our next rehearsal, which I did on my way home that day. Like me, Steve wasn't really into the type of stuff The Embankments were playing but, also like me, he was a quick learner and fitted in seamlessly. More gigs followed at the Kensington, and we were invited to support Dance Factor 7 at The Richmond. DF7 had a decent drummer, Viv Blake, who was a bit older than me, also worked at Amex, and went on to join a band that contained the brother of Vince Clarke (from Depeche Mode, Erasure, etc.).

London Calling

Les came bounding excitedly into rehearsals one Saturday and announced that we'd got our first-ever gig in London, at The Moonlight Club in West Hampstead. He'd spoken to the promoter who was going to arrange flyers on bus stops, lampposts, record shops, etc., and there would be members of the music press present. An 8-piece support band was going to come up with us, so with them, the 5 of us (plus our equipment) and, no doubt, some of our increasing fanbase from The Kensington/Richmond, we decided to hire a coach which would be driven by Cliff's mate, Dave Vinall. We arranged for Dave to pick everyone up from outside St Peter's church in central Brighton and, after waiting for ages for our non-existent fans to not turn up, we set off with just us, the support band, Cliff and Dave on board. Never mind, the club will be packed if the promoter has done his stuff.

My first impressions of The Moonlight Club weren't great. We all had to lug our equipment into the building swerving the dogshit on the top step outside. We set up and waited for the masses to arrive. And waited. And waited. No one had yet turned up, so the support band went on and played their set. Still, no one came, so we had no choice but to play our stuff with only Cliff and Dave in the audience as the support band joined us on stage for a jam. It was a complete disaster, and we never got the chance to play in London again.

Although The Moonlight Club was a bit of a dive, I subsequently learnt that Joy Division had played their last ever London gig there and The Stone Roses played their first London one in the same place. So I'd been in the same toilet as Ian Curtis and Ian Brown, albeit, not at the same time. Which was the only crumb of comfort I could take from the debacle.

Changes

Gigs at The Kensington and The Richmond continued for a while until we sacked our singer, Mark. He'd owed me money from the coach hire to The Moonlight Club gig and kept promising to repay it but never did. He worked in a late-night restaurant in the Old Steine and one night, accompanied by Cliff, I paid him a visit. His female boss initially refused to hand it over from his wages until I 'persuaded' him it was in his best interests, whereupon she paid me what I was owed, and that was the last I saw of him. It was my first experience of 'doorstep' debt collecting, and stood me in good stead when I did it for a living many years later. But for now, our band was singer-less. Which was a bit tricky!

Thankfully, Mick Clare arrived on the scene. He was quite a bit older than the rest of us but had previous experience singing in bands and slotted straight in. By now, we were starting to write our own material and had moved away from covers by The Beat, Specials etc., so much so that we changed our name to Nothing From Nowhere, something I came up with when I was in one of my more positive moods! We even started to use some of the songs I'd written back in my mailroom days in 154 Edward Street, although we could never set any music to one of my best ones, Protein, which was a shame. The new songs started to go down well when we played them live, with one in particular, 'Poppy Day', written by Steve, Les,

Martin and me before Mick joined. It was a catchy little ditty and by far the most commercial song we'd written. I thought it had 'hit' written all over it. It was so good we decided to record it at a session at Nick Tribe's Blue Box studio in Wilbury Mews, Hove, and headed over there one Friday evening to do just that. We needed another song to record to maximise the time and cost of recording and settled on 'I Apologise', a very dancey tune in which my synth played a prominent part. I remain convinced to this day that if it had ever been released as a single or 12-inch, it would have been a massive hit in the clubs (although probably not the crappy ones the mailboys continued to frequent!).

It was a very long night but, for all of us, a fascinating insight as to how records were made. Firstly, Martin's drums for 'Poppy Day' were recorded, then Les' bass, Steve's guitar, my keyboards and, finally, Mick's vocals. Nick insisted on several takes for each instrument and then mixed and produced the final version. It sounded fantastic! We then did the same for 'I Apologise'. Because the track was so synth-centric, I think Nick recorded the drums first and then my synth, as it would help with the rhythm section for Les and Steve. Mick's vocals were again recorded last with a lot of echo; it was all mixed by Nick, and, hey presto, we had our first 2 track demo. Daylight was coming up as we left the studios around 5 am, knackered but elated.

The End of My World As I Knew It

Shortly after recording the demo, we were invited to support The Skelatal Family at the Zap Club on Brighton seafront. They were from West Yorkshire and were becoming a big noise on the indie scene. It was a massive chance for us to get noticed – so naturally, we didn't!

Martin had, by now, left school and obtained a job on The Tube, a Friday night music show hosted by the likes of Jools Holland and Paula Yates, which was filmed live in Newcastle and which was a showcase for indie bands in particular. His job entailed him travelling up by train early on Friday morning, setting up all the drum kits for the bands who would be appearing that evening, dismantling them after each set and catching the mail train back to London/Brighton in time to be at our rehearsals at Grapevine on Saturday. For his age, he was an excellent drummer but, possibly due to his age, he got a bit over-exuberant at times. Whenever we rehearsed or played live, he kept the beat going perfectly but would always have to add an extra one or two beats too many at the end of each song. This started to grate with the rest of us – well, probably not Les, as he was too stoned to realise- and we warned him to cut it out. Things came to a head during one particular rehearsal when, after one hi-hat too many, Steve threatened to kill him! And he meant it. As I've mentioned before, Steve is the most passive bloke I've ever met, so if he was threatening to kill someone, they must have seriously pissed him off. Which, of course, Martin had. Martin wouldn't back down, Les sided with him and that was that. Les rang me a couple of days later to tell me it was all over – ironically, on the same day, we were due to support The Skelatal Family! Steve formed the Midniters, Mick had some minor success with Hot Knives, and I've no idea what the other two eventually did. It would be another 38 years before I wrote or recorded another song.

I was absolutely gutted as all I'd ever wanted to do from an early age was to be in a band and on stage. I'd had 5 minutes of it, had recorded a demo (that was never released), played a gig in London where one of my heroes had played before me, and I'd genuinely loved every minute of it (apart from the extra hi-hats!). Seeing the crowd dancing to our music and none of them giving a toss what I looked like was such a buzz, and I wish it had never ended. As it turned out, the year we split was the year I had my 2nd (big) operation, so I would have been out of action for a large part of it. Another one to be filed under 'what could have been.'

Break It Up, Break It Up

The Amex Social Club had a number of sports teams affiliated with it. Snooker, pool, football and cricket. Rod Clarke and Mick Green were heavily involved with the latter and, as it was the only sport I was half decent at, I gave it a go. Matches against other local sides around Sussex would take place on a Sunday. I still couldn't bat to save my life, but I could bowl and field quite well, usually at point or, more often than not, on the boundary. My opportunities to bowl became more limited with the introduction of Mark Ricksen, who was about 6ft 7 inches tall and could hurl the ball down from a great height with wicket-taking success. Most of my involvement then consisted of stopping the odd boundary in the unlikely event that the ball came my way and getting cold. It was a good social event, and I went on a tour the club organised to Norwich where my sole contribution was, dressed only in my Y-fronts at 2 am, to stop a fight between two very drunk girls who took one look at my (lack of) clutter, pissed themselves laughing and went off into the night, arms around each other and besties once more. I deserved the Nobel Peace Prize for that!

The Man in Black

The football section of the club played a big part in my life for many years, initially as a player, and then as a manager. At first, we played solely in the Sussex Sunday League under the leadership of Rob Dunkerton, who was a decent right-back and even better as a manager. The Sunday players all had to work for Amex, although this changed when we joined the Saturday Leagues and became more competitive. The Sunday side was full of great characters who bonded on and off the pitch (particularly off!). In addition to Barry, Kev, Nobby Purser and Paul White, we had the likes of Andy Cole (no, not that one!), Ashley Wright, Tony Whittingham, and Lee Barnett. And my old mucker from Stringer, Neil Cornford, who was lethal in front of goal but did bugger all elsewhere on the pitch! Rob's great skill, apart from his Churchillian speeches at half time, was that he had an eye for talent and for who was crap. Sadly, I fell into the latter category, although I did make an occasional appearance and scored a couple of goals, including one with my head. I don't remember too much about it as my eyes were firmly shut, but I was told it was a worldy (or, more accurately, belonged in another world!). I was usually a sub, which I didn't mind as I knew my limits, and it meant I got to chat with Caroline and her friend, Jo Ambler, who came along to watch (as Jo was going out with James at the time). I was also a linesman on occasion and, due to the dearth of reliable referees at our level, went on a course where

I qualified to be a referee. This was invaluable whenever our appointed ref failed to show up and prevented the club from being fined for not providing a ref. I'd don my ref's kit, and the game could go ahead. I'd always bend over backwards to give certain decisions to the opposition so I couldn't be accused of being a 'homer', which used to drive Rob mad, but he knew it had to be done. Cries of 'who's the wanker in the black?', could frequently be heard, to which I would respond with my non-bow cello playing hand movements!

Magazine

Thankfully, Rob began to recruit a better standard of sub, so I was no longer required in that role. I would still go along and write up a report of the match in my own publication, 'The Grunt', so named after the noise I once made winning a penalty. The Grunt was very loosely based on Private Eye, which I would read from cover to cover every fortnight when it came out, and was a satirical review of that Sunday's game, including player ratings, player profiles, etc., which I would hand write when I returned home after the game/pub. I'd then arrive at work at 7 am the following day when no one else was around, photocopy each page (which could sometimes run to 10 pages or more), and end up with 20 copies of the whole magazine, thus satisfying my distribution list. Each magazine would be stapled and placed in an internal envelope addressed to the recipient and be ready for collection by the mailboys on their 9 am round. And then I'd start my day job!

The phone calls would usually start around 11 am, often with uncontrollable laughter from the person at the other end who had found that week's edition particularly amusing. One particular player would ring me at home on the Monday evening enquiring as to why I'd only rated him a 6 when he thought his performance merited at least an 8. After an hour and a half of me explaining what he'd done well and not quite so well, which included, on one occasion, an unusual injury whereby he'd split his anus, we'd eventually compromise on a 7.

Vienna

The Social Club decided to enter a couple of football teams into a European Banking tournament to be held in Vienna. At first, it meant nothing to me, but Rob then told me I was in the squad. The club kitted us out in 2 different styles of tracksuit, various other accessories, and a snazzy holdall, and we travelled by coach to the Austrian capital, where we played a few games against teams from European banks and credit card companies. I didn't play for more than a few minutes, but it was in their international stadium, which was a slight upgrade on Wild Park!

The trip wasn't my first experience of going abroad. I'd obviously been part of the group scaring the shit out of the locals in Dieppe, and the Social Club had previously run a coach to Lake Lucerne, to where I travelled with James and Caroline. The views were absolutely stunning, both of the mountains and the lake itself. Everywhere was so clean, and I felt a bit guilty dropping my fag butts on the pavement!

Another Social Club jaunt took us to Antwerp, where we ended up in a gay bar and an old bloke, wearing a white glove and watching James through a mirror, started knocking one out. We left there a bit sharpish!

I also had a couple of holidays abroad with Barry, firstly via coach to the South of France, and then by plane to Kos in 1986, before the last of my three big ops. Despite my chronic fear of heights, I've always loved flying, and the trip to Kos didn't faze me.

Further overseas trips under the guise of 'work' took me to Phoenix in the States (twice), all major European capitals plus Milan and Barcelona numerous times, and South Africa, where I wangled a day trip to Soweto, which was eye-opening!

Saturday's Kids

Amex FC decided to enter two teams into the Brighton Saturday League. Rob was the manager of the first team, and Chris Isherwood agreed to manage the seconds. A lot of our Sunday League players were dual-registered, but we could also sign non-Amex employees as well. Chris packed in managing after a few games, and I volunteered to take it on. For my first game in charge, I put myself in goal and within the first 10 minutes, we went 1-0 up with Scott Carroll scoring against a team who were a division above us. Piece of piss, this management lark! 80 minutes later, I trudged off, having lost 8-1 which included a bullet header from 25 yards that I never saw as it flew past me into the top corner of the net. I pretty much packed up playing there and then and concentrated on managing. We did quite well in the years I was in charge, reaching a Cup Final, which we lost (thanks to Nobby Purser) and another, which we won when my captain, Lee Knight, deliberately broke the nose of our opposition's most dangerous player very early on. Lee was a lovely bloke, hard as nails, who had served in The Falklands War and who had a sweet left foot. He formed a formidable central midfield partnership with James, who could run all day and liked a tackle.

Post-match drinks for both Saturday teams always took place at The Hanbury Arms on St. George's Road in Kemp Town. The pub was run by Alan and Heather, who were the respective parents of Tony Whittingham and Scott Carroll, and they always looked after us. It was a proper old-school boozer, and most weeks, a van would pull up outside with row upon row of top-of-the-range tracksuits, trainers, etc., at unbelievably cheap prices. No questions asked!

Go West

In the mid-80's, I started to go and watch Bristol City games, not because I'd fallen out of love with the Albion – I hadn't – but if City had a local derby and Brighton were playing up north, I fancied the shorter trip. The first such game I went to was City v Plymouth, a proper West Country battle. I travelled with Rory and Dave Sheppardson – who may or may not have featured in the Anal Split story- and, as soon as we drove past Bristol Meads station, it was going off. And that was at 11 am! Both Rory and Dave were handy and liked what they experienced, so much so that we went to a few more City games that season, including at Swindon, Aldershot and Brentford, where the sheer weight of numbers of the City fans kicked the gate down and we all got in for free.

We also had a couple of good away days with City at Wembley as they reached consecutive finals of The Freight Rover Trophy in 1986 and 1987 against Bolton and Mansfield, respectively. The Bolton one was particularly memorable as it seemed that the whole of the North West had turned up to meet the entire West Country. Which was nice!

Tarzan O'Gram

By 1987, my career at Amex was slowly progressing and I was now working in another admin department with slightly more responsibility. My supervisor was Andi Rooke, a very short, very pretty and very horny lady who ended up marrying Lee Knight. They seemed so right for each other but sadly, it didn't last. Andi had a friend who was getting married and who was starting her hen night in the Social Club one Friday after work. Towards the end of that afternoon, there was a mad panic in the office and Andi and a couple of the other girls came up to me and told me that the Tarzan O'Gram they'd booked couldn't now make it and would I do it. Although I had no particular experience in this part of the entertainment business and, frankly, had the body shape of a pregnant hippo as opposed to some ripped dude who could swing from tree to tree, it was another public performance that I couldn't turn down. That and the free beer they promised to keep me in all evening. We headed over to the club after work, and I had a pleasant time in the Gents' toilets with three young ladies painting chest hair on me - (as I was completely bereft of the natural stuff)- with their mascara and dressing me in a loin cloth which they'd managed to find at short notice. (I'm not entirely convinced that I wasn't their Plan A to begin with, but I wasn't complaining!). They gave me the nod to enter the main bar area where the unsuspecting bride-to-be was waiting with her back to me, but not for long as the rest of the bar exploded with laughter and, frankly, some rather unpleasant comments. I read out a poem I'd hastily put together, made a rather impressively loud Tarzan roar, and proceeded to lift the poor girl over my shoulder and carry her around the bar. Unfortunately, she was rather a big lass – positively svelte in comparison to me - and it wasn't until the next morning, when the alcohol had worn off, that I realised that I'd done my back in!

Hanging on the Telephone

My role in Andi's department involved dealing with more complex customer queries and writing detailed replies to them after comprehensively researching their issues. It also involved taking and receiving telephone calls from third-party companies (usually banks) to further assist in their resolution. One day, I took a call from a young lady who worked for Midland Bank in Oxford Street, London. It related to a 'high-worth' Saudi Arabian customer, and I was able to resolve her query to her satisfaction. She rang again the following day under the pretext of clarifying the outcome of the previous day's call but, as she admitted later, she liked the sound of my voice and just wanted a chat. An hour later, I was getting evil looks from Andi as my productivity was clearly suffering so I asked the young lady if it would be ok to ring her at home that evening to continue our conversation. To my amazement, she agreed and gave me her home number (no mobile phones in those days). Her name was Caroline Haughey.

I rang her that evening and spent another couple of hours chatting to her. She was three years younger than me, lived in Hertford and had recently split up with a long-term boyfriend. I, of course, was very, very single, which presumably appealed to her. These calls continued every night for a few weeks until, towards the end of August, she dropped a bombshell; could she come down to

Brighton for the bank holiday weekend, stay at 28PR and get to know each other better? I replied in the affirmative but pointed out that I was already booked on Rory's coach to watch the Albion play Northampton on bank holiday Monday and couldn't miss that, so we'd have just the Saturday and Sunday together. (Despite my desperation, I wasn't forgetting my priorities!). Mum and Dad weren't keen. 'Where will she sleep? Where will you sleep?' 'My bed, the sofa', I told them, but the thought that I'd have a female in the house gave Mum one of her (numerous) migraines. Eventually they relented, and I agreed to meet Caroline at Brighton Station on a sunny August lunchtime. She told me what she'd be wearing, and I told her I'd have a red carnation in my button hole and meet her under the clock! (Actually, I didn't). I was as nervous as hell as I waited for her on the platform. She soon came into sight, I checked it was her and gave her a hug before picking up her case and heading for the taxi rank. She was quite short with mousey hair and quite pretty. She spent the entire cab ride to 28PR looking out of the window rather than paying me any attention, which I didn't think was a great sign, but as it turned out, she was even more nervous than me. We arrived at 28PR, I introduced her to Mum, Dad and Fi, had a drink and a bite to eat and took her case up to my room to show her around, whereupon she proceeded to take all her clothes off and lay on the bed! In a blind panic, I looked out of the window and could see that Mum and Dad were at the top of the garden, so I only had a few minutes, which was ample for her. I was predictably rubbish, though! I took her to some pubs in the town and to the pier, all the usual touristy stuff and did the same on Sunday. The following day, after I'd watched her catch her train at the station, I caught Rory's coach to Northampton, where we drew 1-1.

We spoke on the phone every night during the next week, and she invited me up to her place for the following weekend. I caught the train to London after work on the Friday and met her outside her bank in Oxford Street. We went for drinks and a meal and caught the train to Hertford, where I met her parents and stayed at their house that weekend. Both parents were from adjoining villages in County Donegal, smoked like a Welsh holiday home, and were very devout practicing Catholics. Hmm. Neither Caroline nor her younger sister, Trisha, went to church all that often, although they had both attended a girls-only convent school, which must have been a breeze compared to my RE teacher at Stringer, Hickman, and his Winfield plimsolls!

Shortly after we met, on October 15th, 1987, it was a bit windy. When I got up the following morning, there were no buses running up or down Lewes Road, so I had to walk to work. The scene of devastation as I approached The Level was apocalyptic. Most of the trees had come down and were laying across the road, on the tops of cars and on houses. The landscape had changed forever. I was due to visit Caroline after work that day and couldn't get there as there were no trains or any other kind of public transport. That slight wind had turned into a hurricane.

The pattern of staying at each other's every weekend continued for some time. Mum still wasn't keen, Dad just grunted periodically, and I think Fi was happy that I'd met someone at long last. The pain of the recent operations seemed to have been worth it.

On February 14th, 1988, having borrowed money from Barry to buy an emerald ring as I was skint, I proposed to her in a restaurant in Brighton, and she accepted. Too soon? Probably. Too desperate? Definitely! Mum wasn't in the slightest bit impressed, but her parents were delighted. The date was set for April 29th, 1989, at her family (Catholic) church in Hertford.

Later, in 1988, the Social Club ran one of their coaches to the Loire Valley in France on which Caroline and I both went. France as a country is staggeringly beautiful in places; it's just the locals who are a bit of a nause! When we were younger, Cliff formed the 'Kick A Citroën Today' club, of which Steve and I were willing inaugural members.

Never Mind the Bollocks

Also in 1988, at the request of Amex, I spent a couple of weeks in Phoenix in the USA, notionally working on user-testing a new computer system they were introducing to support the launch of a credit card in the UK, but the system was rarely available to test, and it was the one of the best free 'holiday's' I ever had. One night, I went with a couple of American colleagues to a bar in the Scottsdale area of the city. Upon entering the bar, I noticed the Never Mind The Bollocks Album cover up on a wall. I had a couple of drinks and asked the barman if he had the actual record in his bar. He said he did and asked if I liked the Pistols. I told him that not only did I like them, I was a roadie for them when they toured the UK. He and the locals in his bar were initially apprehensive, but I told them that I knew all the tunes off by heart, having heard them so often when I was on the road with the band, and if he played it, I'd sing along to it. He was still a bit sceptical but started to play the record. From the opening vocals on Holidays In The Sun to the last words of EMI, I was word-perfect on every song and as the album progressed, the bigger the crowd of locals grew around me. When I reached the end, they whooped and hollered (as only yanks can whoop and holler). They were completely convinced that I had indeed been a Pistols roadie, and I never bought another drink all the time I was out there and went into that bar. I don't think they fully realised that I'd have been 12-13 years old when the Pistols were touring but, like most Yanks, they were pretty gullible!

Harold Shipman

Back in England, I had to do the usual pre-wedding churchy stuff and attended a couple of masses in Caroline's church in Hertford, which was horrific. The congregation just looked fearful and nervous the whole time. In fact, the last time I'd seen people look that nervous, they were sitting in Harold Shipman's waiting room!

The other equally horrific event was having a meeting with her Monsignor, the bloke who would be marrying us. I had to agree to all sorts of shit like bringing any kids up in the catholic church, which made me think of a bloke I knew in Bradford – Asif!

Our House

We started saving for a house, and with the availability of a cheap staff mortgage from her employers, we found and bought a 2-bed semi-detached house in Maresfield Road, Whitehawk. It was near the top of the hill, and out the back, had stunning views of the marina and the English Channel. Given its location, it was really cheap and very affordable and had a bright yellow burglar alarm, which was never required. The location was ideal for The Hanbury and nights out after football. At first. Caroline used to join us there and made a couple of friends, including Kev's other half, Karen, but eventually her interest waned as other things/people became more important to her. By now, she'd transferred to the Church Road, Hove branch of the bank.

Mum hated the house but realised that if we were going to be married, we needed a marital home. If she was ever out in the town and bumped into a friend who would ask how I was getting on and where I was living, she would reply, 'North Kemp Town'! She really was such a snob.

Wedding Bells

I asked James to be my best man and he accepted. The stag night consisted of a pub crawl around some of the more obscure pubs in Brighton not far from the Grapevine Studio we used to rehearse in. I deliberately selected these pubs for their real ales and alternative music. In one, I could have sworn I heard Killing Joke being played (which hopefully pissed the mailboys off!).

A couple of days before the wedding, James and I checked into the White Horse hotel in Hertford. Mum, Dad, Fi and all our guests from Brighton came up a day later. We all had a quiet drink and a meal the night before – The Last Supper, you could say! The wedding went by without any dramas, the reception was ok, and we caught a cab to Heathrow for our flight to our honeymoon in Budva the following day.

Tito

I'd chosen Budva in Yugoslavia (now Montenegro) for two reasons; it was dirt cheap, and it was very close to the Albanian border. I'd had a fascination with Albania since my teens. Here was a tiny country in Western Europe that had fallen out with the Russians, the Chinese, the Yanks, the British, and all of its neighbours –basically everyone–, which had been run by a communist dictator (Enver Hoxha) since the end of the second World War, and which was almost totally self-sufficient. Oh, and they had secret police (the Sigurimi) who made the Gestapo look like Girl Guides!

Imagine my utter delight and excitement when, after arriving at our honeymoon hotel in Budva, the first thing I saw was a poster advertising a coach trip to the Albanian border. I booked us both on one of those before we'd even checked in!

On the day of the trip, my excitement and anticipation were off the scale as we boarded the coach and set off. As it drove closer to the border, I could see the locals (on the Yugoslav side) all dressed in what looked like period costumes with no cars in sight, just loads of horses, mules, and carts. This wasn't for the benefit of tourists; this was how they dressed and lived. The coach took us up into the mountains overlooking Lake Skadar, and the views were stunning. The border was heavily fortified by barbed wire, and on the

Yugoslav side, there was an armed guard in a tower. Further down the mountain was his Albanian counterpart. There was a big sign which basically said, 'Don't go past here, or you will be shot'. Having survived a paper round in Newick Road, that didn't faze me, so I reached through the wire on to what was technically Albanian soil and picked up a rock. Without getting shot. Bloody Health & Safety rubbish! Despite numerous house moves since, I've still got that rock in my garage.

Also on the border was a massive rock carved out of the mountain upon which someone had painted the Yugoslav flag and 'TITO'. President Tito died in 1980 but had held Yugoslavia (and most of the Balkans) together like a powerful glue for decades; sadly, the 'glue' evaporated a couple of years after we were there, resulting in the horrific Balkans war in which the Serbs, Croats, Bosnians etc., took their medieval feuds out on one another. In every shop or restaurant, there was a photo of Tito. Not the Pope, or Jesus, or anyone else. Just Tito. He was bigger than God's Dad in that country!

I spotted a fantastic photo opportunity and, standing in front of the rock with the flag and TITO behind me, I raised my clenched right fist and gave it a 'come the glorious day, brother' pose, and Caroline (wearily) took a couple of photos.

The rest of the honeymoon thankfully sped by and on the Monday after our return, she took all the wedding and honeymoon photos into her local branch of Boots to have them developed and was told they would be ready for collection on Wednesday. On that day, I raced home in eager anticipation. She had, indeed, collected the photos and I was forced to sit through the wedding one's 'oohing' and 'aahing' at appropriately (disinterested) intervals. And then we got on to the main event, the honeymoon photos. Only there was a slight problem. I'd outsourced all aspects of the honeymoon photography to Caroline which included putting the film in the camera. Unbeknown to me, the daft bint had put it in back to front, so when I got to the photos taken on the Albanian border, and in particular, me standing in front of the big rock, you can imagine my disappointment to see my left hand in a clenched fist with 'OTIT' above my head. And people wondered why the marriage didn't last long!

Ireland

Our first married Christmas was spent with her parents in County Donegal, at Killybegs and Kilcar, from where they originated. The scenery was stunning, and her family were very welcoming as were all the locals – except one. County Donegal isn't known as 'Bandit Country' for nothing. The vast swathes of farmland and outlying, remote farm buildings made it easy for the IRA to store weapons and explosives for future use on unsuspecting Army checkpoints or, more likely, the security services or members of the public.

On New Year's Eve, we went to a local pub, and there was a fantastic atmosphere with Irish bands playing, people dancing on the seats, and everyone having a great time. I went to the bar to buy a round of drinks for our crowd and as I turned to walk back to our table, I accidentally bumped into a lady. 'I'm so sorry', I said, whereupon she smiled sweetly and said, 'no problem'. 'Yer focking will be', came a deep, menacing voice from behind me, and he meant it. I could sense that my Newick Road one-liner might not be appropriate here, so, without turning round, I beat a hasty retreat back to my seat and didn't move again all night.

Most Irish people I've ever met have been great fun and in The Undertones case, great musicians. Parts of the country, though, were stuck in a time warp. On behalf of Amex, I once had to attend court in Mullingar to give evidence against one of our customers. Mullingar is in the middle of the country and not particularly appealing. A bit like Leicester really! The court hearing was due to start at 10 am and I arrived in plenty of time. There were hordes of locals standing around outside the courthouse and when I entered the court, there was standing room only in the public gallery. It wasn't a particularly high-profile case, and it dawned on me that they all had nothing better to do than rock up at court on a Friday morning to see what was going on. And their clobber! Albanians wouldn't have been seen dead in it (and they're not particularly choosy!).

Cheat

The summer of 1990 was most notable for Italia'90, for which the Social Club erected a huge screen in the main hall, and it was packed with Amex employees and friends watching it. The mood in the club and in the country generally was on the rise the further England went in the tournament. The mood in Maresfield Road was also changing, but not in a good way. Caroline had made a bunch of friends at her new branch of Midland Bank and was spending more and more time with them. One in particular. Although we had a two-week holiday in Marmaris, Turkey in August, things didn't seem great between us although she refused to open up and say why. Upon our return, she suddenly bought a car without any kind of discussion, and I guess it gave her a bit more freedom. She used it to drive her new male friend to a race meeting at Silverstone one Sunday, even though I'd arranged for us to attend an event at Withdean Stadium, to which I subsequently went and got very pissed. I tried to lock her out and went to bed but she managed to somehow get in and slept in the spare room. Things came to a head in January 1991. Her 'friend' worked with her at the bank and played in goal for non-league Woking, who had a decent run in the FA Cup and were drawn away to West Brom in the 3rd round. Caroline told me she was staying at her parent's house that weekend, but I sensed that she would be at The Hawthorns watching him play. When I got back to The Hanbury after that afternoon's Amex FC match, I rang her parents to ask if she was there. 'No love', her Mum said, 'she's gone shopping in London'. 'She fucking hasn't', I replied, 'she's at West Brom'. 'I don't think so dear', she said, but I could tell I'd sown some seeds of doubt in her mind. Caroline returned to our house after work on Monday, lying through her arse and swearing blind she'd been shopping in London. Conveniently, she'd accidentally left all her shopping at her parent's house! As a result of winning at West Brom, Woking were drawn away to Everton. Before that took place, certain things happened.

One Thursday evening, Caroline came home from work and went straight to bed, saying she had a migraine. A few hours later, there was a knock at the door and two of her female friends from the bank, who I had only met a couple of times, were standing there. They asked for Caroline, and I explained she was in bed with a migraine but invited them in and went up to see if she was up to seeing them. She wasn't, and I relayed this to them, whereupon they asked if they could pop up and see her briefly, and I said they could. They came back down after a few minutes, thanked me, and left. It was a bit bizarre, but I soon found out why.

After work the following day, I had a very long session at the club and arrived home around midnight. The house was in complete darkness, so I assumed Caroline must have gone to bed. There were a couple of ornaments missing from the mantlepiece and as I looked around in my drunken daze, I noticed other things were missing as well (photos, pictures, etc.). I went upstairs into our bedroom, and there was no sign of her. I opened her wardrobe, and all her clothes and shoes were gone, the same in the chest of drawers, in the bathroom, etc. She'd left and taken everything of hers with her. Blimey! I sobered up fairly quickly and found an envelope she'd left behind which contained a letter explaining that I was paying too much attention to my football than her – (she'd run off with the pizza-faced Woking goalkeeper FFS!)- and so she was off. The envelope also contained a Woking home programme for that season, which showed that she'd sponsored his kit, as well as a rental agreement for a flat in Small Dole, a tiny village in Sussex, to where she'd moved.

And then it dawned on me why I'd had that visit from her colleagues the previous evening, who obviously knew what she was planning to do. She was very capable of lying and over-dramatising things, and it was completely feasible that she'd told them I was a wife-beater who wouldn't take the news well, so they visited to check I hadn't actually knocked her into next week!

I had a driving lesson booked for Saturday morning, which I rang to cancel. I also rang both sets of parents to tell them what had happened. Hers were shocked and drove straight down from Hertford to check I was ok, which was really nice of them. Her sister came down the following weekend and drove me to Small Dole. The flat was above a vet's practice, and Caroline was in but wouldn't answer the door, not even to her sister. I posted the envelope she'd left behind through her letterbox, and that was the last I saw of her. Thankfully, we didn't have any kids. I thought of my friend in Bradford and smiled!

Three Lions

Although she never mentioned it, one thing that may have concerned Caroline was that I might become a lot more involved in football than just running the Amex FC Saturday team. After England's exit from Italia 90, the Manager, Bobby Robson, announced that he was stepping down from the job. I immediately sensed an opportunity and wrote to the FA, enclosing my application. I listed my achievements to date with my Saturday side, which consisted of one promotion and two cup final appearances of which, thanks to Nobby, only one resulted in our lifting the cup, but I thought I was in with a chance. Upon our return from holidaying in Marmaris, there was a letter from Graham Kelly, Chief Executive of the FA, in which he thanked me for my interest and stated that they hoped to make an announcement regarding the position shortly. Bugger! This was in the day before mobile phones; he had clearly been trying to contact me at home without realising I was in Turkey, and he was under pressure from his bosses to quickly make an appointment, so he had to settle for Graham Taylor. And look how that turniped out! Another one to be filed under 'what could have been'!

I Want To Break Free

1991 didn't start too well, and it didn't end well either. In November of the previous year, Dad developed a cough that he couldn't shift. His doctor sent him for tests, which came back confirming he had asbestosis. 'About a year', he was told when he asked how long he had left. He and Mum were naturally shocked. Fi and I were summoned to hear the news, and there was plenty of hugging and tears. During his last year, Mum took him to various Gardens (Leonardslee, etc.) as they shared a (rare) interest in them, but as the year wore on, he became progressively weaker. I helped Mum move a single bed from upstairs and put it in the dining room so he could look out over the back garden that he and Mum had created and lovingly nurtured. There was a downstairs toilet at 28PR which he used until he was too weak to do so. Mum used to wash him and look after him until he was admitted to a hospital in Boundary Road, Hove and from there, taken to Coppercliff Hospice in Colebrook Road near Withdean Stadium in November. Mum, Fi, and I used to regularly visit him, and during our visit on Friday, November 29th, a nurse told us that it wouldn't be too long. The three of us stayed the night with him, and a bed was made up in an adjoining room in case any of us wanted a break. As the night wore on, his breathing became more and more irregular and at 08:40 hours on the Saturday morning, as I was holding him, he slipped away. Mum and Fi were understandably very tearful, but I wasn't, as I wanted to hold it together for them both. The date was November 30th, St Andrew's Day, which was a tad ironic.

Completely numb, we caught a taxi back to 28PR and sat around in a daze. My Amex team was playing a league game in Stanmer that afternoon, and I'd tipped my Assistant Manager, Mark 'Harvey' Proctor, on Friday that I might not be able to make it, so he agreed to run the side for me. I decided to take the family labrador, Sebastian, for a walk into Stanmer but didn't want the team to be distracted by my being there, so I walked through the woods until I was high up on the bank (close to where I'd snogged Carol) and watched the ant-like shapes running around below. We drew 1-1 and their goal was miles offside!

Dad died in the same week as Freddie Mercury. Freddie died on Sunday, and Dad died the following Saturday, although that's where any similarity ends, as he wasn't a massive Queen fan. Having said that, since he passed, I've often had a dream where Dad is wearing a black wig and a leather skirt and pushing a hoover around singing 'I want to break free', but I think that's more of a nod to Mum than anything else!

Love of My Life

By now, I was working at a different Amex building, Sussex House, in Burgess Hill. At the time, I thought the cold concrete outer façade of the building looked like a 4-star Albanian hotel, but having since stayed in one of those, I now realise it was more like a Romanian one!

There had been mergers between several Amex departments, with some moving to Brighton from Burgess Hill and vice versa. I'd only been to Burgess Hill once before and didn't think much of it, apart from the ridiculous number of Indian restaurants per size of the population. I was put in charge of a team that included Margaret Hume and Sarah Woolmer. Margaret was 20 years older than me and clearly the matriarch of the team. She had an unbelievable work ethic and was still working part-time at a chemist's well into her 80's. Sarah was immaculate with a huge mane of blonde hair and was very attractive. Her then-boyfriend was a black belt in karate, so that quickly put paid to any romantic notions I may have had. They both helped me settle in, and I quickly began to like the place. I still couldn't drive so Andi, who had also been transferred to the same building, used to give me a lift to and from Brighton. I was now renting a 2-bed flat in Beaconsfield Road, having had to sell the Maresfield Road house when Midland Bank 'regrettably' informed me that they could no longer provide the cheap staff mortgage as their staff member was no longer living there. I 'regrettably' informed them that the reason she was no longer living there was because she'd gone off shagging another of their staff members, but they weren't having it, and I had to sell up. I initially shared the flat with Fi, which was a bit weird at first, but we got used to it.

Around the time of Dad's death, a young girl from an adjacent department in Sussex House caught my eye. She had dark hair, was as thin as a pencil and very pretty. Her name was Diane Tomsett ('Di'), she was 19 and single, which I was amazed to learn. Despite my recently failed marriage, I was all set to ask her out but then she wasn't around for a while. It transpired that her very young niece had died shortly after Dad did, so that delayed things a bit.

The pub nearest to Sussex House was The Potters on Station Road. From the early seventeenth century, brick and tile manufacture were the main industries in the town, and this is reflected in some of the road names (Kiln Road, Potters Lane, etc.). Each Friday after work, a number of us would head to The Potters to drink and play pool before catching a train or taxi back to Brighton and on to more pubs down there. Occasionally, Di and her friends would be in the pub but apart from the odd 'hello', I wasn't at all confident that she'd be remotely interested in me. The department Di worked in was managed by Nobby, he of the Amex FC Cup Final costly error, and I reckoned he still owed me. His birthday is the day after mine, so we decided to have a joint 'NB/NP' birthday bash starting at The Potters one Friday and heading down to Brighton afterwards. (Only Nobby and I will <u>ever</u> know what it stood for!). We knocked up some flyers and put the word around. He knew I was interested in Di and made sure she and her friends were in the pub at the start of the evening. I managed my usual 'hello' when I saw her in there but not much more than that, although she did confirm she was joining us in Brighton. A big group of us set off in numerous taxis and our first port of call was the Druids Head in The Lanes, where my mailboys nights out used to start. Fairly early on, I plucked up the courage to approach Di and said that as I was likely to be pissed and incoherent later, would she like to go for a drink with me after work one night the following week and was astonished when she said she would. Thereafter, we were inseparable for the rest of the evening, chatting, snogging, and having a great time getting to know each other. The pub crawl ended, and I ensured she got into a taxi to take her back home to Burgess Hill. I was back on the bike, so to speak, although I had no idea how to ride it on account of having lived on a hill when I was very young!

Walk On the Wild Side

Di must have given me her home phone number as I rang it the following day on the pretext of checking that she'd got home safely (but, in reality, I wanted to ensure she wasn't having second thoughts about our forthcoming date having had the chance to sober up). Her Mum answered, and I asked for Di. 'Oh, you've just missed him', came back the reply. Him!? Him!? My mind flashed back to a time when I took a train to London and there, sitting opposite me, was a beautiful Oriental woman with massive tits. She kept bending down, and all I could say to myself was, 'Please don't get an erection, please don't get an erection' but, sadly, she did! Could Di be a transvestite? I mean, I'd felt the strapline of her BRA the previous evening, but that didn't mean anything in this day and age. 'Er, could I speak to Diane, please?', I asked, whereupon her Mum giggled and said, 'Oh Diane, yes of course', and handed the phone to her. It transpired that her brother, Bryan, had a friend called Dai, who had indeed just left their house. Phew! I'd been starting to sweat like GG in a creche!

Diane came along from Burgess Hill

Down to Brighton just for a thrill

When I rang her on the phone

Her mother said that 'she' was a 'he'

I said 'Hey Di, Take a walk on the wild side'

I said 'Hey honey, take a walk on the wild side'.

(With apologies to the late, great Lou Reed!)

Breakthrough

We chatted for a bit, and no, she wasn't having second thoughts, so we arranged to meet for a drink after work the following Tuesday. Of course, we saw one another at work on Monday and smiled and chatted. The Tuesday date was at the Railway pub opposite Burgess Hill station. I had hair back in those days, although it was receding badly, and I used to brush what was left in the front backwards so it looked slightly less shit than if I'd left the uneven 'fringe' to droop forwards. On the morning of my big date, I stuck Queen's 'Breakthrough' on my cassette player and danced around in front of the bathroom mirror, singing it with my hairbrush for a microphone. The evening went well, and we just seemed to click. More dates followed and she agreed to come and stay at the flat one weekend. We walked into town and spent virtually the whole day in The Sussex pub in The Lanes. Di clearly shared my enthusiasm for the wet stuff, and we arrived back at the flat absolutely hammered. After a few more weeks, she agreed to move in with me, by which time Fi had moved out so we had the place to ourselves. It was a decent-sized flat at the top of a long, steep hill with a bus stop outside, which was useful when neither of us was sober enough to walk back up the hill after a session in the town. It was also close to Preston Park station, which was handy for getting to and from work in Burgess Hill. There were a few pubs nearby, including the Park View in Preston Drove and the Preston Park Tavern. One evening, we were on our way back from the latter, having imbibed our usual quantity, when we approached a corner leading into our road. A bloke suddenly came round the corner whistling and stood in front of us. I squealed like a girl and hid behind Di. Thankfully, she's a black belt in Origami and was able to deal with the situation!

Not long after that, we were burgled. Our ground-floor flat was one of four in a converted Edwardian house. Access through the communal front door was fairly easy using a credit card, and the thieves had smashed open our flat's front door with brute force. Neither of us were in at the time, and the scrotes nicked some of Di's jewellery. Surprisingly, they left behind the trophy I'd won impersonating GG back in 1973. Perhaps they knew!

Sit Down

Di's family were very welcoming despite me being a lot older than her and a divorcee to boot. Her Dad, John, was Sussex born and bred, who could turn his hand to anything from car mechanics to all forms of DIY – building ponds, kitchens, bathrooms, etc. Di had two older brothers, Paul and Bryan, and two older sisters, Lesley (Lou) and Jacqueline (J). With the exception of Lou, they all lived in the same house in West Street, Burgess Hill, in which her Mum, Ann, had grown up. Di and I were, by now, considering buying a house together but needed to save a few quid, so we moved into her family home while we saved up. Eventually, we had enough for a deposit and as we were both working full time earning decent combined salaries, managed to obtain a mortgage.

We found a 2-bed mid-terraced house in Dunstall Farm Road, not too far from her parent's house, had our offer accepted and moved in. It was a fairly new house, approximately 20 years old, and had a large eucalyptus tree in the back garden. But no koalas! It was an ideal starter home and had a parking bay out the front into which I parked my newly acquired car (having recently passed my driving test at the first attempt). Di and I became engaged and set a date for 1st October, 1994, at Haywards Heath registry office, with the reception held in nearby Clair Hall. Money was tight, so I arranged for Margaret Hume and her friend, Janet Hill, to do the catering. Janet also worked for me at Amex and was the office gossip, often poodling around, talking to all and sundry without actually doing much work. Like Margaret, she was 20 years older than me and was known as 'One Foot' from the TV series 'One Foot In The Grave', which was very apt!

As I was beginning to forgive him for losing us the cup final many years ago, and as he'd played a big role in bringing Di and me together, I asked Nobby to be my best man. He organised a relatively low-key stag do (as the wedding was the following day), consisting of a few pubs around Burgess Hill starting, obviously, at The Potters, followed by a curry in one of the multitude of Indian restaurants situated in the town. He stayed at our house that evening, and Di stayed at her family home. The following morning, I couldn't get off the pan! I swore Nobby had spiked my onion bhaji, but he denied it. He had to go out and collect some things best man/wedding related and didn't have a key to get back in. I had to throw the front door key out of the bathroom window and resume my pan-sitting!

That Petrol Emotion

The wedding went well. Di looked lovely in a white hat, white jacket, and skirt. I looked even lovelier in a petrol-blue suit. I wore it in case I started blubbing and could blame it on That Petrol Emotion! (*I think that takes me up to about 470 Undertones references so far!*). Mum and Fi attended as well. Fi had only met her future husband, Nick, a few days before the wedding, but we were very tight for space and couldn't accommodate him on one of the tables. Margaret and Janet did a great job with the catering, and I bought loads of English wine at £3 a bottle from Asda. It tasted lush – honest!

More guests arrived for the evening but as Di and I started our slowy to get things going, I had to suddenly rush off as the spiked onion bhaji made an unwelcome reappearance!

We stayed at our house that night, and the following day, I drove us down to Arundel, where I'd booked us a hotel room for the night. And then we were off to Australia!

Down Under Part 1

Mum had very kindly paid for and booked our honeymoon Down Under, but there was a slight snag. She'd booked herself a ticket too as it would almost certainly be the last time she would see her brother and sister. Di wasn't overly thrilled at the thought of going on honeymoon with her mother-in-law, but she agreed to put up with it. Thankfully, Mum's travel phobia kicked in, and she cancelled her ticket and accommodation. She had taken out full cancellation insurance as she anticipated that she wouldn't be able to face it. Di breathed a sigh of relief!

We landed in Sydney, where we were met by one of Paul's daughters, Barbara, who lived in the Kings Cross area of the city, and who put us up for a couple of nights kipping on her lounge floor. She took us around several of the sights – (Opera House, Harbour Bridge, etc.)- and also to a Vietnamese restaurant, which was my first experience of that kind of cuisine. I quite enjoyed it, although I gave the sweet & sour labrador a wide birth! We also visited a couple of the beaches, including Bondi, which looked a mess and was full of junkies' needles, and Manly, which utterly magnificent. From Sydney, we flew up the coast to a small airport at Coffs Harbour, from where we were picked up and driven to Paul's place in Scotts Head. His house had been specifically built for him by his son-in-law, Allan (Janet's husband), and was absolutely stunning. At the top of the road, there was a path through tall grasses, beyond which lay miles and miles of white sand and the Pacific Ocean. Di and I absolutely loved the place and spent all day there one Saturday without seeing more than 3 people all the time we were there. Which was handy as I was still very large and feared I might get harpooned, as there are a fair few Japanese over there!

From Scotts Head, we travelled to Brisbane and stayed in a backpacker's hostel. I like my creature comforts too much, so it wasn't for me having to share a bathroom with a bunch of hippies. Brisbane itself was a bit dull, with loads of concrete and a man-made beach. It's not that far from the ocean, so that must be the definition of 'what's the point?'. Thankfully, we didn't spend too long there and flew up to Cairns, which seemed to be solely inhabited by permanently pissed Abo's – so Di and I got on well with them! We went on a glass-bottomed boat on the Great Barrier Reef which was ok but no different to watching the brightly coloured fish and rays, etc., in an aquarium or on TV.

On the last leg of our honeymoon, we flew across to Perth, where Bet, Dick and their family lived. Bet and Dick had just celebrated their 50th wedding anniversary. After Di and I had left Scotts Head, Paul and Gladys had flown over to Perth to celebrate the event with them. We arrived a couple of days after the party and stayed at Sue's house. Bet's other daughter, Joy, lived nearby with her husband, Ian, and it was a great family get-together. Unfortunately, due to a combination of swimming and flying, I got a chronic ear infection, which left me in agony. The rellies obtained some antibiotics for me but they didn't help much, and my memory and awareness of Perth is almost non-existent, although the port of Freemantle seemed quite pleasant. And then the honeymoon was over, literally, and we flew home. Time to start a family!

Reproduction Part 1

On the face of it, 1995 didn't seem to have a lot going for it. No World Cup or European Championships. The perfect time to start procreating without any distractions. So we did. And it didn't take long before Di discovered she was expecting with a due date in January 1996. It was an exciting time, going to pre-natal appointments, watching her bump grow, etc. Barry proudly announced that his then-wife, Gill, was also expecting later in the same month as us. Our 'due date' was 18th January, and Di and I agreed that if it was a boy, we would call him Charlie, but there was no sign of him arriving on that day. Instead, Barry rang and triumphantly announced that he was the father of a baby boy who had arrived on our due date. I naturally congratulated him and asked what his son was called. 'Charlie', he replied. 'But you can't, that's what we're calling ours if it's a boy', I wailed (a tad childishly), whereupon he laughed and put the phone down.

On 22nd January, Di was admitted to the maternity unit at Princess Royal Hospital in Haywards Heath as the signs were that the birth was imminent. I sat with her throughout the night, holding her hand, mopping her brow, telling her how nice her hair looked, all the things she really wanted to hear. At 02:08 hours on 23rd January, 1996, she gave one final push and out came our first baby.

I had one quick look at his clutter to make sure it was a boy, and just as importantly, his face to ensure that he hadn't inherited my facial issues, and gave Di lots of hugs and kisses as she cradled Charlie John Owen. After ensuring they were both ok, I went downstairs to the payphone and rang Mum. I broke down with the relief that Charlie wouldn't have to go through all the years of shit that I had to because of how he looked. He was perfect!

As any new parent will tell you, life becomes a bit different when you have your first baby. For me initially, it was the sheer enormity of being responsible for this little human being and the continuation of life, something that has happened for thousands of years. The old lady at the bus stop, the bloke sitting on the park bench reading a newspaper, the teacher, the pupil. They all started out as babies. As did Charlie. The shock of sleep deprivation is the thing that gets you the most, and the inability to stop your baby crying, combined with the lack of sleep, leaves you thinking thoughts that the calm, rational you would never think. He wasn't a bad baby. On the contrary, he was really good but would have his moments, which all babies do. Thankfully, with Di's family close by, we had a great support network, and Mum and Fi helped out when they could. Charlie was very healthy, which was the most important thing, and his first year – full of 'firsts'- flew by.

Build a Bonfire

O n the face of it, 1997 didn't have much going for it either (no World Cup, no European Championships, etc.), so we thought we'd create another baby. Before we did, a couple of fairly significant events took place.

The date 26th April, 1997, is permanently etched in every Brighton fan's memory as it was the day we played our last ever game at our beloved Goldstone Ground against Doncaster. The ground had been sold by our wanker of a chairman, Bill Archer, owner of Wickes DIY, who lived in Mellor, Lancs (which, ironically, was the surname of the scorer of our winner in my first game watching us against the scum – Mellor, that is, not Lancs!). Archer had no interest in our club, had bought a controlling stake in it for £56.25 and saw it as a prime site for retail development, which it eventually became. With a (local) silent partner in Greg Stanley, and a vocal puppet figurehead and failed Liberal Democrat MP, David Bellotti, the three of them proceeded to drive our club to the verge of extinction and didn't give a toss about the consequences as long as they made money out of it. Stephen North and Paul Hodson's outstanding book, 'Build A Bonfire', explains the events far more eloquently and in much greater detail than I can here and is essential for every Brighton fan to gain a full understanding of what those 3 tossers tried to do to our club. I had a silent party for one when I learnt that Belloti and, subsequently, Stanley had died. I'd imagine there will be an open-top bus parade and a national holiday when Archer goes!

Anyway, back to 26th April, and a poignant and tearful farewell to the Goldstone. A game I couldn't go to! After Dad died, Mum enrolled on an Open University course, something she'd wanted to do for years, but Dad kind of held her back. She travelled to various parts of the country attending lectures but most of her studying was done at home or in libraries. She obtained a Bachelor Of Arts (Hons.), which was a fantastic achievement, and Fi and I were incredibly proud of her. At least, I was until she contacted the OU and (probably) demanded that the awards ceremony for her degree be held at the Brighton Centre on – you've guessed it- 26th April, 1997!

Mum had always hated me having anything to do with football as I was 'obsessed' and 'besotted' with it. I probably didn't help that misperception by constantly throwing a ball up against the side of the house and volleying it into the garage doors at the top of the drive, breaking a window or 6 in the process. I was just like any other sport-mad kid, but being that much older (and deeply disappointed that I wasn't a girl), she just didn't get it.

And so there I was, with Fi at Mum's awards ceremony, wishing I was 5 miles away in Hove in the pissing rain, collecting clumps of turf and the odd turnstile or two and saying goodbye to the old place.

The week before that final game, when I knew I wouldn't be able to attend, I contacted the club and spoke to Matt Hicks, who was involved in the player liaison/kit collecting side of things. I explained that I couldn't go to the Doncaster game, my 15-month-old son would never be able to set foot in the ground, and would it be ok if I took him out there one evening so he could at least see it.

Matt was great and confirmed it would be fine, so on the Thursday after work, I picked up Di and Charlie and drove to the ground, having had the foresight to take a ball with us. Matt let us all in, and there were the 3 of us with the whole ground to ourselves. Charlie ran around the pitch in his Albion kit and kicked the ball past me in the North Stand goal a few times, and I held him as he sat on one of the crush barriers in the North Stand behind which I used to stand for many, many years. Di snapped away on her camera and those photos are amongst the most cherished in my possession.

The Great Escape

As a result of beating Doncaster in that last home game, we needed a draw at Hereford in the final league game of the season the following week. Lose and we would be relegated out of the football league and in all possibility, existence altogether, so dire was the financial and off-field situation of the club at that time. Hereford had to beat us or else it would be they who were relegated. I managed to get hold of a ticket from somewhere and so, with 2,999 other Brighton fans, set off in a minibus containing Nobby and Mad John, amongst others, on the morning of 3rd May, 1997. There was a fair bit of booze and other stuff floating around, and the journey seemed to take forever. We eventually stopped at Ledbury, where it was rumoured that Cardiff might be popping by for a chat, although I don't remember seeing them, and after a while, we continued on our journey and managed to park reasonably close to Hereford's Edgar Street ground. Before we alighted the minibus, Nobby had dropped something in Mad John's drink. Mad John was a lovely bloke and wouldn't hurt a fly but was a bit, er, mad on account of the medications he was taking for various things. Nobby's little 'gift' clearly sent him over the edge as he never made it back to the minibus after the game, and wandering around Hereford on your own, given the circumstances, was definitely not advisable.

Somehow, he made it back to Brighton in one piece but sadly died in 2004 from his various ailments.

The game itself was crap; there was too much riding on it to be a classic, and there were hordes of OB in riot gear with one of their helicopters hovering overhead throughout. At half time, we were 1-0 down thanks to Kerry Mayo's own goal and had one foot in non-league/non-existence. The mood in the away end was a tad sombre, to put it mildly, however we all leapt around like uncontrollable loons when Robbie Reinelt equalised in the 62nd minute. There followed half an hour of 'hearts-in-mouth' stuff before the final whistle blew, and we were safe. Grown men in tears hugging complete strangers, the relief was palpable. The OB spread across the entire width of the pitch to prevent the seriously pissed-off Hereford fans from getting to us, and once we were safely back on the minibus and waited a while for Mad John to never arrive, we headed home.

Reproduction Part 2

Knowing that the Albion were safe for another season at least, Di and I started the procreation game again. As with Charlie, it didn't take long for her to fall pregnant, and our second baby was due in August 1998. We decided to move to a bigger house and found a 3-bed, semi-detached property in Condor Way, also in Burgess Hill. It was very close to the first 2 schools the kids would attend and the perfect location for bringing up a young family. Our moving in date was set for 28th August. Georgina Marie Owen duly arrived on 26th August, healthy and bouncing but squeezed a shit out as she entered the world, so she had to be kept in overnight. However, this should have given Di plenty of time to recover and give me a hand moving the washing machine, fridge freezer, etc., two days later. Or so you would think. But oh no. Family and friends did manage to help with the move and our newly enlarged family was in its new home. Where we remain to this day.

Freeloader

My role at Amex had moved into the world of debt collection, and specifically, the management of the debt collection agencies and Solicitors in the UK and throughout Europe, which involved frequently meeting these companies in their offices. Two of the UK agencies were based in Preston and Leeds, which was handy for watching Albion games in northern grounds. For instance, if we were away at Carlisle on a Saturday, I'd arrange a meeting with the Preston agency for the Friday before, stay in a local hotel that night, and then head up to Carlisle the following day. Hartlepool away on a Tuesday night? No problem. Schedule a meeting in Leeds during the day, drive up to Hartlepool for the game, then back to a Leeds hotel still buzzing from the 0-0 draw! And all on expenses. Some of the agencies, knowing about my passion for all things Albion-related, would arrange for me to have a ticket in the home end if I was in the vicinity for a 'meeting' on the Friday before the game and would usually accompany me to it. I'd have to sit on my hands and behave myself at such places as Preston, Bradford, Halifax, and Burnley. Especially Burnley! And I'd not pay a penny! Corporate hospitality is by far and away the greatest invention of all time.

Tony Bown was a larger-than-life character who worked for a top firm of Solicitors in London, and he was always taking me to weird and wonderful places, including Sir John Mills' 90th birthday party celebrations at The Dorchester Hotel, an audience with Eric Sykes at a book launch at Café Royal, and to a clay pigeon shoot in aid of Dame Vera Lynn's charity in a remote field in Sussex. The reason I once ate 22 fist-sized profiteroles in one sitting was due to Tony. He took me out for a meal at a top London restaurant and after polishing off the starters and main course, it was time for dessert. I'd spotted these huge profiteroles on another table and decided to go for them. Tony did likewise and bet me that he could eat more of them than me, and the loser would pick up the tab for the whole meal. Tony was a massive bloke, even bigger than me, and I was well into the 20-stone region, but I do like a challenge and so agreed to it. The first plate containing 4 of these massive things came and went down very easily; the next 4 took slightly longer to eat, the next 4 longer still, and the 4 after that were a challenge, but neither of us would back down. We reached the grand total of 22 each, whereupon the restaurant told us that they'd run out of profiteroles, but would we like some Tiramisu? 'No thanks', we both bloatedly replied and split the bill.

Eddie Stobart

Another couple of cracking freebies were provided by a pair of wide boys, Duncan and Robert Beat, who worked for an insolvency company in London, and who were forever badgering me to provide them with authority to act on Amex's behalf in bankruptcies involving our customers. They were also massive Spurs fans and had their own box at White Hart Lane, where they invited me to watch an FA Cup tie between Spurs and Notts County. Don O'Riordan was playing for County and had previously played for Carlisle, a team I'd always had a soft spot for on account of their kit sponsors being Eddie Stobart. In my journeys up and down the motorways with a colleague (or even the kids) in the car, I'd always indulge in a bit of 'Eddie Spotting', trying to be the first to 'spot' the green, yellow, and red livery adorning their lorries in the distance. The problem was that John Smith's brewery had a very similar livery, which could cause issues when trying to claim an Eddie 'spot' too early. I had an array of Eddie-related stuff; boxer shorts, a mug and even a calendar. As thousands of mechanics up and down the land changed the month on their Pirelli calendar from March to April and exclaimed, 'Phwoar, look at the tits on that!', I would calmly do likewise on my Eddie calendar with an excited 'Phwoar, look at the side trailer on that!'.

The vast majority of Eddie's were on the northern motorways as the company was based near Carlisle, and I never lost at Eddie spotting. The closest I came was when I was returning back down south with a colleague, Duncan Brooks, who, to be fair, was doing well and was a couple of 'spots' ahead, but he'd made the schoolboy error of claiming a John Smith's lorry as a 'spot' and had to suffer a 30-minute penalty of not being able to claim any 'Eddie spots' in that time. We were approaching Toddington Services towards the bottom of the M1 and I knew that once we were past there, we'd soon be on the M25/M23, and the chance of more 'spots' would diminish. Under the guise of needing a piss, I turned into the services and proceeded to drive around the lorry park claiming a further 4 'spots' as I did so. Duncan was helpless to do anything about it as he was still suffering his penalty. This took me into the lead; we left the services, and as anticipated, as soon as we hit the M25, there were no further 'spots', and I was able to maintain my unbeaten record. But it was too close for comfort!

Back in the Spurs box, the wide boys insisted on draping Spurs scarves and hats on all their assembled guests except one. 'I'm not wearing that shit', I told them, and as I was a potential client, they relented. Their box was very close to the south end of the ground, and in the 41st minute, County were awarded a free kick just outside the penalty area. Up stepped Don O'Riordan to smash the ball past the Spurs keeper and put County 1-0 up. I'd had a few by this time and to piss off my hosts and all their soppy scarf-wearing guests, I yelled in delight and punched the air. Only I was standing where the hard foam ceiling started to descend, and my fist connected with it and left a large imprint in the ceiling (which was still visible when they invited me back there for further games!). Oh well. Spurs went on to win 2-1, with a certain Paul Gascoigne scoring the winner. The game was live on BBC TV and, after the game, Des Lynam and Bob

Wilson came into the box to chat to the wide boys' guests, as did Phil Beal, who was a legend at Spurs and who played a handful of games at the Albion at the very end of his career. Whilst Des was delighted to chat all things Albion-related with me, Beal was less so. He was crap for us anyway!

The Boxer

I must have given the Beat brothers some work as they invited me to the Chris Eubank v Michael Watson fight at White Hart Lane in September 1991. I'd previously watched a couple of Eubank's fights locally when he was starting to make a name for himself, including one against Kid Milo from Birmingham at the Brighton Centre, which Barry also attended. In the run-up to the fight with Watson, the promoters had tried to portray Eubank (a Brighton fan) as a Spurs fan, and he did a photo shoot wearing their kit, as Watson was a genuine Arsenal fan, so they tried to cram the football rivalry into the fight. I took Nobby and Sarah Woolmer with me as my guests and we watched it in a box on the halfway line at the ground, which provided a fantastic view of the ring (and the afters!). It was a typically brutal contest, and Watson was miles ahead on points until the 11th round when Eubank, sensing it was shit or bust, floored him, from which he never got up. And who never really recovered. Eubank, understandably, was never the same fighter thereafter. Once the main fight was over, the unofficial 'undercard' began between all the Spurs and Arsenal fans in the crowd, and the security didn't stand a chance. This free for all only ended when a group of Brighton fans in the North Bank made themselves heard, whereupon the Spurs and Arsenal fans made a beeline for the Brighton lads. We certainly got value for money that night and didn't have to pay for the ticket!

Once everything had died down, the three of us – plus the Beats-headed into town but got thrown out of Stringfellows as the wide boys had partaken in too much Colombian marching powder for the bouncers' liking, and so we ended up in a bar called Moscow in Soho until 4 am. By then, it was too late to catch a train home, so one of the Beats put us up in his flat in Maida Vale, from where the three of us crept out later that morning with me nicking his programme from the night before on the way out. Old habits and all that!

Shrek

Another freebie occurred on my 39th birthday when I visited a firm of Solicitors in Leeds, Eversheds, who were working for me. After our meeting, they put me in a car together with my contact there, Peter Wordsworth. I didn't have a clue where we were going but we ended up at a small private airfield outside the city, where Peter and I boarded a helicopter and flew north, setting down in the grounds of Durham Castle. The view from the helicopter was fantastic, and at one point, I could see both the east and west coasts of the country at the same time. Given my fear of heights, I was surprised I enjoyed it so much, although I preferred the more compact safety of a plane. At the Castle, a chauffeur drove Peter and I to the Stadium of Light in Sunderland, where England were due to play Turkey in what was the debut appearance of Wayne 'Shrek' Rooney. Instead of having a go at the Turkish fans, the Sunderland and Newcastle lads were more interested in having a ruck amongst themselves, and it was a bit lively both inside and outside the ground.

The B-52's

My boss throughout all of this was Mark Fearnside ('Fearny'). He was a couple of years older than me and joined Amex from the Co-Op, where he'd been pricing up carrots and onions. (No, not really; he'd been running their credit card debt collection operations). He was probably the most numerically astute bloke I've ever met and could look at a bunch of numbers and identify trends and patterns in seconds. He was also great fun and the best boss I ever had. He was passionate about all things Leeds United and had a broad Yorkshire accent on account of him being born there – well, he was actually born in Sunderland but moved to Leeds as a small child- so, unlike the 'plastic' southern-based Leeds fans, he actually had a genuine reason to support them. Oh and he loved a freebie as much as I did.

Fearny had been a true punk when it was happening for real and saw loads of bands the first time around when they played in or near Leeds. We shared a particular passion for The Clash, and I was envious that he'd seen all these great bands as they were starting out. He confessed to me that the only time he'd ever cried was when I messaged him to tell him that Joe Strummer had died on 22nd December, 2002. We shared numerous trips in the UK and abroad, always with plenty of fun, alcohol, and other substances. Like me, he smoked like a Beagle and was a great bloke to be around.

Another couple of blokes who worked in the same department as me were Jim Jasicki and Mark Finney. Jim was the son of an American serviceman and was massively into American Football. Together with his older brother, Chas, they were prominent in setting up the Brighton B-52's American Football team. Mark Finney was one of those irritating blokes who was ridiculously excellent at every sport he played. Snooker, pool, football, golf, you name it. He was a lovely bloke, a genuine Chelsea fan (from pre-Roman Abramovic days) and great fun on our many nights out.

Millenium

The Millenium came and went without the disastrous crash of all things computer-related at midnight on 01/01/2000 that had been predicted and which had seen thousands of computer programmers earn millions in the run-up to that non-fateful day. Planes didn't suddenly fall out of the sky, ATM machines at banks didn't (sadly) start spewing out banknotes, and Take That didn't (sadly) stop making records. There wasn't a glitch anywhere. Well, apart from my Casio calculator, which stopped working. But that's because the battery had run out!

Bad Day

On 11th September, 2001, I met with an agency in South London and drove home, arriving back around 3 pm. Di was at home with Charlie and Georgina, watching TV. The programme was interrupted by breaking news that a plane had crashed into one of the World Trade Centre towers in New York, and the live pictures showed the flames and smoke coming from the building. As it did so, I saw a second plane crash into the other tower. 'Bound to be women pilots', I remarked, but it wasn't one of my better one-liners. As the hours and days unfolded, the full extent of the carnage became clearer, and the world became a very different place.

The Art of Bluff

My travelling around for work wasn't just limited to visiting agencies and Solicitors. On occasion, our section of Amex (Risk Management), would put on conferences in such places as Athlone (Ireland) and Cadiz in Southern Spain, where our UK and European colleagues would gather to sit through dull presentations about achievements, targets, etc., and then proceed to get pissed and cause chaos which ensured we were never invited back. Most of the presentations were so boring that it was difficult to stay awake, particularly after the previous evening's consumption. Fearny and I would usually have to present something debt-collection-related. He would go on first and come up with some amazing and amusing anecdotes, which would get the audience stirring, but he was only ever the warmup act to the main event. Me!

The English contingent would hurriedly come in from the bar to join their European counterparts when they saw me go up to the stage as they knew what was coming.

'Hello', I would start, 'for those of you who don't know me, my name's Stuart Owen. For those of you who do know me, you know I'm a fat bastard!'. Ripples of laughter from the English contingent, the Germans turning to one another with an expression that said, 'Vot is dis?', and I was off and running. The 'set' would usually include a few mother-in-law gags, constant piss-taking of myself, the Germans, etc., anything basically that avoided talking about debt collection targets and trends, of which I didn't have a clue. The Art Of Bluff!

Occasionally, one of the blokes in the audience, who had downed a few beers, thought it would be funny to heckle me and try to put me off. Big mistake!

Heckler: 'Oi, you fat bastard, your tits are bigger than my wife's'.

Me: 'Yeah, I know, she tells me how jealous she is when I'm shagging her!'.

Sometimes, in comedy, you have to be cruel to be kind!

I obviously loved being on stage, so making 'presentations' to complete strangers held no fears, but it wasn't the same for everyone. A couple of young ladies who worked for me, Jaime and Kim, were shit scared about presenting in public. I would coach and try to help them in that regard by saying, 'When you get up on that stage, look at the women in the audience. They're no different to you. They piss and shit exactly the same way you do'. (That probably also applied to some of the blokes, to be fair!). I hope it helped them.

Putting On the Ritz

The owner of a debt collection agency in Leeds was Lester Newman. Like Fearny, he was a Leeds United fanatic, and the three of us got on well. He was also exceptionally generous and when I was up there for a visit, would take me for lunch at The Flying Pizza, a fabulous Italian restaurant in the Roundhay area of the city. Pictures adorned the walls showing the various celebrities who had visited the place over the years. It was a magnet for sports stars and entertainers and so it was only natural that I should be there! Christopher Biggins was in there on one occasion when I visited, as was Jimmy Savile on another, holding court at a table with all his sycophants and hangers-on. Now then, now then!

In 2001, Leeds had a decent run in the Champions League and were drawn against AC Milan in the group stage. Lester asked if Fearny and I would be interested in going, and we replied in the affirmative. The trip involved catching an early morning flight from Leeds/Bradford airport to Milan, so we stayed in a local hotel overnight and caught the flight down to the Italian city. We were met from the plane by the Carabinieri, who never let us out of their sight all day and 'kettled' us in a Milan park for hours until we boarded the buses to take us to the San Siro stadium, which at that time, was still impressive. The game finished 1-1, and we flew back to Leeds/Bradford airport straight afterwards.

In the next group stage, Leeds were drawn against Real Madrid. Again, Lester asked the question and again we replied in the affirmative. Only this time, it was a bit different! Lester was putting us up in the Madrid Ritz for 2 nights! Fearny and I flew over from Gatwick and met Lester and his wife, Sandra, at the hotel. Opulence wasn't the word (Grease was!). It was utterly magnificent. This time, we were able to do some sightseeing, which didn't go much beyond an Irish Pub near Plaza Mayor, which Leeds fans had taken over. The Spanish OB watched from a distance but weren't anywhere near as over the top as their Italian counterparts had been. The Bernabeu stadium was also impressive, and the atmosphere inside was terrific. Leeds were unfortunate to lose 3-2 in a cracking game, and we were kept back for ages afterwards, during which time the then Chairman, Peter Ridsdale, and then Manager, David O'Leary, together with all the players, came back out to the pitch in front of the Leeds fans and gave a rendition of 'Marching On Together'. It was a great night and a fabulous trip and must have cost Lester a fortune but that's the kind of bloke he is. This was at a time at Amex when the rules stated that you weren't allowed to accept a gift greater than £25 in value. I think it cost just that for one beer in the Ritz!

Another event I attended with Lester was an evening with Tommy Docherty and Bernard Manning at The Queens Hotel in Leeds. The 'Doc' was full of funny anecdotes from his lengthy time in the game. Manning wasn't everyone's cup of tea, but his delivery and timing were exceptional. After he finished his set, I went for a piss, and he was in there. He was a tiny bloke, not much over 5 feet tall and as I knew he was a massive Man City fan (and this was before they were 'ruined' by oil money), I made a gag about them, which he liked. He asked me who I supported and when I said 'Brighton', he laughed even louder! Bastard! His set had so much material in it and when I got back to my hotel room in the early hours, I jotted down as many as I could remember in one-word bullet points and, unashamedly, used some in future 'performances'.

Back Home

On the evening of the Twin Towers disaster in New York, the Albion lost 2-0 at home to Southampton in the League Cup at Withdean Stadium. The atmosphere was incredibly subdued in view of the events earlier in the day and it felt that no one really wanted to be there. Withdean was our 'temporary' home (if 12 years can be called temporary) after 2 years in exile in Gillingham following the 'sale' of the Goldstone. I managed to attend half a dozen games at Gillingham, but it was a balls ache to get to and I admire those fans who went far more frequently than I. At Withdean, Neil and I obtained season tickets in the South Stand which, like most areas of the ground, was uncovered and open to all the elements. We remained in that stand until our sons started going a few years later when we took up residency at the back of the Family Stand.

Neil and I would take turns driving to the game, parking initially in the (then) Black Lion Car Park (where Barbara Gaul was shot dead in 1976), and then walking south along the A23 until we reached the ground. Withdean was a converted athletics stadium with one main stand and several uncovered ones. It also had portacabins in which both teams and officials changed, and which also served as 'corporate hospitality'. As football grounds go, it was a shit hole. But it was <u>our</u> shit hole. Opposing teams would be 1-0 down psychologically before they set foot on the pitch, so unused were they to their surroundings. As a result, our home record was decent during the first few years we were there.

Buffalo Girls

One day, we were walking from the pub car park to the ground for a particular home game when Neil, aware of my reticence for any kind of public speaking, asked if I would be his best man at his forthcoming wedding to Dawn. I'd been a best man once before at the wedding of Jon Barnes, who used to play for the Amex FC Saturday and Sunday teams, and his wife Selina, but my speech wasn't one of my best as I rambled on about Margaret Thatcher and the Poll Tax riots, neither of which were remotely relevant to the blushing couple. I told Neil that I would be delighted to but that he was mad!

Having known Neil since our school days at Stringer, I had plenty of material. At each subsequent home game that season, during our long walk to the ground, I would run him through the one-liners or stories I'd come up with during the previous week. If he laughed, they were in; if he didn't, they weren't. I was slightly surprised that he chortled at my stories about him wetting the bed and that when we were at Stringer, he was in a class so bereft of any educational talent it would, in modern parlance, be classed as 'special needs'. This went on until I had enough material for my speech. When it came to delivering it on the big day itself, some people in a similar position might have written it on a sheet of paper.

Not me. I'm a bit more upmarket than that, so, as I'd done after the Bernard Manning gig, I wrote one-word bullet points on the back of a Hamlet cigar box!

It was my responsibility to organise Neil's stag do, which was held in Newcastle. We actually stayed nearby in Gateshead, but it was only a short cab ride to the city centre and, in particular, the Bigg Market. I'd not been to Newcastle before and was blown away by how good it was. It has to be the best night out anywhere in the country. The blokes weren't looking for a ruck every 5 minutes, and the women were off the scale in terms of being out for a good time. And canny with it. One bar in particular, Buffalo Joes, had leather bikini-clad waitresses dancing on the tables, their tassels flying everywhere. The sight of their bikini bottoms temporarily took me back to my childhood, but theirs were leather, whereas mine were nylon. And chafed. A lot! Most of the old Amex FC crowd made the journey up, nothing untoward happened to Neil so I'd done my job.

What's The Frequency Kenneth?

On the face of it, 2001 didn't have too much going for it as there were no major football tournaments, so…, you can guess the rest. Actually, although we weren't intentionally pro-creating, Di fell pregnant again (and was carrying our third child when the Twin Towers went up). The baby was due in February 2002, so we did the usual pre-natal stuff, and Charlie and Georgina were excited at the impending arrival of a brother or sister. Di experienced a touch of diabetes during her pregnancy, so it was decided that she would attend the Princess Royal Hospital on Friday, 15th February, to be induced. The following day, the Albion were due to be playing Huddersfield in a top-of-the-table clash at Withdean. The deal with Di was that if she'd had the baby by noon on Saturday, I could go to the game, which I thought was very reasonable of her (although there were echoes of the death of Grandma Hicks and the missed Hereford game in 1975 in the back of my mind!).

I drove Di to the hospital on Friday afternoon, whereupon the nurses informed us that there were a couple of 'natural' births being attended to, but they should be able to start inducing Di later. Time ticked by, and still no inducing. We were well into the evening by now when suddenly, one of the nurses appeared and told us that they'd had yet more 'natural' births come in, so they wouldn't be able to start inducing until the following morning. I was obviously concerned that this wouldn't have a negative impact on Di's health, but I was also mindful of the noon agreement. I can't honestly recall which thought came first! They made Di comfortable for the night and I returned home having the foresight to tip Neil off that it was unlikely that I'd be at the Huddersfield game.

The following morning, I drove back to the hospital and found Di in the same bed, uninduced and obviously no baby yet. I was by now resigned to missing the game but I put on a brave face and read the newspaper. Eventually, the inducement process began, and Di started to get twinges and the usual stuff, but 12 o'clock came and went. Around 2.30 pm, she started showing proper signs of labour and was moved into the maternity room. Upon entering the room, I spotted a radio. I turned it on, and it was tuned to Classic FM, presumably to play soothing music to mothers-to-be in the last throes of labour. Fuck that! I tried to tune it into BBC Radio Sussex, who I knew would be providing live commentary of the Huddersfield game, but it had been a long time since I'd tuned a transistor radio, and I couldn't find it. There was a male nurse nearby called Kenneth, so I asked him what the frequency was. He told me, and I found it. Sorted!

Marvellous

The game kicked off at 3 pm as usual, and from the commentary, I could tell we were playing well. We duly went 1-0 up with a goal scored by Junior Lewis, and that was the half-time score. Huddersfield started the second half strongly and it seemed only a matter of time before they would score. At 4:30, with approximately 75 minutes gone, disaster struck. No, they hadn't equalised, but Di was rapidly entering the latter stages. Due to the diabetes she'd suffered during her pregnancy, the nurses now had to rig her up to a special machine, and I could no longer clearly hear the radio as there was more interference on it than there had been at Stoke Mandeville! I was distraught/ecstatic at the imminent arrival of our third child and sure enough, within the next hour, out came a baby boy who just happened to be named after our goal scorer that day. No, not Junior – sake! Lewis James Owen had arrived safely in the world. Also within that hour, I discovered that we'd held on to win 1-0. So a day that had started out so disappointingly turned out to be marvellous.

Scumday Bloody Scumday

As a football-loving Dad, there can be fewer prouder moments than taking your son to his first match, and aged 5, Charlie made his watching debut at Withdean against Darlington (well, we've all got to start somewhere!). He seemed to enjoy it, although he did wander up and down the steps from time to time, but I didn't mind and thought back to all those years ago when my Dad inflicted a lifetime of highs and lows upon me. Charlie had got the bug, and his appearances increased as he grew older, which included a 3-2 home defeat against the scum on 20th November, 2005. Leon Knight put us 1-0 up in the 22nd minute and after a moment or so of joyous celebrations, I saw Charlie with blood pouring out of his nose. It transpired that I'd punched the air in my celebration but had unfortunately connected with his hooter, causing the claret to flow. 'You never forget your first goal against the scum', I told him, followed by 'don't tell your mother!'. The same fate befell Lewis at his first scum game many years later, but both boys agreed it was 'character building'.

Thieves Like Us

After a while, it became cheaper for Neil and I to obtain season tickets for ourselves and our boys in the Family Stand, where we stood at the back. There was a tall, well-built bloke who stood a few spaces along in the same row. He was a screw at Lewes Prison but nice enough with it. Lewis would occasionally get bored during games, so he would walk along the row and start dipping in the screw's pockets, earning the nickname 'Fingers'. I had to give back to the screw whatever Lewis had nicked, together with an apology and faked external disgust but, inwardly, I was pleased he was carrying on a family tradition. As far as I know, he's not yet been caught nicking a Yorkie!

Lewis was the most troublesome of the three kids. Charlie and Georgina were no bother, but Lewis, who was ultra-competitive from an early age, was desperate to catch them up and didn't react well when he couldn't. He was forever hurting himself, entirely accidentally, which usually resulted in a hospital visit. In view of the number of times he ended up there, it's a constant source of amazement that we never received a visit from Social Services!

Never Mind the (Swollen) Bollocks

When Lewis was 2, Di and I decided that we'd stop at 3 kids, and it was agreed that I would have a 'gentleman's operation' to prevent that from increasing to 4. I quickly realised that our NHS are absolutely brilliant; I went in for my operation and came out with Diabetes! Impressive stuff!

I was booked in for the op on a Thursday, and I would be off work until the following Monday, so I decided this would be a good time to try to give up smoking. Whenever I'd tried previously, I needed to be in a situation where I could lay down and sleep whenever I felt a craving coming on. The 4-day period around my op seemed to be a good time to try again and break the back of the addiction phase. I would, however, be giving up coffee and alcohol at the same time as I associated smoking with drinking one or the other (or both). The weekend before the op would therefore be my last decent session, so I caned the vodka and Red Bulls like it was going out of fashion. I had to attend a pre-op on Monday at the hospital, where they did loads of tests, cholesterol, blood, etc., and I had to provide a urine sample. The nurse conducting these tests asked if I suffered from diabetes. I told her I didn't and asked why. She informed me that my blood sugar level was ridiculously high, and I explained about caning the vodka/Red Bulls the previous weekend. She wasn't convinced and told me that I would need to undergo another pre-op on Thursday and if there was no improvement, the operation wouldn't proceed. The next pre-op showed that my blood sugar level had reduced significantly since Monday but was still a bit high, and it was recommended that I contact my doctor as soon as possible after the operation, which I duly did. After conducting further tests, he concluded that I did indeed have Type 2 Diabetes. Which was nice!

The gentleman's operation was successful, although I subsequently got a hernia from carrying my grotesquely swollen testicles in a wheelbarrow for a couple of weeks! The cessation of smoking lasted 3 months before I regressed, and I haven't tried again since.

Sammy Davis JR

One of my last sanctioned overseas trips was to Johannesburg. Senior Management were hell-bent on outsourcing a load of telephone-based jobs to 'cheap' call centres in India and The Philippines. They may have been cheaper than their English or European counterparts, but the quality of the calls (and levels of service the customers experienced) was crap. One of the big hitters in the UK debt collection industry, Cliff Poole, set up a similar outsourcing operation in Jo'burg where communication links, plus the ability to speak English in a way that our customers could understand, were far better. I was asked to visit their office on a couple of occasions to deliver debt-collection training techniques to the locals. I was a bit apprehensive as I'd heard that Jo'burg was a bit rough; the centre of it was indeed very moody and made Whitehawk look positively idyllic in comparison! I stayed in a heavily fortified villa in Sandton, which to be fair, was one of the posher parts on the outskirts, but I was driven in a car with blacked-out windows absolutely everywhere and was told, in no uncertain terms, not to travel anywhere on foot. I usually like a challenge, but even I saw the sense and necessity of the advice.

During a day off from delivering the training, I was fortunate to visit Soweto. The trip itself was postponed a couple of times as the

Afrikaans lady, who was coordinating things for me, received a phone call on 2 consecutive evenings informing her that the situation down there was a bit too moody for it to be safe the following day. We eventually got the green light and set off in a minibus. To say it was one of the most interesting places I've ever visited would be an understatement. The level of poverty and deprivation was immediately visible as our driver received clearance to enter the township. He took us on a tour around all the key sights, including Nelson and Winnie Mandela's original house, which was almost next door to Archbishop Desmond Tutu's place, and these were in a slightly 'posher' part of the township. He also took us to Regina Mundy (Queen of the World), the church where in 1976, during the student uprisings, many students fled to shelter from the police bullets and teargas (with the police following them inside the church where they continued firing). We were allowed off the minibus and entered the building where we were met by the priest, a small, over-excitable, black man who looked a bit like Sammy Davis Jr. He welcomed us and gave us a potted history of the church and what had happened in 1976. He pointed out the bullet holes in the ceiling and walls which, he said, were caused by the police when they followed the students into the church. 'Two sides to every story', the Afrikaans lady whispered in my ear. There was a stained-glass window which, on the outside, depicted a white Mary holding a white baby Jesus; on the inside, both Mary and Jesus were black. Sammy Davis Jr. bounced over to me and excitedly asked if I thought Christ was black or white. 'You're asking the wrong bloke', I replied, 'I'm an atheist and couldn't give a toss!'. He looked very despondent as it clearly wasn't the response he was expecting.

We left the church and continued our driven tour until we reached some of the shanty shacks. Again, I was allowed off the bus and introduced to a woman who lived in a shack which was no more than 12ft long by 12ft wide and which had a bed, a sink, and a bucket in it. She lived there with her three children, and this was replicated in mile upon mile of similar shacks – quite an eye-opener! One of her children came up to me before we left and pointed to a plane which was flying overhead at the time. He was probably the same age as Charlie, and I told him that I was due to fly home on one of those later that day. He was a happy little boy, smiling and dancing around, but I realised that unless something miraculous happened, he would probably never get to travel on a plane in his life.

It really was a different world and a very humbling experience.

Money, Money, Money

By 2005, Amex was no longer a fun place to work. The cyclical round of redundancies was rumoured to be imminent, our freebies were no longer sanctioned, every expense item was heavily scrutinised, and our American bosses were becoming more involved in day-to-day decisions, forcing through unpalatable (and often unworkable) changes. We were also 'invaded' by a group of people from another country.

A bunch of Indian blokes had come over and were having a huge say in how things were done. They were incredibly bright and possessed numerical and analytical skills that I'd never seen before, but they had no people or man-management skills, and I sensed it was time for me to go. Fearny had taken his redundancy package a few months before; the package offered to me was too good to turn down, and so, after 25 years of mostly happy memories, meeting great people and seeing places I'd never ordinarily have been able to see, I decided to go. I left on 30th November, 2005, which was the 14th anniversary of Dad's death. The saying 'too many chiefs, not enough Indians' was almost right. By the time I left, there were too many fucking Indians!

Down Under Part 2

I was about to enter the world of the self-employed, but before I did so, I used some of my redundancy payment to take Di and the kids to Australia for 3 weeks. Before leaving Amex, I had asked their Travel Department to book me flights, hotels, car hire, etc., in various places throughout Oz and they did a great job. We flew to my favourite place over there, Sydney, and stayed in the Holiday Inn close to the Harbour Bridge. It had a heated rooftop pool, into which the kids loved going at night, and they especially loved the sight of hundreds of bats flying above us from the Botanical Gardens close to the Opera House. We went round the usual tourist attractions; the Opera House, a zoo, the Botanical Gardens as well as sightseeing in the city itself. Another highlight was catching the ferry to Manly, which looked even better than the first time I went there.

From Sydney, we caught a short flight to Melbourne and stayed in the 5-star Park Hyatt Hotel, where the highlight for the kids was sitting in the bath and watching TV on small screens on the walls in there. Melbourne is a lovely city, very 'anglicised' due to the number of churches and cathedrals and greenery around the place. The climate, too, feels more English than the other cities over there. I hired a car and drove a couple of hours north to Cobram, a small town where Bet's daughters, Sue and Joy, had moved after Dick, and then Bet passed away in Perth. Joy kindly put the five of us up, and

Joy's daughter, Amber, and Amber's daughter, Jordan, also lived there together with Joy's husband, Ian. I'd always liked Amber ever since she visited 28PR as a youngster and made Fi's life hell!

Cobram itself was pleasant enough, but there wasn't a great deal to do there. It's situated right on the border with New South Wales and has the Murray River flowing nearby, into which all the kids paddled in the evening sun, taking care to avoid the shopping trolleys and cow's carcasses! After a few days there, I drove us back to Melbourne for our flight to Coffs Harbour. We were a bit strapped for time, so I was doing around 120/kmh when, out of a central reservation and hidden by bushes, appeared a police car. I pulled over, accepted the bollocking and fine (which remains unpaid to this day) and was allowed to resume our journey. The kids were wetting themselves in the back, which took Charlie's mind off being carsick, and I felt quite proud to be classed as a 'crim' in the land of the 'crims'!

We duly arrived in Coffs Harbour and the part of the visit I had been dreaming about. Literally! Since Di and I had visited Paul and Gladys in Scotts Head on our honeymoon, I had dreamt that one day, Charlie would walk up his front path, knock on the door, and when Paul opened it, ask 'Are you my Dad's Uncle Paul?'. And that's exactly what happened, although he had Georgina for company. And as he spoke in a quiet voice and Paul was a bit deaf, he had to repeat himself. Di videoed the whole thing, and I was a bit emotional as this particular dream had come true. Paul, and particularly Gladys, were quite frail by now – she moved into a nearby home shortly after we visited, where she passed away. They were great company, and I was glad the kids were able to meet this wonderful man. Whilst we were at Paul's, we took the kids to experience his vast beach and all swim/paddle in the Pacific Ocean. As when Di and I were there before, it was completely deserted and there were no Japanese whaling boats in the vicinity. Which was a relief!

Palm Cove, north of Cairns, was our final destination, and being in the tropical rainforest, was absolutely sweltering. The hotel had a great outdoor pool in which Lewis swam for the first time. The beachside bar/restaurant we visited each night had geckos running up and down the walls whilst we ate. Amex Travel had booked us all on a trip on the Kuranda railway up the side of a mountain in the rainforest. The trip up was fine, but they'd also booked the return journey by cable car. I've always had an intense fear of heights (apart from flying itself), so I was shit scared on the way back down, using language which the kids would have heard for the first time, which caused them to rock the bastard cable car even more so that further profanities were emitted! Di, of course, did nothing to discourage them and just took pleasure in videoing the whole episode. When we got back to the hotel, room service were great about my request for urgent laundry requirements!

And then, all too soon, our trip was over, and we left the tropical heat to return to freezing Heathrow.

Australia is such a beautiful country and I've barely scratched the surface. Georgina has since been back three times, and Lewis also went over there on his own for a couple of months. My last visit was in June 2009, when it was becoming apparent that Paul didn't have too long to live. I flew down there, spent a couple of days with him and flew back having said our goodbyes. He passed away a few weeks later.

All by Myself

In self-employed world, I'd set up an investigations company with the idea of driving around listing assets of companies and/or individuals who might be worth suing to recover debts they owed. For a fee, I would provide this information to the debt collection agencies/Solicitors with whom I was familiar in the UK and who had said, prior to my leaving Amex, that they would provide me with work. After a few weeks of waiting for the phone to ring, no work was forthcoming, and there was no response to the messages I left with my contacts at these companies. Fuck! I needed to do something. I searched around and found a couple of companies that provided me with a small number of instructions, which involved driving vast distances to collect small debts. It wasn't cost-effective, but it was a way of getting my name out there.

After a while, I started to receive more doorstep debt collection work from Southern Water, attending properties in Burgess Hill, Haywards Heath, and Lewes to collect outstanding debts from customers in their homes. The work combined two skillsets I had honed at Amex. Debt collection with a customer service approach. The hardest part was getting the customer to answer the door in the the first place and talk to me. Once they could see I wasn't a double-hard bastard who was there to steal their kids, things could progress. My initial knock would often turn into 2 or 3. By the third one, the door would very slowly open, and I would introduce myself and why I was there. Before they could shut the door, I'd tell them a mother-in-law gag! The door would open a bit more, and I would usually see an incredulous face behind it. 'If you don't pay me something tonight', I'd continue, 'I'll tell you another one'. And the ice was broken. I generally enjoyed this type of work and got on well with most of the customers. I was invited to some of their parties, had a drink at Christmas with them and one lady even invited me to her wedding reception! I also diversified into other areas, which included accompanied bailiff's visits (usually to repossess vehicles), serving court papers on companies or individuals, and mortgage arrears counselling. I even got sacked from one job for laughing at work although, to be fair, I was driving a hearse at the time!

It may come as a bit of a shock to those of you who know me but I consider myself to be a diverse, modern guy and as a result, I also got a job in the Wild West of America as a non-binary gold prospector as I was told there's money in them/their hills!

Temptation

At the age of 43, I had a mid-life crisis (although I'll be amazed if I live to 86!). I had an affair with a woman from whom I used to collect in respect of an old credit card debt. She turned out to be a complete 'head the ball' and seriously did my own head in. I modified the old saying that 'the grass may look greener over the other side of the fence, but it doesn't mean it's any easier to cut it!'. I moved out of the family home and into a rented 2-bed property in Rastrick Close at the southern end of the town. My selfish behaviour caused a huge amount of distress to Di and the kids, which I shall regret forever. My new housemate was Dave Jefferies, who was 6 months older than me and who had a variety of different jobs while I knew him. He was also a big Burgess Hill Town fan and was very accommodating whenever the kids came to visit me. Although she was incredibly hurt by my moment of madness, Di was brilliant regarding access to the kids, and they would come and stay with me each weekend when I'd bend over backwards to make the most of my time with them. There was a small park nearby, which had a large wall with a crossbar and posts painted onto it, where I would take the kids to have a kickabout. I also took them on holidays to the South of France and Portugal with Fi and her family, and whilst they were obviously upset at what I'd done, it doesn't seem to have affected the wonderful adults they have become, which is mainly down to how Di brought them up. With the occasional assistance from me in the profanities department!

After the affair ended, I started to suffer a mental and financial breakdown. Although I was self-employed and didn't earn if I didn't go out to work, there were many days when I couldn't face getting out of bed and would cry constantly at the most trivial thing. I ensured that Di, the kids, and Dave were completely unaware of this but couldn't see a way out of the mess that I had created. One New Year's Eve, Dave was away for a few days, I didn't have the kids, and I tried to drink myself into oblivion. I was startled out of it by Mum ringing me around 5pm on New Year's Day, frantic with worry as she'd been ringing me all day and I hadn't answered. I wasn't coherent enough to tell her what had been going on, but very slowly started to see a bit of light at the end of the tunnel.

Where Were You When We Were Shit?

After 12 years at our 'temporary' home at Withdean Stadium, and after years of campaigning, petitioning, marching, etc., the Albion moved into a newly built stadium at Falmer, not far from 28PR. It was initially called the American Express Community Stadium as my former employers had decided to get involved and had their name and logo displayed on the stadium walls, as well as the teams' shirts. The phrase 'Where were you when we were shit?' was never more apt. Back in the 80's and 90's, when the club was skint and came so close to going out business, Amex didn't want to know, despite being the largest private employer in the city and for whom a significant number of fans worked. Even their local rival, TSB Trustcard, had put a few quid the club's way by sponsoring the shirts for a couple of seasons. And yet, here they were years later with their name and logo emblazoned everywhere. I found it nauseating, but it was not untypical of all the corporate bollocks that was to follow. Fellow fans, commentators and the like have always called the stadium 'The Amex', but to me, it will always be 'Falmer'. Petty, perhaps, but I really can't give them any credit for their involvement with my club as I feel they could have helped out a lot sooner.

Stand

As the new stadium was being built, I would take the kids down there when we visited Mum. There were 'peep' holes around the perimeter fences through which we could see how it was taking shape. It was an exciting time after the years of struggle and uncertainty that had preceded it, and once completed, was an absolutely magnificent modern football arena. It was just a shame about the shit blue box on the wall outside! As a season ticket holder at Withdean, I qualified for a priority invitation to choose our seats and applied for season tickets at the new ground. I selected three in the very back row of the North Stand where, sadly for Lewis, there didn't appear to be any screws' pockets in which he could have a dip! Neil chose seats for himself and his family high up in the impressive West Stand, where the view was fantastic, but there wasn't a 'bad' view anywhere in the place. After a couple of warm-up games, the scene was set for our first league game at our new ground on 6th August, 2011, against Doncaster, who had been our last-ever opponents at the Goldstone Ground. The atmosphere inside the stadium was superb, and as kick-off approached, the three of us took our seats (although no one ever sat) despite the stadium having a 'no standing' policy. The stewards initially tried to enforce this but were told to piss off and never bothered trying again. I'll admit there was a tear in my eye for Dad and so many other fans who were no longer with us and unable to share this wonderful day.

Billy Sharp hadn't read the script and put Doncaster 1-0 up. The mood amongst the fans was subdued until substitute Will Buckley equalised in the 83rd minute, and the same player scored a 98th-minute winner, sparking more scenes of unbridled joy and more tears! There have been many more big games and big occasions at the stadium since then, but those who were there on that day will never forget it.

Reach Out

Work was still plentiful, and I knocked (pun intended) the doorstep debt collection stuff on the head to concentrate on the more remunerative work I was doing. My relationship with Di had improved – she really is a remarkably tolerant and stoic woman- so much so that she allowed me to move back home, which the kids were thrilled about. We had a couple of family holidays in Corfu and another in Crete. The Corfu ones were a bit frustrating as you could almost reach out and touch Albania, so close was it to the island.

Words and phrases such as 'reach out', 'cascade' and 'engage' have become used over the last 20 years or so as a result of 'corporate-speak', and have a different meaning from how they were originally used. These changes seem to have originated from America, a country that can't even spell 'theatre' or 'centre' properly! To my mind, the only person who should be allowed to use the phrase 'reach out' is a member of the Four Tops! 'Cascade' is an equally horrific word in its modern context and conjures up thoughts of an awful Paul McCartney song about Waterfalls! The worst one for me, though, is 'engage', usually used by pretentious pricks as follows:-

PP: 'I'd like to engage with you'.

ME: 'That's nice, where's the ring?'

PP: 'The what?'

ME: 'The ring. You don't usually get engaged without a ring'.

PP: 'Oh, it's not that sort of engage'.

ME: 'Well fucking talk properly then!'

(I can do irony with the best of them!).

Tom Jones

Another bugbear of mine regarding the bastardisation of the English Language, is the way kids (in particular) can't be arsed to write properly when texting or messaging each other. 'Yh m8', 'K', and 'wtf'. At least 'lol' has a fucking vowel in it, I suppose, as does 'wtaf'! It's rubbish but indicative of the world we live in, innit!

I'll confess, however, that even I've slipped into this modern malaise. A while ago, a woman I know, whose name was made famous by a Tom Jones song, sent me a message which contained photos of 3 women with huge tits, to which I replied Y, Y, Y, Delilah!

North Korea

Three season tickets at the Albion were becoming too expensive to afford, so I cancelled mine and Lewis's, and we started watching our local side, Burgess Hill. I kept paying for Charlie's so he could continue going to Falmer, and when he couldn't make a game, either Lewis or I would go instead, but that wasn't often as we were having too much fun travelling around the non-league grounds of Sussex, Surrey and Kent watching Burgess Hill. Our manager was Ian Chapman, who had played over 300 games for the Albion in the 80's and 90's, and his assistant was Stuart Tuck, who also played nearly 100 games for the Albion. As a management team, they were outstanding, and it helped to have a very talented squad at their disposal. The club's attitude towards fans could not have been more different from that at Falmer. At Burgess Hill, they were genuinely pleased to see you and grateful for your entrance fee. At the Albion, they couldn't give a toss if you couldn't make a game that had been rearranged at the request of the TV companies; they'd already got your money through paying for a season ticket, so tough. To rub salt into the wounds, I would be included in that game's 'attendance' irrespective of whether or not I'd actually been able to attend, as the attendance number was based on tickets sold, not bums on seats. Never was this absurdity more apparent than when, a few minutes before the end of the game, the stadium announcer would gleefully thank the crowd of 28,747 for attending when in reality, there were less than 22k there. It all became a bit too North Korean for my liking!

We are the Champions

Burgess Hill had one of their best-ever seasons in 2014-15 when we romped away with the league title, accruing 109 points in the process. We also had fantastic runs in the FA Cup and FA Trophy, winning at higher league Sutton and Aldershot respectively. Lewis and I went to most of the games home and away and got to know Ian and Stuart quite well as I'd always stand close to Ian's dugout and occasionally let him know how the Albion were getting on as he was still a massive fan. The whole experience of following Burgess Hill around the South East was great fun, and a million miles away from Falmer, which was rapidly becoming twinned with Pyongyang!

Bicycle Race

Apologies to any cyclists reading this. Actually no, fuck 'em! Throughout my constant travels up and down the country, and particularly locally, they were the bane of my life, riding 2 abreast down narrow country lanes in their poncey Lycra outfits, thinking that they owned the road without paying a penny for the privilege of riding on them. The only good thing about potholes is that they occasionally fuck cyclists up! When I used to take the kids down to Mum's on a Sunday, I would drive up Ditchling Beacon on the way there. Every week, without fail, there would be at least half a dozen cyclists slowly making their way up what is, admittedly, a very steep hill with numerous tight bends, all grimacing in pain and all causing a massive backlog of cars unable to overtake them due to the impossibility of seeing round the cyclist and round the bend. I'd wind the window down on the rare chance that I actually got past one of them and shout, 'If you want to ride a bike, go and live in fucking Holland!', which amused the kids so much they started doing it themselves. Being the bad parent that I am, I did absolutely nothing to discourage them.

If I thought Ditchling Beacon was bad, it was nothing compared to Amsterdam, which Lewis and I visited in November 2023 when the Albion played over there. The number of cyclists on their roads was ridiculous, with no apparent rules and a complete and utter disregard for pedestrians. I did get a couple of funny looks from them when I shouted out, 'If you want to ride a bike, go up Ditchling fucking Beacon'! Maybe it got a bit lost in translation. Hate 'em! Unless you've bought this book, in which case I can only apologise for any offence caused!

We're On Our Way

The 2016/17 season was a memorable one for the Albion. After a few near misses in the playoffs, we finally achieved promotion to the Premier League for the first time under the guise of Chris Hughton. Charlie still had his season ticket in the North Stand, and I bought tickets for Lewis and me in the South Stand for the match against Wigan, which we won to seal promotion. A large number of fans went onto the pitch at the end to celebrate, and Lewis and I walked across it to meet Charlie by the north goal. I was pleased for the boys, who celebrated wildly, and also for the other fans who had never seen us play in the top flight before, but I was disillusioned with the modern game and all the corporate crap that went with it.

Never Mind the (Extra) Bollock

In 2020, disaster struck. No, not Covid, although that wasn't great. No, I grew an extra bollock – sort of! I made a cup of coffee one morning, wasn't fully concentrating and spilt a large amount of boiling water on my bare leg. (I was wearing shorts at the time as it was at the start of a very hot summer). A huge blister quickly formed, not far off the size of a testicle, and remained a fluid-filled ball for some time until I got bored with it and popped it! No one knows if it had any bearing on what happened to my legs the following year, but it was in the vicinity.

Thunderbirds Are Go

Covid was a bit of a bummer, and I, together with tens of thousands of others, were indebted to the Arsenal Manager, Mikael Arteta, for possibly saving our lives. We were due to play Arsenal at home on March 14th, when the pandemic was really taking off. Charlie couldn't go so we agreed that I would have his ticket. On the Thursday before the game, Arteta went down with Covid symptoms – there was a chance it had spread to his players, so virulent was it at the time- and the Premier League postponed the game. Had they not done so, I and 30,000 others would have been there spreading the virus amongst one another and the consequences don't bear thinking about. So, thank you, Mikael, even if you do look like a Thunderbird puppet!

The Sweetest Girl

One impact of Covid was felt very close to home. Di's eldest sister, Lou, worked in a care home in Crawley, which had no protective equipment for the carers who worked there or the residents who lived there, several of whom had died from the virus. Lou displayed symptoms and was signed off work by her doctor. We kept in regular contact with her by phone and texts and she seemed to be improving. One day, Di came home early from work in floods of tears and announced that Lou had died. Her son, Kieran, having not heard from her for a couple of days, let himself into her house in Crawley and found her dead in the bath. We were all devastated as Lou was a wonderful, kind-hearted woman who had suffered traumas in her life with the death of her young daughter, Kirsty, shortly before I met Di, and her gentle giant of a husband, Nigel, who passed away a few years before she did. Lou was particularly kind to me when I returned to the fold after my mid-life crisis. All the family were able to attend her funeral in Crawley but had to sit several yards apart from one another due to the restrictions in place at that time. She was a lovely woman and is still very greatly missed.

I Get Locked Down (But I Get Up Again)

As the pandemic took hold, more was becoming known about it and how it could be passed on. Facemasks started to be worn by everyone, which did me a favour as no one could see what an ugly bastard I was! Di, as a carer, had to wear masks and disposable aprons. Lockdowns started to be imposed, and various rules about the number of people who could meet indoors and outdoors were introduced by our then Government, led by Prime Minister Boris Johnson, who all set a fine example to the nation – not! There were nightly broadcasts from 10 Downing Street involving Johnson and 2 medical advisers and various slogans introduced by some genius in the Government's marketing department, including 'Hands, Face, Space'. One slogan which wasn't publicly aired emanated from the subsequent discovery that not only had Johnson and his cohorts completely disregarded the very rules they had brought in (some of which were enforced on the public by the OB), they had handed out contracts for crap and useless Personal Protective Equipment to their chums who made millions of pounds in the process. 'Fucking Lying Bastards' would have been a more appropriate slogan!

Johnson's Government imposed the first national lockdown on 23rd March, 2020, the day before Mum's 89th birthday. She was on her own at 28PR and naturally worried about the virus as she (and indeed I) was classed as 'high risk' on account of the various ailments she had (diabetes, in my case). I was buggered if my dear old Mum wasn't going to see anyone on her birthday, so I drove down there and stood on her front steps and chatted to her without going in. The roads were absolutely deserted, and it was quite an eerie and frightening time.

Our kids had mixed fortunes during the Covid lockdowns. Charlie and his partner, Megan, were staying at her Mum's house elsewhere in Burgess Hill, so they were stuck there for a while, although they did risk being arrested by Johnson's Stasi when they visited me for my birthday and stayed on the drive without coming in. Georgina and her then-boyfriend, Ben, moved into a flat on the eastern side of Burgess Hill just as the first lockdown took effect and were virtually trapped there. Lewis moved his then-girlfriend, Heidi, into our place, so at least Di and I had some company. We kept in touch with all of them through Zoom calls, as we did with Fi, Ian, and her boys. It was a scorching summer, so I spent most of it in the garden, getting a great tan with my extra bollock! And without noticing it, losing loads of weight.

From a work perspective, Covid brought about significant changes to the way I worked. By now, I was almost solely dealing with insurance claims and the lockdowns meant that I could no longer go into customers' houses to take the photos/videos of the damage for which they were claiming against their policy. Equally, claims were still being made as pipes weren't talking to one another and saying, 'there's a pandemic on, we won't burst just now', so the insurance industry was in a bit of a quandary as to how to deal with them. My client devised a way around this whereby I would do everything on my phone by way of a 'virtual' visit. This enabled the claims to proceed and meant that I kept earning an income. It was a lifesaver for me, particularly with the problems lying in wait for me the following year.

Yes Prime Minister

Prior to the lockdowns, a couple of celebrities I visited for my insurance work were the former World Middleweight boxing champion, Alan Minter, and the politician, Sir Keir Starmer. Minter, had a flat in Littlehampton in which a pipe had burst, but seemed punch-drunk and not particularly lucid. This wasn't surprising in view of the brutal hammerings he suffered at the hands of Marvin Hagler in the 80's, which effectively finished his career. I remember watching him beat Vito Antuofermo on BBC's 'Sportsnight' to win the world title in March 1980, which he retained against the same opponent three months later.

Starmer was very pleasant. I met him and his sister at his late parent's house in Oxted, where a fire had completely wrecked a summer house his father had built for his disabled mother, in which they spent many an hour looking out over their paddocks watching donkeys trundle about. Whilst I was filming the burnt-out shell, something nudged my arm and I turned to see one of the donkeys who had come to see what was going on.

Being the consummate professional I always am, I didn't let on to Minter or Starmer that I knew who they were. Similarly, neither of them mentioned my GG impression from 1973, which I was a tad disappointed about to be honest!

Driving Home for Christmas

The deserted roads during the Covid lockdowns were similar to those I used to experience on Christmas Day. During the period when I was living in Rastrick Close and before I moved back home with Di and the kids, she used to take them around to her parent's house for Christmas lunch. I was at a bit of a loose end, so Mum put me in touch with Hove Methodist Church, who used to provide a Christmas lunch for their parishioners and those who were likely to be on their own on Christmas Day, and I offered to help out by collecting a few of their guests, taking them to the church hall, and going back afterwards to take them to their homes. After I'd dropped them at the meal, I'd drive over to 28PR to see Mum and have a bite to eat with her so that she had company on the day.

The guests were usually old and had mobility issues, but I'd ring a couple of days in advance to let them know what time I'd be picking them up. When I arrived, the old girls had clearly been up all morning, putting on their excessive amounts of lipstick, neatly setting their wigs on their heads, and really looking forward to the meal and meeting similar folk. By the time I collected them after the meal had finished, they'd clearly had one too many sherries; the lippy was plastered all over their faces, and their wigs were at 45-degree angles. They were thoroughly pissed but had obviously enjoyed themselves. After I'd dropped the last guest off, I'd drive back to Di's and have my Christmas with the kids there.

As you know by now, I'm not churchy in the slightest but I felt good about taking time out to help people less fortunate than me. Shame the buggers never tipped me!

Bring On the Dancing Horses

When the kids were younger, I tried to get them involved in sports. They could all swim from a young age; Charlie had a sweet left foot, which he'd demonstrated by putting the ball past me in the North Stand goal at the Goldstone; Lewis was initially a good sprinter, winning a couple of races at his school sports day but, eventually, like Charlie, began to play football for local boys teams, and Georgina also had a dabble with girls' football, although she was more interested in kicking the other girls instead of the ball! I was conscious of the amount of time I was spending with the boys and their football, both watching the Albion and playing for their teams, and I needed to find something solely for Georgina. I hit on the wonderful idea of horse riding as all young girls love to ride a horse, don't they? Don't they? Hmm.

I found a place out at Horsted Keynes in the Sussex countryside and took Georgina along for a ride. The boys came too but were under strict instructions not to laugh! She was suitably attired in a (borrowed) riding helmet and Wellington boots and had a gentle trot around the paddock on her horse. She seemed to enjoy it, so we went back the following week. This time, she sat astride a very small, very old horse who had clearly seen it all before and knew how to have fun. He slowly plodded around the paddock with a weary, resigned look but an occasional twinkle in his eye. Suddenly, without warning, he stopped dead in his tracks, throwing Georgina off in the process. And that was that! Unfortunately, the boys continued their lifetime habit of never taking a blind bit of notice of anything I said and pissed themselves laughing. Georgina went back to kicking girls' shins!

The Boss

L ewis was a half-decent footballer as a youngster and had an unsuccessful trial for the Albion (which he wasn't aware of). He played up a year for his first team, Marle Place, and then moved to Hassocks in the neighbouring village, where he started with the first team before dropping down to the seconds. I used to take him to every game, more often than not running the line for them as none of the other parents could be arsed to do it. The standard of Lewis's team was abysmal; he was by far one of the better players but could do nothing to prevent weekly defeats with scores against in the tens and, on one occasion, in the twenties, mainly due to a goalkeeper who refused to move or dive if the ball wasn't kicked straight at him. There were a handful of boys who, like Lewis, could play a bit, but they were all thoroughly demoralised by their weekly thrashings. After a 21-0 defeat, the coach departed and with 4 games left until the end of the season, I agreed to become Manager with Charlie, who by now was a qualified coach and working part-time for the Albion In The Community programme, going round schools and delivering after-school coaching to the pupils there, as my coach. We lost the last four games, but goals conceded were in single figures, and we scored a few as well, so I could see some progress. I agreed to stay on for the next season, but whilst Charlie could sporadically help out, I needed a coach who could attend every training session and the matches. Whilst I'm a decent Manager (as borne out by my experience in men's football 20-25 years before), I'm not a coach. Step forward Neil, my old friend from school, Amex FC and watching the Albion.

Neil was a good player who, as a youngster, had a trial with Stuttgart Kickers in Germany and was an outstanding coach who could probably have had a good career as one if he'd decided to go down that route. He agreed to coach the boys, and we reported back for pre-season training. Neil's methods weren't to everyone's tastes, but we soon sorted the wheat from the chaff (and there was plenty of chaff!). Those who wanted to learn and develop stayed. Those who just wanted to piss about and waste our time didn't. My role, in addition to dealing with some of the admin, was to liaise with parents of existing players, as well as the parents of boys who I was interested in signing and who I felt would improve the team. The latter job was probably the hardest part at first, as most parents (and their sons) knew of our crap reputation and wondered aloud why their sons would want to play for a bunch of losers like us. I managed to convince a few that we were on the up and that their son could play a big part in it. We had a couple of pre-season friendlies, which went quite well, and we could already see an improvement thanks to Neil's coaching.

Our first league game of the season was at Lewes, who had finished mid-table the previous year; we had obviously finished bottom by some distance. The game started, we had a reasonable shape and then something strange happened; we scored a goal and went 1-0 up. Our parents on the touchline cheered but it was slightly reserved as they were obviously awaiting the traditional onslaught and feast of goals from our opponents. And then we went 2-0 up. The cheers were accompanied by looks of incredulity. Lewes pulled a goal back, and 'here we go, we knew it was too good to last'. Then, we scored again, resulting in joyous scenes amongst the parents. I hadn't yet been able to replace our crap keeper, and lo and behold, he let another one in, but the final whistle went and we had won 3-2. The first win for our team in their history! Some of the parents were in (joyful) tears, the boys were all proud of what they had achieved, and Neil and I were delighted at how quickly we'd improved them. We won quite a few more games that season and finished 5th in the league. We also reached a cup final for the first time, narrowly losing 1-0 to a team who had finished 2nd in the same league as us.

During the next close season, my recruitment job became slightly easier as parents of potentially new players could see that we'd made progress the previous year, and there was less stigma about playing for us. I managed to find a new goalkeeper, and the next 2 seasons saw even more progress, culminating in finishing 2nd and being promoted to the top division for our final season (as the boys were now 15/16 and couldn't continue as a 'junior' club). The gulf in class in the top division showed as we eventually finished bottom, although we were always competitive and performed well in most games. Our final game was The Matthew Harding Cup, and was held at Hassocks FC's county league ground. Matthew was the vice-chairman of Chelsea and lived locally but tragically died in a helicopter crash in 1996 at the young age of 42, and Lewis and I used to watch one of his sons, Pat, play for Burgess Hill. We won the trophy 3-0 which resulted in the boys winning a medal in their last ever game for the team. All a far cry from 21-0 drubbings!

TV Star

In the 2018-19 season, the Albion had a good run in the FA Cup, culminating in a semi-final appearance at Wembley where we lost 1-0 to Man City. We played Millwall in the quarter-final at the New Den, which was considerably more hospitable than the Old Den, where Mick Ferguson nearly got us killed by scoring the winner in 1985! Upon entering through the turnstiles, there was a Southern Counties Radio presenter interviewing Albion fans about what the FA Cup meant to them. (Southern Counties Radio had replaced Radio Sussex, which in turn, had replaced Radio Brighton, and my mind momentarily flashed back to that Brian & Michael LP!). The presenter came up to me and asked the question he'd been posing to the other fans. 'I went veggie when we lost the final in 1983', I answered. His eyes lit up as I was possibly the first person who had said that to him. 'Really?', he asked. 'Yep, straight up. My head was all over the place, so I turned veggie'. After taking my contact details, he murmured something about possibly getting in touch if we reached the final – we didn't, and he didn't- and I never heard anything more from him.

Shortly after Argentina won the World Cup in 2022, and Albion's Alexis Mac Allister played a key role in the win, I received a phone call out of the blue from someone at the BBC asking if I'd like to give my thoughts on what it meant to have a Brighton player winning the World Cup. I'd overcome my public shyness by now (!) and replied in the affirmative. He set up a Zoom call. I duly expressed my thoughts and delight, and approximately 15 seconds of it was broadcast on that day's local BBC TV news programme. Many people got in touch afterwards to say I had the perfect face for radio – and they weren't wrong!

Long Hot Summer

During the Covid summer of 2020 when I gained my extra 'bollock', I started to lose weight and muscles from my arms and legs. I hadn't changed what I ate or drank so it was a bit of a mystery as to what was causing it. I spent the long hot summer dressed only in shorts, and Di and the kids frequently took the piss out of my saggy-skinned arms and old man's legs. I wasn't in any pain at the time, so I assumed it was part of the ageing process.

I started to experience some discomfort in my legs during the early part of 2021, and in May, I had to drive to Rotherfield in East Sussex for an insurance job. On the way there, I started to feel a pain in my chest, which got progressively worse. I was pissed off when I got there to find that they wanted a proper assessor to take up their flooring and locate their leak, and as I was just a humble photographer/videographer, I just wouldn't do. I didn't have any other jobs scheduled out that way, so it was a complete waste of time. The journey back home was excruciatingly painful. My legs were hurting, but that was nothing compared to the pain in my chest, which got worse the further I drove. I started to panic, fearing I was having a heart attack, but was determined to get home. I eventually pulled up outside our house, went to get out of the car and collapsed on the road. Fortunately, a neighbour opposite, Jackie, rushed out of her house, helped me up, and virtually carried me indoors together with Georgina, who wasn't working that day. They immediately called an ambulance, and I laid on the sofa. After a while, the pain in my chest subsided, although there was still a pain in my stomach. A first response paramedic arrived and conducted a variety of tests, attaching several wires to my bare chest – the Tarzanogram chest hair having long since washed off - blood pressure, etc., and they all seemed to be fine. I advised her that I was feeling ok and just wanted to have a kip, so could she cancel the ambulance? She replied that it was already on its way as it's standard practice in urgent cases such as mine and that I should go to the hospital to get properly checked out. I felt a bit of a fraud getting into the ambulance, but the 3 female paramedics who arrived with the vehicle insisted that I must go to hospital.

Crispy Ambulance

I'd never been in an ambulance before, and I was very underwhelmed. The journey was as bumpy as fuck, the windows were all frosted so I couldn't see out, and there was no ashtray! It was a bit rubbish really. I desperately wanted to sleep but the paramedics wouldn't let me and kept talking to me to prevent me from nodding off. One of them asked what I did for a living. 'I'm a gynecologist', I replied. Not even a flicker of a smile from any of them. Really tough crowd!

They checked me in at the hospital's reception, and I underwent more tests, including having those electrodes on my chest again, blood tests, etc. This went on for several hours until around 4 pm, a nurse came into the cubicle and told me that one of the blood tests hadn't been taken properly and would need to be done again before a doctor could see me and assess the results. She took another sample and told me to take a seat in the waiting area until the doctor called for me. I had to get up off the comfy bed I'd been laying on – although they still wouldn't let me sleep, kept talking to me and weren't in the slightest bit interested when I told them about my extra bollock- and go and sit on the hard, uncomfortable chairs in the waiting area. After sitting there for a while, the pain in my stomach moved upwards and into my chest. I then worked out that my posture in these chairs was almost identical to how I'd been sitting when driving. Eureka! I'd sussed it. A few years before, I'd suffered from Diverticulitis – something Mum used to get regularly- which is a particularly painful condition in the gut. I reckoned I'd got another bout, and my posture had pushed the pain up into my chest when driving. I shared this with the doctor when I eventually saw him. He agreed it sounded likely and referred me to the Digestive Diseases department - sponsored by McVities- in Brighton, who eventually brought it under control with various medications. Piss easy, this biology lark, <u>despite</u> Mrs Booth and Chesterfield FC! So now I was all sorted – or was I?

Bon Jovi

Shortly after the pains in my legs started and way before any diagnosis, I had a weekend break in a cottage in West Meon on the West Sussex/Hampshire border with Fi, 'Saint' Ian and her boys, Harry and Fraser. Di and Lewis couldn't join us, but Charlie drove Georgina, Megan and me down there. Parts of the cottage were over 200 years old; it was quaint and in a very quiet village; perfect for some much needed relaxation – or so you'd think.

Due to Fi and the boys living in Essex, we hadn't seen as much of them as we did when they were younger. Harry was born 5 months before Lewis and was superb at sport from an early age, playing cricket for Essex colts, and was also good at football and rugby. He was academic too and was clearly going to become a politician or barrister (or both) as he could chat shit for England! Unfortunately, when he was 9, after multiple tests, scans, etc., he was diagnosed with a brain aneurysm and was seriously ill in Great Ormond Street Children's Hospital. Thankfully, one of the brilliant surgeons there tried a procedure at the last minute which worked and undoubtedly saved Harry's life. It was a horrendous time for Fi, Nick (Harry's dad), and all the family and after many years of treatment, he eventually recovered, although he could no longer play any contact sports so had to make do with watching West Ham with

Nick as that was their team. Poor kid - as if he hadn't suffered enough!

Fraser was born in 2006 and also suffered his own health issues over the years. He too was into sports (football, cricket and, more recently, golf) and from a young age, was very clued up with meaningless sports-related stats about who did what and when. In this respect, the yawn emoji was probably invented with him in mind! Initially, to wind Harry up, he supported Millwall, then Everton (as they were top of the league one week) before settling on Manchester City as he was determined that no one could ever accuse him of being a glory hunter!

The cousins had always got on well so a quiet weekend away seemed the perfect opportunity to catch up, together with getting to know Ian better as he and Fi hadn't been an item for long at that time. He was a big bloke, massively into heavy metal, which had rubbed off on Fi as she started to wear a black leather jacket and dyed her hair blonde, presumably going full on for the Suzi Quatro look! Ian also enjoyed outdoor activities – (no, not dogging – as far as I knew!)- and was heavily involved with local scout groups in Colchester, camping and hiking over the hilly terrains of Essex! Unfortunately, he assumed that everyone else shared his passion for such jaunts.

On the Saturday morning of our weekend break, Ian excitedly gathered everyone around and announced that he'd found a pub which, according to his top of the range GPS thingy, was a 20 minute walk away along a disused railway line, and we could head there for lunch and drinks. Bearing in mind I was by now struggling to get up and down stairs, a 20 minute walk wasn't my idea of a good time but I agreed to go as the alternative would have been for me to stay at the cottage and sleep as the meds I was on were causing me to do this every day, and it would have been a waste of my time away with Fi and everyone. Like something out of an Enid Blyton story, we set off through woods until we reached the old railway line, the path alongside which was relatively flat, making it slightly easier for me to walk, and grimacing with the increasing pain, I kept going. And going. And going. All the time, Ian was insisting that 'it's not far now'. After an hour and a half of 'walking', Megan had the sense to check the sat nav on her phone and discovered that we were only halfway there (which appealed to Ian as he quite liked Bon Jovi!). Fuck! By now, I was in absolute agony but caught between a rock and a hard place. If I turned back, it would take me an hour and a half (at least) to get back to the cottage, so I might as well continue suffering for the same length of time and reach our destination, which I duly did.

Eventually, like a mirage in the desert, the pub appeared in the distance and was a very welcome sight. The beer garden was packed save for one wooden table with wooden benches around it. Unfortunately, due to the amount of weight and muscle I'd lost over the past year or so, I now had two bits of string for arse cheeks so when I sat on the bench, it was effectively bone on wood, which was more painful than the 3 hour walk my badly damaged legs had just endured! Unusually for him, Ian was very quiet and contrite and after a pint and a bite to eat, very kindly pegged it back to the cottage with Fi and Harry to collect his motor, and came and picked the rest of us up. When it subsequently transpired exactly what was wrong with my legs, it was evident that Ian's 20 minute/3 hour hike had been more painful than being 'Shot Through The Heart!'

Requiem

No sooner had the Diverticulitis been identified and the pain eased off, the pains in my thighs started to increase to the point that I was in absolute agony with them. I visited the local doctor who poked and prodded them and said, 'Quads'. I told him I didn't realise I was pregnant, and he told me to take paracetamol (the usual cop-out). There was some pain in my back as well as my legs, so I thought it might be sciatica and tried acupuncture for the first time with a local Chinese lady. She told me she would cure me within 10 sessions (at £45 a pop) but was absolutely hopeless and inserted one needle in my thigh (which knowing what I now know, caused me unsurprisingly to hit the roof; it hurt so much). She even forgot to take one needle out of my foot, which I only discovered when I got home and took my shoe off! Oh how we laughed at my next session!

The pains got worse and resulted in me being unable to sleep at night, so I would lay on the sofa in the lounge so as not to wake Di. It got so bad that I considered ending it all if this was how things were going to be for the rest of my life. I worked out where and how but not when. By now, I couldn't walk anywhere without pain, so Di borrowed a wheelchair and pushed me around on the rare occasions when I could go out, including a visit to see another doctor who referred me for x-rays (which didn't show anything untoward) and an MRI scan focusing on my back as he thought it might be spinal related. I'd never had one of those before and quite enjoyed it. I had to lie completely still with my whole body encased in this machine, the noise of which was so loud I had to wear headphones.

The loud humming of the machine was identical to the intro to Killing Joke's 'Requiem', and I found it immensely difficult to refrain from tapping my fingers to where I imagined the drum roll would kick in! The scan on my spine didn't show anything particularly averse so they sent me for another one, this time on my legs. The nurse asked if there was anything I particularly wanted to listen to, and I immediately discounted The Undertones as it would have been nigh on impossible not to drum along to Teenage Kicks or attempt the bass intro to Tearproof, so I asked for Radio 6 and spent a pleasant 30 minutes listening to Johnny Cash live at Fulsom Prison. I'd never heard any of his stuff before and quite liked it.

Pol Pot

Whatever they found on the second MRI scan caused me to be sent to a neurologist for various tests, but he was still none the wiser as to what was causing the pain. Di and the kids were still pushing me around everywhere in the wheelchair; the incredibly strong medication I was taking only had a minimal effect on easing the pain, and I was off my nut with the side effects. My legs and arms were now just skin and bones with absolutely no muscles anywhere, and my weight had plummeted from its original 15 stone when this all started. At one point, I was losing 1lb a day and went down to 10 stone 10lb at its lowest point. I felt dreadful and looked so much like a skinny Cambodian that even Pol Pot would have felt sorry for me!

Club Tropicana

A nd then Di found out what it was. She googled my symptoms and came up with the possibility that it was Diabetes Atrophy, a fairly rare spin-off of diabetes. The muscles in my thighs had completely wasted away, exposing (and permanently damaging) the nerves that were touching the bones, which would explain why it hurt so much. At our next appointment with the neurologist, we put this theory forward; he looked it up and agreed it was a strong possibility. He immediately put me on a huge course of steroids to rebuild the muscles around the damaged nerves. I hoped they might also give me a good chance of winning the shot put in the 2024 Olympics! Initially, there didn't seem to be anything happening, but then, on the 5th day of taking them, WHAM! No, not Club Tropicana. WHAM! As in all the steroids kicked in at once, and the pain and discomfort was temporarily worse than it had been when the nerves were exposed. Gradually, the muscles returned, providing some protection to the thighs. After a few more visits to the neurologist, during which he conducted more tests which showed that my thighs had stabilised, there was nothing more that he could do, and I was discharged with the understanding that they would never fully recover but hopefully wouldn't get too much worse, at least not for a long time.

I haven't been able to drive since the day I fell out of the car onto the road and due to the continuing pain I still get in my right thigh, I doubt if I will again as I wouldn't be able to brake suddenly without losing control of the vehicle as the pain kicked in. Di and the kids have been great in taking me to places I need to get to (doctors and hospital appointments, 28PR, etc.), and I'm very grateful to them.

Walking on Sunshine

2 4th March, 2022, was Mum's 91st birthday. It was a lovely sunny day, and I tried walking without the need for a wheelchair or crutches for the first time in nearly a year. With Di's help, I managed to get out of the wheelchair and take a few steps. It hurt like mad, but I was determined to do it as a birthday present for Mum. She had been so supportive but so worried when they didn't know what was wrong with me. One of the kids took me down to see her, and I somehow managed to walk slowly up her high front steps with a walking stick and into her house to tell her. She was thrilled, and I hope it made her day.

Friends Will Be Friends Part 2

One of the good things that came out of my illness was the kindness and support of my closest friends. Kev Brimley came up to see me every Friday at one point after Barry tipped him off that I wasn't doing too well; Barry, Steve and Cliff all came around regularly to check up on me. Caroline, my old drinking buddy, popped up from Brighton, Margaret dropped by, and Neil was also a regular visitor. He even arranged a surprise for my 58th birthday by getting me a ticket in the disabled section at Falmer for a thrilling 0-0 draw with Norwich and wrote a piece about me, resplendent with a photo of me in my wheelchair, in the matchday programme, which was incredibly kind of him. The disabled section was right next to the away fans so although the game was crap, I enjoyed myself flicking the 'V's and giving wanker signs to the Norwich fans. It felt like I was back and feeling human again.

Another bloke became a good friend out of all this. Mark Durant, AKA Scum Mark, worked for the same insurance client as I did and took on work in my area when I wasn't able to drive to prevent the client from passing it on to someone else. He would drop in for a cuppa when in the area, and we'd have a weekly chat about stuff. He was a West Ham fan originally on account of being born over that way, but he switched his allegiances to the scum as he liked their stripey clown's outfit!

All these people gave me a boost when I needed it, and I'm very lucky to know them.

Goodbye, Farewell

1 5th April, 2022, was Good Friday, and Di, myself, and the kids all went down to 28PR to see Mum. Every Good Friday for as long as I can remember, we would visit her for fish and chips (from the chippy at the bottom of her road) with a cheese and onion pasty for me – obviously – and eat them in Mum's lounge. Sometimes, if Fi and her boys were down, they'd join us, and it was a family tradition. On this particular Good Friday, Di took a photo of Mum, myself and the kids (with me looking very out of it on account of the strong meds I was still taking), and we had a good time as Mum was on form. She used to keep a diary for every day of the year going back to 1973, and her entry for this day read, 'Stuart, Di and children came for fish and chips. Di took a photo of us all. I wonder if this was for posterity?'. Very prophetic was Mum.

A week later, on 22nd April, Mum had to go into hospital for routine tests. She'd been in Atrial Fibrillation for several years and regularly attended hospital to have these tests performed on her. 'Bring an overnight bag just in case you have to stay in', she was told when she rang to check the appointment was still going ahead. She was in good spirits when Fi and I visited her there later that day, but she was having to stay in that night as there were more tests they needed to perform. 8 weeks later, on 22nd June, Fi and I demanded that they discharge Mum and that we would take her home. The change in her was indescribable. She went in alert, chatty, fully with it and came home a complete shell of that and almost unrecognisable. They'd put her in a ward of 'nearly deads' – very old people who were clearly on their way out - who spent all day asleep with their mouths open, or would periodically shout out a load of rubbish in the middle of the night. Whenever Mum had been in the hospital previously, she absolutely thrived on talking to patients and nurses about their backgrounds, etc., and such conversations stimulated her and kept her brilliant mind working. There was none of that where she was now, and we could see her visibly deteriorating mentally with every visit. The doctors were unable to fully explain why she was being kept in there but wouldn't discharge her as they hadn't put a care package in place. Fi and I told them we'd care for her and took her home.

In the days leading up to this, I'd arranged for a hospital bed, oxygen machine and commode to be delivered to 28PR, into which I'd temporarily moved. It was agreed that I would stay there during the week to look after her, and Fi would come down from Essex at weekends so I could go back home for a break. The bed was set up in the dining room so, like Dad, she could lay there and look out into her lovely garden. For the first couple of days, she was more like her old self (bossy!) and seemed to be happy back in familiar surroundings. Cliff and his sister, Lesley, kindly visited her/us as they had experienced several years of looking after their own virtually bed-bound Mum and were able to pass on some useful tips. Mum was quite lucid and chatted away with them. By now, she had virtually no mobility as her legs had given up, so she had to be pushed on the commode from the lounge to the dining room and vice versa. Helping her on and off the commode became more of a challenge with every passing day, as was getting her on and off the bed and getting her dressed. Fi and I needed help, but it was a bloody long time coming! She was continuing to go downhill, frequently dozing by day and hallucinating at night until, in one of her rare lucid moments, Fi and I managed to get her to agree to go into a home as we were way out of our depth, and it was making her distressed when she saw that we couldn't cope. A very pleasant lady from such a home in The Drive in Hove came to visit and assess her, agreeing that she would admit her to the home. On Tuesday, 5th July 2022, just under 2 weeks since we brought her home from hospital, an ambulance came to collect her, and Mum left 28PR after 59 years – for the last time.

Almost as soon as she set foot in the nursing home, Mum changed. She hated the place, couldn't stand the nurses who were rude to her – (they weren't)- and wanted to go home. She was becoming more delirious by the day, and it was heartbreaking to see. Would it have been any different if we'd been able to get her out of that hospital any sooner? Probably not. I visited her each day for the first few days, courtesy of the kids and on the Friday, Keely, Fi's old friend from way back when, drove from her home in Hove to collect me from Burgess Hill to take me to see Mum. Keely went in first to see her as they'd always got on well and Mum was a regular sounding board for advice for her and so many others over the years. When Keely came out, I went in but Mum was very incoherent, and I doubted she knew I was there. Keely then drove me back to Burgess Hill, which was incredibly kind of her. The following day, Saturday, 9th July, was an absolutely scorchingly hot day. Georgina dropped me at the station, and I caught a couple of trains to get to Hove. The route from the station to the nursing home was relatively flat so I was ok slowly walking it. When I entered Mum's room, she had deteriorated from the previous day, constantly rambling and asking questions like 'Will I be able to sit on the council again?' and such like. I kissed her goodbye and as I was leaving the room, looked round to see her for the last time. She was staring straight ahead, mumbling something random. I walked back to the station and caught the train home.

Fi came down by train from Essex the following day and visited Mum. I couldn't (and wouldn't) dissuade her from travelling as it was her Mum too, and it was important that she saw her. Fi texted me on the train home. 'That's not my Mum', it said, and I could only agree with her.

I moved back into 28PR on Monday and arranged for the hospital to come and collect the bed, oxygen machine and commode over the next couple of days. I didn't visit Mum that evening but planned to on Tuesday evening. At 4.30 am on Tuesday morning, 12th July, 2022, my mobile rang. A nurse from the home informed me that Mum had passed away 20 minutes earlier. I immediately rang Fi, who drove down from Essex, and Di so she could let the kids know. I caught a cab to the home and went into Mum's room. She was laying there with her mouth open and, rather disconcertedly, one eyelid was also open and refused to close. One of the nurses had laid a small flower on her chest and she looked very peaceful with no more pain. She was 91 and had led a very full life, achieving a great deal.

Fi arrived after a while. We hugged, and I left her alone with Mum before thanking the nurses and leaving. I felt the same kind of numbness I had felt when Dad passed away. We then went and had a coffee at Costa on Lewes Road, where Fi could get yet more loyalty points, and worked out who would do what. Fi registered the death later that day and arranged the funeral and the wake. I took on all the financial stuff, contacting all relevant parties, as well as selling 28PR later in the year. I stayed on in the house for a couple more days, overseeing the collection of the hospital equipment, and we then both set about sorting out the vast number of items that Mum and Dad had accumulated over the years. It felt really strange being in there and knowing we'd never see either of them again.

Don't You Forget About Me

The funeral was held at St Andrew's church on 27th July. There weren't as many there as I thought they'd be, but then I realised that most of her peers had departed over the years. Uncle Paul's eldest son, John, came down from Oxfordshire with his daughter, Rachael; Cliff, Steve, Barry and Kev came too, as did Scott Bell. Fi's friends, including Paul Hartley, were also there. The service was going well; Fi read out a tribute, Charlie and Harry read poems Mum had chosen and being top billing, I went on last. Just before I started to speak, I started coughing and asked the verger if I could have a glass of water, which he duly provided. I had a couple of gulps and the coughing stopped. I now had a microphone in one hand and a half-empty glass of water in the other. The problem was there was nowhere obvious for me to put the glass while I delivered my set. So I did what any like-minded person would do; I put it on top of the coffin! There were a few gasps, and I could hear the lovely female vicar behind me pissing herself laughing too. I shared a few anecdotes, including the little-known time when Mum had a tenuous link with the world's oldest profession, and we headed off to the wake at The Swan pub in Falmer where, as requested, there was a tray of mushroom vol-au-vents.

Before the wake, the family was driven behind the hearse to the crematorium to say our final 'goodbyes'. The record playing as we left was 'Don't You Forget About Me', and I could have sworn I heard Mum shouting it out!

This Old House

We put 28PR on the market and it sold immediately for way above the asking price, which may have had something to do with the historic blue plaque I'd put up denoting my significant presence! The house was old and in need of some modernisation as it was only a matter of time before the bay window at the front gave way completely and ended up further down the road, but it had lots of potential and the buyer, a keen gardener, fell in love with the back garden. We cleared virtually everything out, but Probate was taking an eternity to go through as I'm sure they thought I wasn't important enough to deal with! In November, disaster struck when a pipe from a tank in the loft leaked, causing a huge amount of damage throughout much of the house. It was going to cost thousands to repair, so we had no choice but to drop the sale price (which would never have happened if the Probate Office had done their job properly!). Our old home was now a soaking, mouldy mess and completely unrecognisable from the place that Fi and I once loved. The completion date was set for 22nd February, 2023. The evening before, Lewis drove me down there to read the meters, and as I shut the front door and walked to his car, I looked back – for the last time.

The Last Time

I felt numb again for the next couple of days. The house in which Fi and I had grown up was no longer somewhere we could visit with the kids on a Sunday, and of course, Mum and Dad were no longer there. Suddenly, I started to write a song about it all. The words came flooding out and using a keyboard I'd given Lewis when he was younger, I set a tune to it. It was the first thing I'd written or played for nearly 40 years, and it was, I guess, my way of coping and letting the emotion out. I played around with the tune and recorded myself singing it on my phone. I handed Steve the lyrics and keynotes when I met him and Cliff for a meal the evening before Lewis took me on a surprise trip to Zurich – a gorgeous but bloody expensive city- and I sent Steve my basic recording when I returned. He had his own recording studio at the top of his garden in Mayfield, East Sussex as he had been recording songs (and videos) for his own band, Killer Tone Jones, for several years. He sent back an initial version, which was really good. We then worked on adding strings, a specific bass line, drums, etc., and the kids took me over there a couple of times until we were both happy with how the music sounded. And then it was time for me to record the vocals.

The trouble is, I've never been a great singer. I had a tryout at one of our Embankments gigs just before we sacked Mark, and the audience just melted (away to the bar!). I wasn't the best, but having written the words and knowing how I wanted it to sound, I gave it a go. Steve recorded it in his studio and after a few takes, added it to the music. He then played the whole thing from start to finish and it sounded fantastic, much better than when I first wrote the words and basic tune. He's an incredibly gifted bloke, and it was tremendous fun working in a studio with him again after so many years.

I sent the final version on to close friends and family and everyone loved it, particularly the lyrics which resonated most with them. So I've got a song out there that people can play and hear me when I'm no longer around. In view of the subject matter, it was aptly called 'The Last Time'.

The Last Time

Close your eyes, for the last time

Say goodbye, for the last time

Laughter, dreams, and memories

When all our days were carefree

Growing up and going out

And coming home, sometimes

I've closed the old piano lid, for the last time

I've closed the battered old front door, for the last time

This old place is no longer mine

Damp and mouldy and seen better days

Someone else can have it now

And create new dreams and memories

I've closed the gate, for the last time

Just one look back, for the last time

I'm never gonna see you again,

I'm never gonna see you again,

I'm never gonna see you again,

I'm never gonna see you again.

Close your eyes, say goodbye.

Close your eyes, and say goodbye.

You've closed your eyes,

For the last time.

Europe Part 1

The trip to Zurich was just what I needed, and it was symptomatic of the kindness of my kids that Lewis organised and paid for it. One of the highlights was attending a game between FC Zurich and Lucerne, where I heard the noise and saw the ferocity of European 'ultras' at first hand. The home fans started setting off flares and making a row a good hour before kick off and continued throughout. Lucerne fans, although much smaller in number, did likewise, and the whole atmosphere was terrific. During halftime, a huge Lucerne flag appeared and completely covered all their fans. Unbeknown to the police or stewards, they used the flag to hide the fact they were setting up flare and firework launchers. As the teams emerged for the second half, the flag disappeared, and hundreds of flares and fireworks erupted, causing the lino and goalkeeper down that end to shit themselves, and it was ages before the game could restart. We didn't know it at the time but it was a taster for things to come with the Albion.

Holiday in the Sun

The first anniversary of Mum's death came when Di, Georgina, Lewis, and I were on holiday in Menorca. I loved the place. Our villa was extremely private, so much so that I burnt my arse! It was a relatively quiet part of the island; the beach wasn't all that, but I didn't mind as all I wanted from a holiday abroad was the sun, a pool and a few good restaurants, and Menorca ticked all these boxes. I set my alarm so that I was awake at 4:10 am on 12th July and sat on the terrace with a coffee and a smoke and had a quiet 'chat' with Mum.

Europe Part 2

Our next European adventure was in November 2023. The Albion had qualified to play in a European competition for the first time in our history, and one of the teams in our group was Ajax of Amsterdam. Although we didn't have a hope of getting match tickets, thousands of our fans would be in the same situation, and it promised to be a great time. I arranged flights and a hotel for Lewis and me – staying at the same hotel as Kev and his son, Liam, who both had match tickets- but Charlie couldn't come with us. Lewis was on a crutch, having had an operation the previous month on a broken bone in his foot, and with my mobility issues, we didn't get around too much. Whilst it was sunny when we arrived, it pissed down continuously thereafter, but we checked out some Irish bars that would be showing the game. As I thought, there were hordes of ticketless Albion fans over there, and every bar was rammed with our lot. Neil had taken his whole family over there, and we met up in one particular Irish bar, in which Kev, Liam and loads of old faces from back in the day were imbibing.

Lewis and I watched our game in a bar in which two thirds of the blokes in there were Ajax fans. We went 1-0 up and I over-celebrated a tad, getting stern looks from the locals. When we scored again, I really couldn't contain myself to the point where all the locals pissed off and we had the place to ourselves. Ah well, shit happens!

Grandad

The reason Charlie couldn't join us in Amsterdam was because on 5th November, 2 days before we flew out, his partner, Megan, gave birth to my first grandchild. Ava Marie Bennett Owen was born at the Princess Royal Hospital in Haywards Heath and was (and still is) a very healthy, beautiful baby girl. It was quite poignant for me as one of the things Dad said when he was told he only had a year to live was that he wouldn't get to see any grandchildren, and here was my granddaughter, a gorgeous bundle of love and joy. Hopefully, the first of many!

Europe Part 3

The Albion finished top of their Europa League group and were drawn away to Roma. Lewis couldn't come as he was travelling around Australia, so I took Charlie and Georgina with me, staying at the same hotel as Neil and his kids. I'd been to Rome a few times before when working for Amex, so I had visited most of the main tourist attractions, but it was Charlie and Georgina's first time. We posed for the obligatory photo outside the Colosseum, and they both went off to the Trevi Fountain. There were fewer ticketless fans over there than there had been in Amsterdam, and there was a different vibe, which wasn't helped by 2 of our lot being stabbed on the evening before the game. One of them was Jack Albion, one of Mad John's sons, and a larger-than-life character but no trouble. Thankfully, both he and the other lad weren't too badly hurt, but it made my piss boil. Every time an English team goes to play in Rome, some of their fans are either stabbed or mugged or both. The authorities turn a blind eye to it and nothing is ever done to prevent it. The game itself wasn't great; we were crap, lost 4-0, and that was the end of the Albion's European adventure for a while. But for me, it was only the warm-up to the main event a month later.

Dreams Can Come True

As I've mentioned before, I've had a fascination with Albania since my teens and always wanted to visit the country (when it was safe to do so). With my 60th birthday looming, I decided I wanted to spend the big day in the capital, Tirana. I booked the whole family (including 4-month-old Ava) on flights and found a four-star hotel, which was fairly central. We flew out on 1st April 2024, and after a 3-hour flight, my feet were finally on Albanian soil. It was very warm compared to the freezing conditions we'd left behind at Heathrow and although Tirana airport was picturesque, set down with huge mountains to one side, our first impression in the taxi to the hotel wasn't great. Not as a result of muggers or beggars or armed guards in sentry posts threatening to shoot us. No, the roads and, in particular, the drivers over there were horrendous! There weren't any rules on the roads; it was a complete free-for-all at roundabouts and traffic lights. If you've ever experienced the chaos on the roads around the Arc De Triomphe, then multiply that by 10, and that's Tirana's roads for you. Somehow, our driver made it to the hotel without incurring any bumps or scratches, but it was very close on several occasions.

Albania and, in particular, Tirana, has modernised significantly over the last 15 years or so, mainly driven by the Prime Minister, Edi Rama, but I was amazed at just how much development had occurred and with the presence of so many cranes around the city, how much is ongoing. I'm not usually a great fan of modern architecture, but the high-rise hotels, apartments, and business centres were all unique in their design and colours, and blended in perfectly with all the older style historic buildings. The people we met were very friendly, very proud of their country and delighted that tourists could now safely visit.

On the big day itself, we went to Bunk Art 2, a museum contained in one of the numerous nuclear bunkers that were built for the dictator, Enver Hoxha, while he was still alive. Inside were a series of underground corridors, each of which contained several rooms showing the history of the country since the end of the Second World War, with graphic photos of hangings and shootings, and each room had a full description in English. It was fascinating stuff. There are loads of other museums in the city for which there simply wasn't the time to visit – maybe I'll save that for my next trip over there. I hoped I'd enjoy it there, but it exceeded my expectations, and it was a great way and occasion to fulfill a dream with all my family.

The Men They Couldn't Hang

On the Saturday before we went to Albania, Georgina had arranged a surprise birthday party for me at Burgess Hill Rugby Club. She'd kept it quiet for months and did a fantastic job arranging for a load of old faces to be there. Cliff and Steve bought me a Dukla Prague away shirt in recognition of the song by The Men They Couldn't Hang, and I was chuffed to bits. I was even more chuffed when it was time to bring in my cake and grinning from ear to ear and carrying it was Lewis, who had flown in from Australia a couple of days earlier than 'planned' so he could be there and also join us in Albania. It was a great evening and the only downside was that there weren't any mushroom vol au vents!

It was quite fitting that Fi and her lot should be at the party as Georgina has definitely inherited my sister's 'blondness'. Amongst many examples of this was the time when George was flying on her own to Australia. An hour or so before she landed, she had to complete the various documentation to be presented at Border Control but realised she didn't have a pen. She was sitting next to a Chinese couple who could see that she wasn't filling in her forms, and kindly offered George the use of their pen. "Thank you", said George, "but does it write in English?". Seriously!

Heroes

As you've seen throughout this book, music has played a big part in my life, and I've cobbled together a list of my Top 10's in four categories which are shown later on. As far as favourites go, I find it difficult to separate **The Undertones** and **The Clash**. The former, with the song writing genius that was the O'Neill brothers, were fun and fast with songs which honed in on teenage angst, of which I suffered plenty. **The Clash** were different gravy altogether and probably one of the most important bands of all time. Their ability to cross over different genres whilst still sounding relevant and pioneering, was a masterful collusion between Joe Strummer and Mick Jones. Strummer was one of the best frontmen ever, delivering a 100 mph performance on stage and in the studio. **Joy Division** only made two albums but were on the cusp of greatness when Ian Curtis committed suicide. His lyrics inspired me (and no doubt countless others) to write and set down our own feelings into verse, and Peter Hook took bass playing to a whole new level. I've no idea why I never got round to seeing **The Smiths** live but the combination of Morrisey's weird and wonderful lyrics, and Johnny Marr's sublime guitar playing really set the sound for the mid-80's. When The Embankments played our first ever gig at Stanley Deason school in 1984, This Charming Man had just entered the charts and was the start of their ascendency into the big time.

But for me, my absolute hero and inspiration from the music world was Dave Greenfield of **The Stranglers**. Dave used to live near The Wilmington pub off Carden Avenue in Brighton and was, in my opinion, the greatest keyboard player of all time. He was the least 'punk' looking of the four of them but was handy and once had to be dragged off John Lydon who he'd pinned up against a wall and was about to knock into next week! His skillful melodies tied everything together for the band and he wrote many of their classic songs. He died aged 71 during covid and I'm not ashamed to say I shed a tear when I learnt of his passing.

If I could go back in time and create the ultimate super-group from my favourite bands, it would consist of the following: -

Drums: Rick Buckler (The Jam)

Bass: Peter Hook (Joy Division/New Order)

Guitar: Johnny Marr (The Smiths)

Keyboards: Dave Greenfield (The Stranglers)

Vocals: Joe Strummer (The Clash)

As far as a band name goes, they'd have to be 'The Dogs Bollocks'.

Top 10's

Singles

1. Good Morning Britain – Mick Jones & Aztec Camera
2. Pure – Lightening Seeds
3. Atmosphere – Joy Division
4. Complete Control – The Clash
5. A Town Called Malice – The Jam
6. Rockaway Beach – The Ramones
7. You've Got My Number – The Undertones
8. Ceremony – New Order
9. Ever Fallen In Love – Buzzcocks
10. Ghost Town – Specials

Albums

1. Hypnotised – The Undertones
2. Unknown Pleasures – Joy Division
3. Give 'Em Enough Rope – The Clash
4. Black & White – The Stranglers
5. Rocket To Russia – The Ramones
6. Power, Corruption & Lies – New Order
7. Jollification – Lightening Seeds
8. All Mod Cons – The Jam
9. Never Mind The Bollocks – Sex Pistols
10. Transformer – Lou Reed

Gigs

1. The Undertones
2. The Clash
3. The Stranglers
4. The Jam
5. Teardrop Explodes
6. The Cure
7. Echo & The Bunnymen
8. Stiff Little Fingers
9. Skids
10. Public Image Ltd

Intros

1. Of One Skin – Skids
2. Tearproof – The Undertones
3. Age Of Consent – New Order
4. Strange Town – The Jam
5. What's The Frequency Kenneth? – REM
6. Pretty Vacant – Sex Pistols
7. Alternative Ulster – Stiff Little Fingers
8. Safe European Home – The Clash
9. Public Image – Public Image Ltd
10. My Life – Billy Joel (obviously!)

And Now, The End Is Near (Or Is It?)

And that's it – the first 60 years. I'm not entirely convinced there will be another 60, but I've crammed quite a bit into my life so far, and my friends, kids and grandkids can now see what I've been up to and I hope you've enjoyed reading it. If just one person with a facial issue takes any kind of inspiration from it, then that will do for me. Unless they're a cyclist!

Huge thanks to Di for putting up with me for all these years and to my fantastic kids, who have grown up to be wonderful adults – despite my parenting skills!

Thankfully, since my illness, I've regained quite a bit of weight, so I'm still a fat bastard!

Photos

Front cover; Me in the back garden of 28PR in 1966 wearing 'those' bikini bottoms and standing inside Coldean's first unofficial swimming pool.

Back cover; top left. The whole family – including 4 month old Ava- in a restaurant in Tirana for my birthday meal, April 2024.

Top right. A very heavily medicated me with Mum and the kids in 28PR on Good Friday, April 2022. The last photo of us all together.

Bottom. With my wonderful, naturally blonde sister, Fi at The Copthorne Hotel, March 2011.

Epitaph

Here lies Stuart

Under this epitaph

He was a fat bastard

But he made us laugh